The Three Best English Translations of the Torah Available Today

Most people today can't read Hebrew, which is the original language of the Torah. Luckily, many English translations of the Torah are available; the following is a list of my three favorites. You can find and purchase Torah translations at the many Jewish bookstores across the United States as well as online (just type "Jewish books" into your favorite search engine). See Chapter 16 for details on translations, commentaries, and other tools to help you study the Torah.

- *The Living Torah* by Rabbi Aryeh Kaplan: This is the most readable of all translations, and its brief footnotes are always illuminating. It isn't a precise, literal translation, but rather a translation that focuses on the ways in which the great Jewish sages have traditionally understood the Torah text.

- *The Chumash: The Gutnick Edition:* If I could have only one translation on a desert island, it would be this one. It's filled with rich insights from classic Jewish commentators and from a brilliant modern spiritual master known as the Lubavitcher Rebbe.

- *The Chumash: The Stone Edition:* This translation has become the standard edition found in most traditional synagogues throughout the world, and for good reason. It's easy to read and the commentaries, which make up half of this volume, are selections from the most authoritative Torah sages throughout Jewish history.

A Few Behavior Guidelines from the Torah

The Torah is a guidebook for living. While it contains hundreds of commandments of all kinds, the Torah is particularly occupied with personal behavior. Here are six of the most important prescriptions from the Torah for a healthy, spiritually sound life (see Chapter 9 for more information):

- **Good works** or **ma'asim tovim** (mah-ah-*seem* toe-*veem*): Always be on the lookout for opportunities to do good things for others and for yourself. Get up on the right side of the bed, be nice, and always be the one who does the right thing.

- **Acts of kindness** or **gemilut chasadim** (geh-meh-*loot* khah-sah-*deem*): Look at the world through eyes of compassion, empathize with the challenges of others, and look eagerly for opportunities to be kind to everyone, especially to those less fortunate than you.

- **Hospitality** or **hachnasat orchim** (hakh-nah-*saht* ore-*kheem*): Invite family members, friends, and acquaintances to your home, be generous and gracious hosts, make sure your guests are comfortable, and treat them the way you'd like to be treated.

- **Charity** or **tzedakah** (tzeh-dah-*kah*): Give generously to charities and to individuals who are in need. Make it a regular habit. Some sages say that there is no good deed more important than giving charity.

- **Visiting the sick** or **bikkur cholim** (*beer*-khoor *khoh*-leem): Visit and/or call people you know who are ill and be sensitive to their needs. Know that visiting a sick person is part of their healing process and makes a big difference.

- **Evil speech** or **lashon hara** (lah-*shone* ha-*rah*): Be careful with what you say, don't be verbally abusive, don't embarrass someone publicly, don't lie, and know that words can be cruel weapons.

The Torah For Dummies®

Cheat Sheet

The Ten Commandments According to the Torah

Did you know that the Ten Commandments according to Jewish tradition are different from the Ten Commandments of various Christian denominations? And did you know that two versions of the Ten Commandments are in the Torah itself — one in the book of Exodus (see Chapter 5) and one in the book of Deuteronomy (see Chapter 8)? Here are the Ten Commandments according to the book of Exodus; see Chapter 17 for more information, including the list that appears in the book of Deuteronomy.

1. **I am the Lord your God.**

    "I am the Lord your God, who brought you out of the land of Egypt, from the house of slavery." (Exodus 20:2)

2. **You shall have no other gods before Me. You shall not make for yourself an idol.**

    "You shall not recognize other gods before Me. You shall not make for yourself a carved image, or any likeness of what is in heaven above or on the earth beneath or in the water under the earth." (Exodus 20:3–4)

3. **You shall not take the name of God in vain.**

    "You shall not take the name of the Lord your God in vain, for the Lord will not leave him unpunished who takes His name in vain." (Exodus 20:7)

4. **Remember and observe the Sabbath and keep it holy.**

    "Remember the Sabbath day, to keep it holy. Six days you shall labor and do all your work, but the seventh day is a Sabbath to the Lord your God; you shall not do any work, you or your son or your daughter, your male or your female servant, your animal or your stranger within your gates." (Exodus 20:8–10)

5. **Honor your father and mother.**

    "Honor your father and your mother, so that your days may be prolonged in the land which the Lord your God gives you." (Exodus 20:12)

6. **You shall not murder.**

    "You shall not murder." (Exodus 20:13)

7. **You shall not commit adultery.**

    "You shall not commit adultery." (Exodus 20:13)

8. **You shall not steal.**

    "You shall not steal." (Exodus 20:13)

9. **You shall not bear false witness.**

    "You shall not bear false witness against your neighbor." (Exodus 20:13)

10. **You shall not covet your neighbor's wife or house.**

    "You shall not covet your neighbor's house; you shall not covet your neighbor's wife or his male servant or his female servant or his ox or his donkey or anything that belongs to your neighbor." (Exodus 20:14)

For Dummies: Bestselling Book Series for Beginners

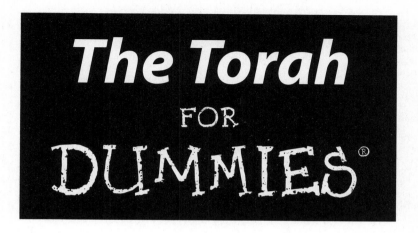

The Torah
FOR
DUMMIES®

by Arthur Kurzweil

BICENTENNIAL
1807
WILEY
2007
BICENTENNIAL

Wiley Publishing, Inc.

The Torah For Dummies®

Published by
Wiley Publishing, Inc.
111 River St.
Hoboken, NJ 07030-5774
www.wiley.com

WILEY

About the Author

Arthur Kurzweil is one of the most popular lecturers and teachers on the Torah, Talmud, Kabbalah, and other topics of Jewish interest in synagogues and at other Jewish gatherings across the United States and Canada. He is a direct descendant of Rabbi Chaim Yosef Gottlieb (1790–1867), Rabbi Isaiah Horowitz (1555–1630), and Rabbi Moses Isserles (1530–1572), three illustrious and revered rabbis and teachers of the Torah.

Arthur is the author of *Kabbalah For Dummies* (Wiley) and *On the Road with Rabbi Steinsaltz: 25 Years of Pre-Dawn Car Trips, Mind-Blowing Encounters, and Inspiring Conversations with a Man of Wisdom* (Jossey-Bass). He's also the author of the best-selling classic *From Generation to Generation: How to Trace Your Jewish Genealogy and Family History* (Jossey-Bass), coeditor of *The Hadassah Jewish Family Book of Health and Wellness* (Jossey-Bass), and editor of *Best Jewish Writing 2003* (Jossey-Bass). He also wrote *My Generations: A Course in Jewish Family History* (Behrman House), which is used in synagogue schools across America.

Arthur is the recipient of the Distinguished Humanitarian Award from the Melton Center for Jewish Studies at The Ohio State University for his unique contributions to the field of Jewish education. He also received a Lifetime Achievement Award from the International Association of Jewish Genealogical Societies for his trailblazing work in the field of Jewish genealogy.

A member of the Society of American Magicians and the International Brotherhood of Magicians, Arthur frequently performs his one-man show "Searching for God in a Magic Shop," in which he blends the performance of magic tricks with a serious discussion of Jewish theological ideas. Arthur lives with his wife, Bobby, in a suburb of New York City.

Visit Arthur's web site at www.arthurkurzweil.com.

Dedication

For Bobby

*"He must have loved me so much
to send me someone as fine as you."*

Author's Acknowledgments

My goal in these acknowledgments is to recognize those people who have helped me, in many different ways, to think I'm qualified to write this book. Who am I to write a book on such a sacred subject as the Torah? And who helped me have the nerve to claim I have the qualifications? I think I know. But before I acknowledge them, I take full responsibility for this book. Any errors are mine.

Many years ago, when my children were young, I asked my teacher, Rabbi Adin Steinsaltz, for some advice: How do I teach my children the Torah? He told me to speak with them about the most difficult and abstract spiritual ideas I knew to exist. I took his advice, and the result has been extraordinary. For the past quarter of a century, I have had the deepest religious discussions, sharing amazing words of Torah with my three children. My decision to enroll my children full time in schools of Torah study (with full secular studies as well) created three knowledgeable Torah teachers surrounding me daily. The experience has been mind-blowing — for me. My Torah education has unfolded every day from the process of learning from my children, each of whom is my teacher. I have insisted upon it.

My greatest thanks, appreciation, love and gratitude go to:

Miriam Kurzweil: You will surely see how important your help with this book has been because there is clear evidence of your hard work, knowledge of the Torah, and eager, unfailing assistance on so many of these pages. I hope and pray you also know how precious, deep, intimate, and profound our countless hours of conversations have been to me over the years. You're awesome.

Moshe Kurzweil: If I were asked 20 years ago to dream my wildest dreams and express what I would hope for in a son, I would have described the person you've become. You're a spiritual searcher and teacher, kind and articulate, gentle, strong, and wise. You and I can speak about God forever. And I hope we will. As I write this, you are in the Holy Land for a year of advanced Torah study. Please keep teaching me.

Malya Kurzweil: As you know, when a question of Torah comes up among some of our family members, the first words spoken are, "Let's ask Malya." You have deservedly earned the reputation of having Torah knowledge that is broad and deep and so often profound. And you have proven to so many people that your talents as a teacher of Torah are on the highest level. How rare and priceless have your words of Torah been for me. You are a treasure.

Heartfelt thanks are also due to:

Rabbi Adin Steinsaltz: You are the Light of our generation. I'm just one of so many who simply don't know where we would be without you. If I have one wish for this book it is that its readers will seek out *your* books and learn from your endless wisdom, understanding, and knowledge.

Saul Kurzweil: My extraordinary father. You personify the spirit of the Talmud. You were always in my mind as I wrote this book and as I tried to anticipate your rich flow of deep and important questions.

Evelyn Kurzweil: My beautiful mother. You personify the words of Hillel when he taught the essence of the Torah, and you are a role model of patience, kindness, empathy, and refinement. Your Hebrew name, Zisil, captures you perfectly.

My editors: Georgette Beatty, Mike Lewis, Elizabeth Rea, and Rabbi Alan Kay. Georgette, your firm and wise guidance, your delicious laughter, and your genuine warmth made the whole process an uplifting one. Mike, thank you for your vision and for your confidence in me. Elizabeth, every question, suggestion, and insight from you enhanced this book. Alan, it is no surprise that your participation inspired me to be more sensitive to others; you are a rare gem. Because I have been in the world of publishing for 30 years, I know the kind of magic that talented editors perform. The four of you are the best!

My editorial consultants: Rebecca Allen — If there's an editorial job to do, you're the one for me. Alan Zoldan — When I need creative help, you're first on my list.

My ancestors: Rabbi Chaim Yosef Gottlieb (1790–1867), Rabbi Isaiah Horowitz (1555–1630), Rabbi Moshe Isserles (1530–1572), Reb Avraham Abusch Kurzweil, Rabbi Shlomo Zalke Rosenvasser, Rabbi Asher Yeshia Gottlieb, Reb Yekutiel Yehudah (Zalman Leib) Gottlieb, and Reb Yehuda Yaakov Kurzweil. May your descendants continue to invest their lives in the study of Torah.

My teachers: Reb Shabtai Zisel ben Avraham Zimmerman of Hibbing, MN, Reb Eliezer Nehemiah HaCohen of Montreal, Ram Dass, Reb Eliezer ben Shlomo of Sighet, Rabbi Shlomo ben Benzion Halberstam (1907–2000), Rabbi Menachem Mendel ben Levi Yitzchak Schneerson (1902–1994), Rabbi Meshullam Zalman ben Shlomo HaKohen Schachter-Shalomi, Reb Yaakov Yehuda ben Yitzchak Zelig Halevi v'Yehudis Siegel, Yosef Puglisi HaMalamud HaGadol, and Rabbi Israel Nobel of East Meadow.

Ken Kurzweil: My brother and friend. You're always there when I need you, with patience and endless support.

Ruth Rothwax: With my love and gratitude. Thanks for your belief in me and for the advice and support you always give freely.

My wife's family, especially the inspirational Estelle and Eugene Ferkauf, Howie and Liz Kleinberg, Josh Kleinberg and Donna LaGatta, Gal Dor, and Orna Dor. Special thanks and heartfelt love to Rachel Dor: I will always be grateful for the very first moment we met, and I am truly impressed by your fertile mind, moved by your sweet soul, and inspired by your thirst for the delicious waters of Torah learning.

Rabbi Simcha Prombaum: Loving friend, gifted Torah teacher, and cherished advisor. I consult you almost daily on all things large and small.

Ed Rothfarb: In every way an artist, fellow seeker, loving friend for nearly 50 years. We went to Hebrew school together, walked to grade school together, and here we are, still celebrating life together and continuing to share our search for spiritual wisdom.

Richard Carlow: Source of infinite joy and delight, loving friend for over 40 years. I can't imagine life without you.

Robin Kahn Bauer: Loving and loyal friend, and fellow seeker for over 40 years.

Rick Blum: Loving friend, Torah buddy, and confidant for over 40 years. Your spiritual journey and love of Torah is a true inspiration to me.

Gary Eisenberg: My spiritual brother. No words can even begin. From the moment we met, it was love at first sight.

Marc Felix: Loving friend, joined at our soul's root.

Marcia Cohen: Loving friend for over 45 years. You've taught me about spiritual devotion, crazy wisdom, and the pure joy of lifelong friendship.

Margy-Ruth Davis: Special friend, Jewish leader, and role model.

Zsuzsa Barta: Trusted friend and beautiful cousin. I knew you and began loving you the moment I met you on that train platform in Budapest.

Dr. Helen Hecht: Loving friend, gifted healer, extraordinary soul.

Reb Tuvia Frazer: Thank you for inviting me in.

Alan Rinzler: Friend, teacher, soul-brother.

Rashi and Shabbos, who sang as I wrote.

Bobby Dor Kurzweil: My wife, my life, my best friend and chevrusa.

Blessed are You, Lord our God, King of the universe, who has kept us alive, sustained us, and permitted us to reach this moment.

Arthur Kurzweil
(Avraham Abba ben Chaim Shaul v'Zisil)
Great Neck, New York, October 2007

Publisher's Acknowledgments

We're proud of this book; please send us your comments through our Dummies online registration form located at www.dummies.com/register/.

Some of the people who helped bring this book to market include the following:

Acquisitions, Editorial, and Media Development

Project Editor: Georgette Beatty

Acquisitions Editor: Michael Lewis

Senior Copy Editor: Elizabeth Rea

Editorial Program Coordinator: Erin Calligan Mooney

Technical Editor: Rabbi Alan Kay

Editorial Manager: Michelle Hacker

Editorial Assistants: Joe Niesen, Leeann Harney

Cover Photo: © Fred de Noyelle/Godong/Corbis

Cartoons: Rich Tennant (www.the5thwave.com)

Composition Services

Project Coordinator: Kristie Rees

Layout and Graphics: Reuben W. Davis, Melissa K. Jester, Christine Williams

Special Art: Pam Tanzey

Anniversary Logo Design: Richard Pacifico

Proofreaders: Laura Albert, John Greenough, Caitie Kelly, Glenn McMullen

Indexer: Cheryl Duksta

Publishing and Editorial for Consumer Dummies

Diane Graves Steele, Vice President and Publisher, Consumer Dummies

Joyce Pepple, Acquisitions Director, Consumer Dummies

Kristin A. Cocks, Product Development Director, Consumer Dummies

Michael Spring, Vice President and Publisher, Travel

Kelly Regan, Editorial Director, Travel

Publishing for Technology Dummies

Andy Cummings, Vice President and Publisher, Dummies Technology/General User

Composition Services

Gerry Fahey, Vice President of Production Services

Debbie Stailey, Director of Composition Services

Contents at a Glance

Table of Contents

Part III: The Torah: An Operating Manual for Planet Earth 141

Introduction

The Torah is both the most sacred object and the most sacred text in Judaism. It consists of the first five books of the Bible: Genesis, Exodus, Leviticus, Numbers, and Deuteronomy. The word "Torah" comes from the same root as the Hebrew word **hora'ah** (hoe-rah-*ah*), which means "instruction" or "teaching." The Torah's purpose, simply stated, is to provide people with instructions for finding and following the path of God and the path to God.

Although the words in the Torah, which is also known as the Five Books of Moses, consists of exactly 304,805 letters, the great sages of Jewish tradition teach that all the wisdom in the universe is hidden within these letters. Jewish tradition looks carefully at these letters and at the words they form, and great sages throughout history have provided — and continue to provide — the proper instruction for analyzing the Torah text and revealing its divine messages.

As my teacher, the renowned Rabbi Adin Steinsaltz of Jerusalem, has said, "Other religions have a concept of scripture as deriving from Heaven, but only Judaism seems to be based on the idea that the Torah Scripture is itself Heaven. In other words, the Torah of the Jews is the essence of divine revelation; it is not only a basis for social, political, and religious life but is something of supreme value."

When you study the Torah, you aren't just studying the word of God. According to Jewish belief, Torah study is actually an authentic encounter *with* God. The Torah can be viewed as a collection of concentrated emanations and trans-mutations of divine wisdom. I'm a Jew who studies the Torah in one form or another every day. I've been studying the Torah for nearly 40 years, and I've come to believe that the Torah is the most profound collection of wisdom and guidance I've ever encountered.

About This Book

It's essential to know that you can't understand the Five Books of Moses simply by reading it like a storybook. A core belief among the Jewish people is that when Moses encountered God on Mount Sinai and received the Torah, he actually received two Torahs — one written and one oral. The two parts together make up what the Jewish people consider to be the Torah.

The relationship between the Written Torah and the Oral Torah has often been compared to the relationship between the United States Constitution on the one hand and both federal and state legislation as well as the decisions of the Supreme Court on the other hand. The written Constitution contains basic principles, but it's the legislation and court decisions that expand upon these principles and give them life. Jewish tradition teaches that the Oral Torah works in much the same way, expanding upon the basic written principles of the Five Books of Moses. These basic principles are constantly being applied to new situations as human history unfolds.

In *The Torah For Dummies,* I explain how both aspects of the Torah work together to form an operating manual for life. Like all *For Dummies* books, you don't need to read *The Torah For Dummies* from cover to cover. Each chapter is self-contained. I've constructed each section so that you can flip through the book, find something of interest, and read it without needing to know what the other chapters say. I've written this book in plain, down-to-earth language, and if I need to mention an essential technical or foreign word or phrase, I make sure to define it the first time I use it.

Even though the Torah is deep and profound, Jewish tradition teaches that the Torah is written in the language of humans and is meant to be accessible and understandable. I've made sure that my explanations and descriptions of the Torah and its contents resulted in a plain-language reference book that will serve you well, even if you have had absolutely no prior experience or familiarity with the Torah.

My goal in writing *The Torah For Dummies* is to introduce you to the Torah, its structure, its contents, and its significance in Jewish life. I also want you to understand how the ideas in the Torah provide the basis of Western civilization and the foundations of Judaism, Christianity, and Islam.

Conventions Used in This Book

Because the Torah is a vast subject with so many parts, qualities, aspects, and subjects, I had to establish a few conventions while writing to make the subject as clear and understandable as possible. As you read *The Torah For Dummies,* please keep in mind my conventions regarding the following:

✔ **The word "Torah":** Don't jump too quickly to define the word "Torah." It has abstract connotations as well as very specific usages. For the most part, when I use the word in this book, I'm referring to the Five Books of Moses. But as you will find out, "Torah" also refers to the oral tradition that has been passed down from generation to generation ever since Moses encountered God at Mount Sinai. In addition, the word "Torah" refers to the entire body of Jewish teachings.

✔ **References to God:** Although the Five Books of Moses refers to God using male pronouns like "He" and "Him," in principle God has no gender and is beyond anything the human mind can grasp on any level.

Occasionally, I refer to God using male pronouns for simplicity's sake, but I try to avoid this as much as possible.

✔ **Pronunciation of Hebrew words:** Many Hebrew words and phrases appear throughout this book in **boldface** text, and because not everyone's familiar with the language, I offer pronunciation help. The syllable that receives the accent is always in *italics*. But you should be aware that there are two ways to pronounce many Hebrew words:

- **Ashkenazic:** This is the Central and Eastern European pronunciation that's used in most, but not all, Orthodox synagogues. An example is **Shabbos** (*shah*-bus; Sabbath), with the accent on the first syllable.

- **Sephardic:** This is the modern Israeli pronunciation that's used in most liberal synagogues and some Orthodox synagogues in the United States. An example is **Shabbat** (shah-*baht*; Sabbath), with the accent on the second syllable.

In this book, I mostly use the transliteration and pronunciation commonly used in Israel, but sometimes I give the Ashkenazic pronunciation, especially if it has become common usage.

✔ **The names of the Five Books of Moses:** I use the common names for each of the Five Books of Moses. For example, the first book, Genesis, is actually called **Bereshit** (beh-ray-*sheet*) in Hebrew and in Jewish tradition. Even though I would love for you to know the "real" names of each book, I've come to the conclusion that using the common names is more useful, especially for a beginner.

✔ **Sages, commentators, and rabbis:** Throughout this book, I use these terms interchangeably. The term "sage" is a common one in Jewish life and generally refers to any highly regarded Torah teacher. By definition, someone whose commentaries on the Torah have come to be accepted among traditional Jews throughout history is known as a sage. Occasionally, I refer to "the rabbis." What I mean by that isn't simply anyone who happens to be a rabbi but rather those rabbis who have earned reputations as luminaries among the Jewish people.

✔ **English translations of verses from the Torah:** The Torah is written in Hebrew; the English translations appearing in this book are mine, but I want you to know that I'm quite familiar with all the available English translations of the Torah and I've often borrowed phrases from them. Generally, my translations are composites of all the available English translations as well as my own translations, and my decisions are based on my judgments as to what's the clearest and most understandable language to modern English-speaking readers.

✔ **Jewish observance:** This book is *not* a guide to Jewish religious observance. If you're interested in following the teachings of the Torah, there are many books available specifically to help you with that. The best way to learn how to live a religious Jewish life is to find a qualified rabbi or teacher who can direct you in the process of learning the way of the Torah.

What You're Not to Read

If you have the time and inclination to read this book from cover to cover, by all means, get to it! However, if you're only looking for the most helpful, most essential facts and explanations, you can skip the sidebars, which appear in shaded gray boxes throughout this book. They're interesting (I hope!) anecdotes and pieces of information that supplement the text but aren't essential for an understanding of the topics being explored.

Foolish Assumptions

When writing this book, I had to make some assumptions about you. First of all, I don't assume that you're Jewish, nor do I assume that you want to be. And although the Torah is just as much about spiritual practice as it is about general spiritual ideas, I don't assume that you want to adopt every practice, custom, and ritual, nor do I assume that you necessarily agree with all the theological assumptions found in the Torah.

Following are some additional assumptions I've made. If you fit into any of these categories, this book is for you:

- ✔ You've heard about the Torah and are curious about it because you know that it's the central book and foundation of Judaism.
- ✔ You know that both Christianity and Islam have their roots in Judaism and the Torah, and you're interested in understanding those roots.
- ✔ You have some familiarity with the Bible and know some of its contents (like Noah's Ark and the Ten Commandments), but you still want more.
- ✔ You're a spiritual seeker, and you've heard that the Torah is the cornerstone of the Jewish path and the hiding place of all the secrets of Kabbalah.
- ✔ You're Jewish but realize that you never received a good Jewish education or you want to supplement, enrich, broaden, and expand your Jewish knowledge.
- ✔ You're not Jewish, but you'd like to understand more about Jewish life, including that of your Jewish friends and neighbors.
- ✔ You've attended a synagogue service and have witnessed the reverence that the Jewish people give to the Torah, and you'd like to know more about it.
- ✔ You've seen popular films like *The Ten Commandments* and *Raiders of the Lost Ark,* and you're curious about the contexts of those films.
- ✔ You've seen a lot of Christian preachers on television quoting from and explaining the Torah from their points of view, but you'd like to know how Judaism understands its holy book.

How This Book Is Organized

I've organized this book so that you can skip around easily. In order to help you get in, get the information you need, and get out without reading cover to cover, I divided the book into parts that give you one piece of the Torah picture at a time.

Part 1: The Torah 101

This part provides you with the basics. You get an overview of the entire subject, in particular the major sections of the Torah as well as some of its most important ideas and concepts. I introduce the main "character" of the Torah — God. There's a lot to say about God, even though, by definition, it's impossible for humans to grasp God. But once you understand the paradox that the Torah expects you to establish an intimate, personal relationship with a God whom you can't conceive of, you begin to understand that God is the basis of everything. And because the Torah is often profoundly misunderstood, I also explore what the Torah isn't in this part.

Part II: One by One: The Books of the Torah

The Five Books of Moses consists of, well, five books: Genesis, Exodus, Leviticus, Numbers, and Deuteronomy. In this part, I walk you through each of the five books, one by one, summarizing the major events and concepts appearing in each. After reading each chapter in this part, you should have a pretty good idea of the books' contents, from stories you didn't know of to ones that sound familiar (like the splitting of the Red Sea or the giving of the Ten Commandments). I'll warn you now that you may end up saying to yourself, "Oh, so *that's* where that comes from!"

Part III: The Torah: An Operating Manual for Planet Earth

Even though the Torah has a lot to say about spiritual topics like God, faith, good and evil, and angels, it's a book of action. Its emphasis is on the world in which people live and function. In this part, I show you how the Torah concerns itself with personal behavior, like honoring parents, giving charity, treating animals with kindness, and just about every personal human activity. I also show you how the Torah has an equal concern for behavior in communal affairs, like the court system, employee/employer relations, and property rights.

Part IV: The Importance of the Torah in Judaism

The Torah scroll is the most sacred object in Jewish life. In this part, I show you how the contents of the Torah form the basis for Jewish holy days and Jewish customs and practices (like eating kosher food), and the way in which the Torah scroll is used during synagogue services. According to Jewish tradition, every Jewish person must either write a Torah scroll or support those who do, so in this part, I provide you with the details of how a Torah scroll is written. Finally, every Jewish person is required to study the Torah, so I describe just how this is done and provide you with some suggestions if you want to participate in the study of the Torah.

Part V: The Part of Tens

Every *For Dummies* book has a Part of Tens. One natural list of ten items relating to the Torah is the Ten Commandments. But it's not so simple: Not only are there two versions of the Ten Commandments in the Torah, but different groups of Christians even count them differently! Another group of ten that I give you in this part is ten famous (and often misunderstood) quotations from the Torah, many of which you'll know.

Part VI: Appendixes

In this part, I include a glossary of terms that you should know for a basic vocabulary about the Torah. And last but not least, I give you a list of the 613 commandments found in the Torah, broken down into positive commandments (what you *should* do) and negative commandments (what you *shouldn't* do).

Icons Used in This Book

All *For Dummies* books feature icons (little pictures that grab your attention) in the margins to serve you well. Think of them as road signs pointing to different kinds of information in the chapters.

This icon alerts you to ideas and concepts that my Torah teachers have given me over the years.

This icon alerts you to concepts, terms, and ideas in the Torah that are of particular importance. Keep the points marked with this icon in mind, and you can't go wrong.

This icon points out helpful information that you can use if you make the Torah a part of your life.

This icon points to misconceptions about the Torah or actions that are strictly forbidden by the Torah. Read this information carefully!

This icon highlights instances when I quote directly from the Torah or some other important Jewish source, often from some of the great sages of Jewish history.

Where to Go from Here

You can begin this book wherever you like. But you may want to start with the following suggestions:

- ✔ If you're interested in all 613 commandments in the Torah, go to Appendixes B and C.

- ✔ If you want to get a good overview of each of the Five Books of Moses, read Part II.

- ✔ If you want to put the Torah's basic principles into practice immediately, read Chapters 9 and 10.

No matter where you start, I can't deny that I'm excited for you. The Torah is awesome. There's a blessing that Jews have said for centuries before studying the Torah as a way of offering thanks to God; the blessing is this: "Blessed are You, Lord our God, Ruler of the universe, Who has sanctified us by Your commandments and has commanded us to get involved with the words of the Torah." This blessing doesn't require you to obey the Torah, believe in the Torah, or follow the Torah. It simply says to "get involved with its words." I hope you do.

Part I
The Torah 101

"Saaay — I have an idea. Why don't we turn down the lights, put on some soft music, and curl up with the Torah tonight?"

In this part . . .

Even though you can begin reading any chapter in this book first, you may want to get some of the basics under your belt. In this part, I cover some of the fundamental elements found in the Torah itself, such as its setup and laws. I also give you a quick overview of the contents of the Five Books of Moses. Perhaps most importantly I devote an entire chapter to God, who is the ultimate author of the Torah; in fact, God is the author of the universe and everything that exists.

Chapter 1

Beginning with Torah Basics

The Torah, also known as the Five Books of Moses, is the most sacred object and the most important text of the Jewish people. As a sacred scroll found in every synagogue throughout the world, it's referred to as a **sefer Torah** (*say*-fehr toe-*rah*; Torah scroll); as a bound book, it's referred to as a **chumash** (khuh-*mahsh*; five).

The Torah is more than a text, though; it's also the spiritual tradition of the Jewish people, communicated by God (the Creator and Master of the universe) to Moses (the greatest prophet of the Jewish people) on Mount Sinai in 1280 BCE and handed down from generation to generation.

You can understand the word "Torah" in a third way as well. Torah is the vast and constantly growing body of teachings and wisdom of Judaism, and in this sense it even includes what a qualified Jewish teacher will teach tomorrow. The "study of Torah" is not necessarily the same as the "study of *the* Torah." "The Torah" usually means the Written Torah, the Five Books of Moses, whereas "Torah" is Torah studies in the more general sense.

In this chapter, I introduce you to various aspects of the Torah, such as its structure, teachings, and study. I invite you to explore this chapter and discover some basics about this unique document of documents that has taught the world about charity; love; the importance of educating children; honesty in the marketplace; the concepts of bankruptcy, courts, and witnesses; and so many other aspects of modern experience that are embedded into the fabric of our lives.

Introducing God, the Torah's Author

Even though the Torah is mainly *about* God, it's also important to remember that the Torah's author *is* God. Although the first line of the Torah says, "In the beginning of God's creation of heaven and earth . . .," it's God who is speaking. God chose Moses to receive and write down a divine message, which is why the Torah is also known as the Five Books of Moses, but the Torah emanates from God. God reaches into the human world with the Torah.

Jewish tradition teaches that God didn't create the world out of nothing. God's creation is an emanation of divine light that God sculpted into all that exists. God is not just "in" everything. Rather, everything *is* God. This is, of course, a paradox. On the one hand, people live their lives feeling separate from God, but at the same time, Jewish tradition teaches that on the deepest level everything *is* God.

In studying the Torah, you'll often encounter paradoxes. Many spiritual teachers teach that when you encounter a paradox, it usually means that you're going in the right direction. The endless struggle to grasp and under-stand what is meant by God is both the most important activity of life and, at the same time, an impossible task. The study of Torah is the way in which Jews participate in this paradoxical struggle. Some of the ideas that students of the Torah struggle with include:

- ✔ Humans are created in God's image.
- ✔ God has many names, but no name can possibly be adequate.
- ✔ God exists.
- ✔ God has no gender.
- ✔ God is unique; nothing is like God is any way.
- ✔ God is everywhere.
- ✔ God is, was, and will be; God transcends time.
- ✔ God is beyond human comprehension.

The Torah is mainly God's communication to people about how to behave. Most of the Torah is directed toward the Jewish people, although it also contains instructions for all other peoples of the world. But for reasons that only God knows, the Jewish people are given extra burdens and responsibilities. God chose the Jewish people, but in no way does this status of being chosen by God imply superiority.

People have responsibilities to God and to each other, and the Torah is filled with instructions about how to fulfill both (see the later section "Living Life According to the Torah" for more about people's responsibilities to each other). Regarding a person's relationship to God, the Torah stresses

✔ Connecting with God through God's commandments

✔ Having faith in God

✔ Maintaining trust in God

✔ Accepting direction from God

✔ Understanding that God directs everything that occurs

✔ Struggling to comprehend God

✔ Communicating with God through prayer

See Chapter 2 for more information about God, the ultimate author.

Examining the Torah's Important Elements

Jewish tradition maintains that the Five Books of Moses contains everything. Yes, *everything*. Although the Torah is a religious document, it isn't a collection of abstractions in spiritual language. Rather, it uses concrete descriptions in the form of laws and stories to express abstract notions. The Torah also deals with all aspects of life, from business, agriculture, and industry to family life, sexuality, and ritual. The Torah directs human conduct in all its aspects. It urges followers to see the whole world as a Holy Temple in which each student functions as a priest whose job it is to constantly purify and sanctify the entirety of life.

The Torah consists of two parts: One is written and the other is oral. Flip to Chapter 3 for a full introduction to the treasures of the Torah.

The Written Torah

As the Torah describes, Moses was the greatest teacher and prophet who ever lived. It's important, however, to always keep in mind that Moses wasn't a perfect being. He had the noble attribute of humility, although he was also self-effacing sometimes, and he didn't always do the right thing. As my teacher has often said, "In Judaism, there are no plastic saints."

At Mount Sinai, Moses encountered God in an intimate way unlike anyone before or since, and Moses wrote down what God told him to write. The result was the Five Books of Moses. It is these five books that are the main focus of *The Torah For Dummies*. Table 1-1 shows you the names of the Five Books of Moses, which come from Greek because a few thousand years ago the Torah was translated into that language. The table also gives you the Hebrew names of the books and their translations.

Table 1-1	The Five Books of Moses	
Greek Name	*Hebrew Name*	*Translation of Hebrew Name*
Genesis	Bereshit	"In the beginning"
Exodus	Shemot	"the names"
Leviticus	Vayikra	"and He called"
Numbers	Bamidbar	"in the wilderness"
Deuteronomy	Devarim	"words"

The Torah isn't the Bible. The Jewish Bible is the book that Christians call the Old Testament, and the Five Books of Moses are the first five sections of the Jewish Bible. The other sections are the books of the Prophets (of which there are eight) and the books of other sacred writings (of which there are 11). In all, there are 24 books in the Jewish Bible, also often referred to as the Hebrew Scriptures.

The Oral Torah

When Moses encountered God and received God's message, the divine transmission included oral teachings that were never meant to be written down. An oral tradition allows for flexibility; too often when an oral teaching is written down, it's taken too literally and loses its power to adapt to changing times and circumstances. It was only after much debate and discussion that the great sages of the Jewish people decided to write down the oral teachings in a process that began a few thousand years ago. This compromise was based on the historical fact that the enemies of the Jewish people were killing so many of the Children of Israel and the sacred traditions were at a great risk of being lost.

The major elements of the Oral Torah include

- **The Mishnah** (mish-*nah*; repetition): A book consisting of six sections, written in Hebrew, that serve as a summary of the oral teachings as handed down by Moses, along with the Written Torah, to the elders of the Jewish people.

- **The Gemara** (geh-mah-*rah*; completion): Additions, written mostly in Aramaic, that serve to analyze the Mishnah, define its fine points, and also illustrate how the Five Books of Moses and the Mishnah are applied to the ever-changing conditions of life.

  The Mishnah and the Gemara appear together in the **Talmud** (tahl-*mood*; learning), which is a set of books consisting of 63 sections and also includes additional commentaries by great teachers throughout the centuries.

✔ **The Midrash** (mid-*rahsh*; interpretation): A few dozen books written over a number of centuries that serve to expand upon the details found in the Five Books of Moses and other books of the Jewish Bible. The various collections of Midrashim (plural for Midrash) teach both divine moral lessons and divine laws.

✔ **Halachah** (ha-lah-*khah*; the way to walk): The term for Jewish law. Jewish laws are either positive ("do this") or negative ("don't do this"), and 613 of them are traditionally found in the Five Books of Moses (see Appendixes B and C for the full list). This number is deceptive because there are actually thousands of Jewish teachings that grow out of the primary 613 commandments in the Torah.

Taking One Torah Book at a Time

There's an ancient Jewish tradition that the entire Five Books of Moses is actually one long name of God. The Written Torah is also traditionally seen as five separate books, each with its own character and content. The following are the Five Books of Moses, which I cover in detail in Part II:

✔ **Genesis:** The book of Genesis focuses on the creation of the universe and the creation of the Jewish family, starting with Adam and Eve, Noah, his son Shem, and ultimately with the patriarch Abraham and matriarch Sarah. The book is filled with many dramas involving the individuals who form the foundation of the Jewish people, most notably Abraham, Isaac, Jacob, Sarah, Rebecca, Rachel, Leah, and Joseph.

✔ **Exodus:** The book of Exodus essentially tells the story of the Jewish people's experience of slavery in Egypt and ultimate liberation under the leadership of Moses and his brother Aaron. This book also describes Moses's encounters with God and the receiving of the divine transmission called the Torah at Mount Sinai.

✔ **Leviticus:** This book of the Torah contains the least amount of narrative among the five. Rather, it's concerned with the rules and functions of a branch of the Jewish family that serves a unique priestly role within Judaism; it's also filled with laws, rules, and regulations of a wide variety.

✔ **Numbers:** The book of Numbers largely concerns itself with the 40-year journey through the desert, from Egypt to the Promised Land (Israel), taken by the Children of Israel. Earlier in the Torah, God promises the Land of Israel to Abraham, and it's Moses's mission to lead the freed slaves — who are the descendants of Abraham, Isaac, and Jacob — to the Promised Land. The book of Numbers provides details of many of their encounters and experiences in the desert and also includes many of the laws incumbent upon the Jewish people.

✔ **Deuteronomy:** The book of Deuteronomy is largely Moses's farewell address to his people. In this book, Moses recounts many of the key experiences of the Jewish people after their liberation from Egypt. He also takes the opportunity to repeat many teachings contained in the first four books of the Written Torah. This book ends with the death of Moses.

Living Life According to the Torah

The Torah is God's instruction book to humankind. For practical purposes, you can see these instructions as two different yet overlapping types: One is the instructions by God about how people should behave as individuals on a personal level, and the other is how people should behave in a community.

Watching your personal behavior

The Torah's instructions to people about personal behavior are based on the assumption that the details are what matters. Sure, it's lovely to say that people should be nice to each other and should love each other, but it has been proven again and again that lofty generalizations like "Be nice" or "Be fair" are never enough. The trend in the Torah is to add details rather than to make broad, sweeping statements. Without specific instructions to follow, people all too often don't really get the picture or behave as they're supposed to. The Written and Oral Torahs together show how the highest, deepest, and most profound ideals from God are applied to the ever-changing circumstances of life.

Head to Chapter 9 for more information on keeping your personal behavior in line with the Torah, including tips on treating both your family and strangers kindly.

Playing well with others in the community

The great American poet Robert Frost wrote, "Good fences make good neighbors." This is a terrific summary of the way in which the Torah concerns itself with communal behavior. As with the Torah's teachings about personal behavior, the details are what matters. While some of the general principles can be summarized as "Be honest," "Be compassionate," "Be a good boss," and "Be a good citizen," it's not enough to give sweet, abstract instructions on how people in a community should behave toward one another. Good rules, good definitions, and good fences serve a community well. The Written Torah and the Oral Torah go into minute detail on the main principles, covering just about every conceivable situation in community life.

Check out Chapter 10 for details on living by the word of the Torah in the community, including information on doing better business, dealing with property rights, and keeping order in the court.

Connecting the Torah to Judaism

The way of Judaism as a spiritual tradition is the way of Torah. The Torah is the link between God and the Jewish people. Jewish belief, Jewish law, Jewish practice, Jewish customs, Jewish holy days, and Jewish values all grow out of the Torah, as you find out in the following sections.

Taking note of the holiness of time

The great Jewish sages teach that it's possible to connect with holiness (which means connecting with God) in three ways: the holiness of space, the holiness of the human soul, and the holiness of time:

- **The holiness of space** focuses on a spot in Jerusalem known as the Holy of Holies; it's surrounded by the Holy Temple. The Holy Temple is situated in the Holy City of Jerusalem, and the Holy City is in the Holy Land of Israel. An example of a constant recognition of the holiness of space is that the Torah instructs Jews throughout the world to face Jerusalem during the three daily prayer sessions.

- **The holiness of the human soul** implies that the human soul can refine itself and make itself holy through the holy behavior as instructed by the Torah.

- **The holiness of time** is expressed through special rituals and prayers that are recited at special times and occasions. The Torah instructs the Jewish people that one of the best ways to connect with God is to observe the commandments that guide them through the various units of time.

The Jewish sages teach that the Torah concerns itself with every moment of life: from the moment of birth to the moment of death, and from the moment you wake until the moment you sleep. Just as God is everywhere in space, so too is God everywhere in time. The Torah instructs its students regarding

- The day (three prayer sessions and other daily requirements)
- The week (the six working days and the Holy Sabbath)
- The month (the observation of the new moon each month)
- The year (many holy days that appear throughout the annual Jewish calendar and are detailed in the Torah)

Chapter 11 has the complete scoop on observing holy days in Torah time.

Following Jewish customs

The Written Torah and the Oral Torah have a lot to say about how Jewish people should conduct themselves throughout each important stage of life, as shown in Table 1-2.

Table 1-2	Key Life Events and Corresponding Jewish Customs
Life Event	*Jewish Custom*
Birth	Circumcision for boys; naming the baby for both boys and girls
Coming-of-age	Bar Mitzvah for boys; Bat Mitzvah for girls
Marriage	Signing a marriage contract; husband and wife both have many rights and responsibilities
Death	Following a detailed, elaborate, and (I must say) brilliant series of steps intended to guide mourners through various stages of mourning

The Torah also has a lot to say to the Jewish people regarding all aspects of life, including

✔ The use of symbols in Judaism, such as

- Mezuzah (a sign on the doorpost of every Jewish home)
- Tzitzit (a sign on the corners of clothes that some Jews wear)
- Tefillin (a sign that actually wraps itself around your head and arm)

✔ The way to eat (eating according to the kosher laws is explained in great detail)

Go to Chapter 12 for more instruction on following Jewish customs according to the Torah.

Witnessing a Torah synagogue service

The best way to understand how the Jewish people revere the Torah is to watch or participate in the weekly Torah service held on Shabbat (Saturday) in the synagogue; I walk you through this service in Chapter 13. The elaborate ritual and public reading of the Torah is filled with solemnity, joy, reverence, and formality. The Torah resides in a special — and usually beautiful — closet found in every synagogue sanctuary. The Torah, in the form of a scroll, starts out literally dressed in the finest royal attire and then is undressed, studied, read aloud, and redressed with the utmost care and devotion.

Since ancient times, the Torah has been read publicly each week on Shabbat. This custom certainly served the Jewish people well when printed copies weren't common like they are today, and the communal gathering of Jews to hear the words of the holy Torah continues to be an emotional high point for Jewish people throughout the world. The Five Books of Moses is divided into weekly sections, and every synagogue community reads the same section each week. The entire Torah is read in the course of one year. On the Jewish holy day of **Simchat Torah** (sim-*kaht* toe-*rah*; the joy of the Torah), the last sentences are read and the first sentences begin the round of the year once again.

Writing a Torah scroll

The Five Books of Moses actually comes in two formats:

- ✔ A handwritten scroll on parchment, essential for use in the synagogue service
- ✔ A book printed on a printing press and readily available to the masses

According to the Torah, it's the responsibility of each Jewish person to handwrite a Torah scroll. Because the task is so difficult, not to mention time-consuming, Jewish law is lenient and permits you to fulfill this commandment in a number of ways, including providing financial support to qualified scribes. Some authorities say that you can also fulfill this commandment by buying books about the Torah. So purchasing *The Torah For Dummies* means that you've already begun to fulfill one of the Torah's commandments!

Flip to Chapter 14 for more information about the commandment of writing a Torah scroll.

Analyzing and studying the Torah all your life

Throughout the ages it has been frequently said that the most important activity in all Jewish life is the study of the Torah, which is the subject of Chapter 15. Many statements in Jewish holy texts support the notion that Torah study throughout a lifetime is of supreme value. Here are a few from the Talmud:

- ✔ In the same way that it's essential to feed a child, it's essential for the Jewish people to study the Torah.

- ✔ A single day of Torah study is more important than 1,000 sacrifices in the Holy Temple.

- ✔ God cries over people who are able but nevertheless neglect Torah study.

- ✔ God studies the Torah every day.

- ✔ Non-Jews who study the Torah to learn of their obligations are as great as the High Priest in the Holy Temple.

Jewish tradition considers every letter, word, line, story, and detail of the Written Torah to be of divine origin and therefore containing an infinity of meanings. In principle, it's impossible to say that any one line, story, or book of the Torah means only one thing. There are levels upon levels of meaning in every tiny detail of the Written Torah.

In principle, it's assumed that everybody hears the Torah differently. This doesn't mean that Torah study is a free-for-all where every and any interpretation is always correct. But as my teacher says, each person has a personal relationship with God, and that relationship is a completely private affair. You can and should work with a Torah teacher and try to understand the Torah through the commentaries of the great sages, but in the final analysis, you have to trust yourself and make your own decisions. As one tradition states, each of us is a letter in the Torah, and each of us must find our letter.

Although the Written Torah is in Hebrew and the Oral Torah is mostly in Aramaic, the good news is that there are lots of English translations of the Five Books of Moses and also English translations of the commentaries that are essential to arriving at a more complete understanding of the Torah (as you find out in Chapter 16). Jewish life is an immersion into the Torah and into the literature that the Torah has inspired. My home library is filled with a few thousand books (literally) on the Torah. *The Torah For Dummies* is one more book for that ever-growing Torah library. In fact, this book is designed to be a doorway that opens into a vast garden of profound Torah knowledge.

A well-known statement in the Oral Torah summarizes the importance of Torah study:

> *Rabbi Tarfon used to say: You are not required to complete the task, but neither are you free to withdraw from it. If you have learned a lot of Torah, much reward has been prepared for you, and your Employer can be trusted to compensate you for your labor. But know that the reward of the righteous is reserved for the World to Come.*

> Mishnah, Ethics of the Fathers 2:21

Chapter 2

Encountering God, the Ultimate Author

In This Chapter

▶ Understanding how God created the world and its people

▶ Discovering some of God's names

▶ Getting a grip on God's nature

▶ Grasping the ways to grow closer to God

▶ Finding out how to communicate with God

*T*he Torah is full of teachings on just about every aspect of human experience. As you find out in Part III and throughout this book, there are teachings about human relations, business practices, ethical behavior, treatment of the poor, family life, sexual relations, holy days, rituals, courts, and criminal law, and that's just the tip of the iceberg.

But at its core, the Torah is a holy book about God and God's relation to the world. The Torah establishes that the source for all teachings, and indeed the source of everything that exists, is God.

It's not easy to talk about God because, according to Jewish wisdom, it's impossible for humans to fully conceive of God. God is ultimately beyond anything that humans can grasp. The study of Torah is, according to Jewish tradition, the way for Jews to travel a path to God. In this chapter, I introduce you to God's creation of the world, some of the ways in which the Torah describes the nature of God, and ways in which you can relate to and communicate with God.

Enter God, Stage Center: Creating a New World (And People to Fill It)

The Torah doesn't waste any time introducing God. The very first sentence of the very first book of the Torah, the book of Genesis (see Chapter 4), begins with the famous line, "In the beginning God created the heavens and the earth." Getting to know God is essential to Jewish life, and as you find out in the following sections, a good way to start gathering this knowledge is to understand the basics of God's creation of the world as described in the Torah.

Switching on the light (and keeping it on)

The first words spoken by God as recorded in the Torah are "Let there be light" (Genesis 1:3). Torah commentators (you meet some of them in Chapter 16) have observed that the light created by God at the very beginning of Genesis is in some ways similar but is really not the same as the light that people know in their everyday lives. The natural light of the world comes from the sun. But when God says "Let there be light" at the beginning of the Torah, this light exists before God's creation of the sun, moon, stars, and planets. Sometimes this original light is referred to in sacred Jewish texts as "Primordial Light." Many Torah commentators over the centuries point out that an understanding of the light in the world can lead to a deeper understanding of the original light.

God's divine light emanates from its divine source. According to the great sages of Jewish tradition, everything in the world ultimately is formed by the primal light at the beginning of the creation story. There's a fundamental view within Jewish thought that makes an important point about creation: Some people in the world believe that God did indeed create the world but that after the creation was finished, God withdrew from the world. In contrast, Jewish sages express the oral tradition within Judaism that God is continuously creating the world, continuously speaking the words "Let there be light."

One illustrious Jewish sage illustrates the point of continuous creation by suggesting that if God were to turn His attention away from the universe for a moment, it would all disappear. As a primary belief, Jewish tradition teaches that God continues to create the world (or sustains it) and is involved in every aspect of it. As the founder of Chasidism, the great Rabbi Israel, known as the **Baal Shem Tov** (bah-*ahl* shem towv; the Master of the Good Name), teaches, "Not even a blade of grass moves without God as its mover."

The use of electrical imagery helps to explain this view of creation. When you turn on an electric light switch, the current flows and illuminates an electric light bulb. If you turn off the light switch, the current is blocked, and the light extinguishes itself. As the great Torah sages say, the world is created by the downpour of divine plenty that's constantly flowing from above; in other words, God never turns off the switch of light and creation.

Using the Torah as a blueprint

Ancient rabbinic tradition offers a startling and profound image regarding the creation of the world. The rabbis suggest that when God created the world, the Torah was God's plan. The Zohar (an ancient mystical commentary on the Torah; see Chapter 3) actually says that God looked into the Torah and made the world accordingly.

This image presents a challenge, because how could God create and look into the Torah before He even created the world? After all, isn't the Torah the sacred text that God gave to Moses? The Jewish spiritual path requires that you establish a unique and intimate relationship with a Torah that is Infinite. The Torah scroll used today is a physical form of the primordial Torah. The image of God looking into the Torah to create the world is also the basis for Torah students' assumption that everything is contained in the Torah. A well-known saying from a sage who lived many centuries ago named Ben Bag Bag can be found in the standard daily Jewish prayer book. Ben Bag Bag speaks about the value of studying the Torah and says: "Turn it and turn it again for all is in it."

A basic assumption of the study of the Torah is that every last letter of the Torah was dictated to Moses by God and has meaning. Even if a word is spelled incorrectly for example, with a missing letter, the assumption on the part of students of the Torah is that this missing letter is not an error but in fact has a reason and has content of its own. After all, the Torah is a book unlike any other book. Many of its most profound teachings are buried deep within the text; the Torah requires ingenuity and brilliance in order to decipher its message. The assumption remains that everything — including the plans for the creation of the world — is contained in the Torah. Jewish tradition teaches that by carefully analyzing the Torah text you can discover many mysteries, even the mystery of God's ongoing creation of the world at this very moment.

Creating the world in six "days"

Early in the book of Genesis (the first book of the Torah), a description of the creation of the world appears. According to the story, it took God six days, or stages, to create the world and everything in it. Students of the Torah don't understand this passage on the literal level.

Why? People measure time in the world by the movement of the sun, earth, and moon. But the Torah narrative doesn't introduce the sun and moon until the fourth day, leading Torah commentators to conclude that the "day" spoken of in the process of God's creation wasn't the typical 24-hour day as humans experience it. Rather, the six days of creation represent six stages of the world's development, and as great Torah commentaries throughout the centuries indicate, the descriptions of these days contain some of the profound secrets of the mystery of creation. The bottom line is that the Torah is neither a sourcebook for scientific information nor a book of history (as you find out in Chapter 3). Rather, the Torah is concerned with eternal spiritual matters and how to make them a part of your life.

Taking a break from creating (and not because God grew tired)

According to the Torah, God created the world in six days and then "rested" on the seventh day. This day of rest, known as **Shabbat** (shah-*baht*; Sabbath), isn't actually considered a real day according to the sages of the Torah. Instead, Shabbat is a special phenomenon, a special gift that God created and gave to the world. Throughout the centuries, Jews have received this divine gift of Shabbat, and convincing arguments claim that the Jewish people's adherence to the rhythm of the week and the culmination of that week in the celebration of Shabbat has been crucial to their survival. (I go into much greater detail about the Torah's conception of Shabbat in Chapter 11.)

Making humans in God's image

This unusual phrase appears in the book of Genesis: "Let us make man in our image, after our likeness" (Genesis 1:26). Many students of the Torah have asked the question, "Who is the 'us' and the 'our' referred to in this line?"

Torah sages suggest that the "us" refers to the ministering angels with whom God consulted. The Talmud and many other Jewish spiritual texts also teach that a person is to be considered a whole world, so when God said "Let us," He was referring to the entire universe. (And "world" and "universe" are synonymous.)

People also have asked how God actually created man. The great Torah commentator **Rashi** (*rah*-she; see Chapter 16) indicates that the verse implies that God first created a mold, or a conceptual archetype, from which to create humans. The great Torah commentator known as the **Ramban** (rahm-*bahn*; see Chapter 16) teaches that humans are a microcosm of the whole of Creation and that contained within each person are elements of everything in the universe.

Physical descriptions of God in the Torah text in no way literally describe God; rather, the words were chosen based on familiar things to attempt to express the inexpressible. So, for example, when you read of God's "eyes," the Torah isn't suggesting that God has physical eyes. It's suggesting that one attempt to know the unknowable God is to try to grasp God as being infinite and therefore as knowing (or seeing) everything. (For more about this concept, see the later section "God stretches out His arm, but He has no arms.")

Given the nonphysical nature of God, the great rabbis ask in what way man is made in God's image. The answer is in the fact that man has free will. Man is given the ability to choose freely and therefore to create and destroy. The Torah sees a human being as the pinnacle of creation, the reason for the creation of the world. Man occupies a unique place in the cosmos of the Torah: He's considered the only actor on the cosmic stage who has a spark of God within, as evidenced by man's power of will and power to create and destroy. One of the profound paradoxes of Jewish theology is expressed in the Talmud by Rabbi Akiva, who says, "All is foreseen *and* free will is given." This paradox is a great challenge but is an essential part of Jewish life and thought: On the one hand, God is in control of everything, and yet, at the same time humans function under the assumption that there is free will. Jewish tradition requires students of the Torah to meditate throughout life on this theological riddle or paradox.

Calling God by Many Names in the Torah

The Torah refers to God by many different names. No one name can possibly represent God, nor can any long list of names even begin to suggest something close to the inconceivable nature of God. As you find out in the following sections, the Torah suggests a number of keywords that, being rich and deep with meaning, may be used as God's names.

Different aspects of God revealed in common names

Each name of God that appears in the Torah invokes its own meaning. Students of the Torah constantly try to reach the unreachable, by which I mean reach with their minds and hearts to more and more vast conceptions of God. As the author of the Torah, God gives Himself many different names, each one revealing a different aspect of the Divine.

The many names of God that appear in the Torah text and that have been used for centuries among Jews include:

- **Adonai** (ah-*doe*-noy): This name of God, which appears in every standard Jewish blessing, is technically the plural form of "my Lord." According to Jewish tradition, you pronounce this name of God only when you're reciting a blessing.

- **Ehyeh Asher Ehyeh** (*eh*-yeh *ah*-share *eh*-yeh): This phrase from Exodus 3:14 in which Moses asks God for His name is often translated as "I will be Who I will be" or "I am that I am." The word **ehyeh** (*eh*-yeh) also can be translated in the future tense to mean "I am what I will be," "I will be what I will be," or "I am becoming what I am becoming." This aspect of the future is noteworthy because the Torah represents God as being beyond time; God knows everything, including the way in which history will unfold.

- **Elohim** (el-oh-*heem*): This form of God's name often refers to God's justice. It's only spoken during prayers and blessings.

- **HaMakom** (hah-mah-*comb*): Jewish theology often refers to God as "the place" of the world, so this term literally means "the place." This is my favorite name for God.

- **HaShem** (hah-*shem*): Torah students worldwide use this name, which means "the Name."

- **Shaddai** (shah-*die*): Often translated as "the Almighty," this name of God often is used in reference to God as the guardian of the Jewish people. It's only spoken during prayers and blessings.

- **Yah:** This is the first part of the Tetragrammaton (see the following section). It's also the source of the Rastafarian name of God, Jah, which often is heard in reggae music.

Many scholars have misinterpreted the names of God that appear in the Torah. In fact, a whole field of biblical studies known as the Documentary Hypothesis developed out of the attempt to prove that the Torah is made up of lots of old documents and stories, thus explaining the variety of God's names. Torah scholars reject this theory based on the understanding that there are profound reasons for the many different names of God that appear in the Torah. Each name reveals a different aspect of the Divine. It's really no different from people's names and how they're used in daily life. Take my name, for example: Depending on the situation, I'm called "Arthur," "Mr. Kurzweil," "Abba" (Hebrew for "dad"), "sir," "Avraham Abba ben Chayim Shaul" (my Hebrew name, used when I am called up to bless the Torah), "mister," "rabbi," and still other names. Each name reveals a different aspect of my activities and relationships in the world.

YHVH: The name of God that's never spoken

YHVH (in Hebrew, it's the letters, "yud," "hay," "vav," and "hay"), which appears over 6,500 times in the Torah, often is considered the most important of God's names and is the one referred to as *the Tetragrammaton,* or *the four-letter name of God.* The pronunciation of this name of God is strictly forbidden because, of all the names of God, it contains the most hidden and profound mysteries. This precious name must be protected and not simply bandied about or used informally. Paradoxically, although this name of God is the deepest and most profound name, it's the one that must not be spoken. This name is so significant and powerful, but ultimately there's no word or name that can adequately represent God. According to Jewish law, only the High Priest in Jerusalem's Holy Temple is allowed to pronounce the four-letter name of God, and he can only do so one day a year — on the holy day of Yom Kippur.

The four-letter name of God has been the subject of much study and the object of intense meditation by Jews throughout history. One explanation of the four letters indicates the following:

- ✔ The first letter, the **yud,** is the smallest letter in the Hebrew alphabet (see Chapter 14 for more details) and represents the essential, original point out of which everything grows.

- ✔ The second letter, the **hey,** expands upon the yud just as the human intellect takes ideas and expands them.

- ✔ The third letter, the **vov,** is the sixth letter of the Hebrew alphabet and refers to the six central attributes of God (and of man) as represented in Jewish theology.

- ✔ The fourth letter, the **hey,** represents the vastness of everything. As the fifth letter of the Hebrew alphabet, it represents the quintessential, or the summation of all creation.

A big name from a big misunderstanding

One popular name for God throughout the world is **Jehovah** (jeh-*hoe*-vah). But Jehovah actually is based on a big misunderstanding. In some ancient texts, an unusual combination of two of God's names were merged. The four-letter name of God was written with the vowels of the word "Adonai" (another name of God; see the earlier section "Different aspects of God revealed in common names") beneath it. In other words. the vowels "a," "o," and "a" were inserted into YHVH, resulting in "YAHOVAH," which was ultimately translated as "Jehovah."

Getting to Know the Nature of God through the Torah

In Jewish tradition, the way to find the path to God is to study the Torah. In addition to all its teachings about behavior and ritual (see Parts III and IV for details), the Torah is also the main source for information about the nature of God. Just as it's impossible to summarize God in a sentence or a paragraph, it's impossible to confine one's understanding of God to one thing or one level of understanding. But by studying the Torah and seeing the way in which it describes God, students begin to understand some of God's nature.

God exists eternally

According to the Torah's view of existence, God is the source of everything, and God is eternal — He is, He was, and He will be. The first of the Ten Commandments, "I am the Lord thy God," is the commandment to recognize God's existence. This simple statement is at the core of all Jewish belief and everything that the Torah represents. (Flip to Chapter 17 for more on the Ten Commandments.)

The Torah sage Maimonides, known as the Rambam, is the author of a masterpiece known as the **Mishneh Torah** (mish-*neh* toe *rah*; the Second Torah). The 14-volume work accomplishes an amazing goal: to document every Torah law and teaching, both in the Written Torah and in the Oral Torah (see Chapter 3). For centuries, Maimonides's Mishneh Torah has been considered an extraordinary masterpiece. Maimonides begins the work by saying, "The foundation of all foundations and the pillar of all wisdom is to know God." His message is that knowing that God exists is fundamental.

God isn't a "He"

The Torah is written in Hebrew, and its references to God often use the masculine form. As in English, the use of male pronouns often has no relation to gender; for example, people talk about "mankind" when they really mean "humankind." In the Torah, God isn't a male, and any effort to conceive of God as a male is limiting and therefore is forbidden according to the tradition of the Torah. Using gender-specific pronouns in reference to God is merely a linguistic limitation.

The rabbis in the Talmud often use a female form in reference to God; when they write of hearing the voice of God, they use the phrase **bat kol** (baht kole; daughter's voice). The term also means "echo," implying that when the

Talmudic rabbis heard a heavenly voice, it wasn't God's actual voice but more like an echo of God's voice. Recall that the Talmud is a recording of the oral tradition of the Jewish people and an explication of the teachings of the Oral Torah that Moses received on Mount Sinai along with the Written Torah (see Chapter 5).

God is a single entity

A prayer known as the **Shema** (sheh-*mah*) is recited twice a day in Jewish life, and its words come from the Torah. Its lead sentence, which is best known among Jews, is **Shema Yisrael Adonai Elohaynu Adonai Ekhad** (sheh-*mah* yis-rah-*ehl* ah-doe-*nahy* eh-low-*hay*-new ah-doe-*nahy* eh-*khahd*; Hear O Israel, the Lord our God the Lord is One). In other words, the daily ritual among Jews establishes and repeats the view of God as One.

As long as there has been a Torah, students have contemplated the meaning of the word **Ekhad** (one). After all, they know that God has many names because no name can contain him (I discuss God's names earlier in this chapter). On the other hand, Torah conception of God is that God is One, and it's forbidden to ultimately conceive of God as having parts. The oneness of God is a profound, deep, and mysterious concept as well as the subject of deep Jewish meditation. God is considered to be a unity, which means that God is a single whole and a complete entity. Ultimately, God can't be divided into parts.

God is everywhere — yes, everywhere

Jewish teachings describe God as omnipresent. With the idea that God is everywhere and both near and far, it's important to make a distinction between the Torah view of God and pantheism. The point of view of the Torah is that everything resides in God, whereas pantheism is marked by the notion that everything is God. As I mention earlier in this chapter, my favorite name of God is HaMakom, which means "the place;" God is "the place" of the world. According to Kabbalah, which is the abstract theology of Judaism (see my book *Kabbalah For Dummies,* published by Wiley), God contracted His infinite self, creating a vacated space within Himself, to make room for the world.

Here's another way to think of this concept: One way that God is described in Jewish liturgy is **Aviynu Malkaynu** (ah-*vee*-new mahl-*kay*-new; our Father our king). This phrase implies that God is both near and far. Your father is close and familiar; you can sit on your father's lap and touch his cheek. A king, on the other hand, is someone whom you may never see in your lifetime.

God stretches out His arm, but He has no arms

Students of the Torah constantly confront a seeming contradiction within the text. The Torah makes it clear that no person can conceive of God, and yet at times it describes God in human terms.

A famous image from the Torah is of the "outstretched arm of God." The Torah says, "I am God, and I shall take you out from under the burdens of Egypt. I shall rescue you from their service. I shall redeem you with an outstretched arm and with great judgments" (Exodus 6:6). An outstretched arm is a very concrete image. Yet it's forbidden by Jewish law to conceive of God in any concrete way or to limit God with any image. So how do you reconcile this image? An important principle of Torah study is that "the Torah speaks in the language of man." This notion, repeated so often in commentaries on the Torah throughout the centuries (see Chapter 16), is a reminder that people use finite images to grasp the infinite, knowing full well the impossibility of the task. These human concrete images make suggestions, but Torah literature throughout the ages warns Torah students to beware of the ways in which concrete images can get in the way rather than clarify.

Growing Closer to God with the Torah's Help

The spiritual path in Judaism has as its main goal the deepening of one's relationship with God. The Jewish answer to the question, "What is the purpose of life?" is pleasure; God creates humans to provide them with pleasure. And what is the greatest pleasure according to Jewish tradition? It's knowledge of God. In the Jewish tradition, the more you know God, the closer (spiritually) you can get to God, and the closer you are to God, the greater the pleasure you feel and experience. As you discover in the following sections, one way to grow closer to God is through the Torah's teachings.

Understanding how awesome God is

The Hebrew term **yir'at HaShem** (year-*aht* hah-*shehm*) is sometimes translated as "a fear of God" but is better understood as "in awe of God." When you think about the fact that there are billions of stars in the galaxy, which is just one of a vast number of galaxies, it becomes clear that the universe is inconceivably gigantic. Thinking, then, that God is the Creator of the universe begins to inspire me to feel that God is indeed awesome.

Today, with advancements in computer technology, I think that grasping the notion that God knows everything isn't quite the challenge that it once was. After all, it's fair to say that we're just at the beginning of the computer age, and yet a small computer sitting on your desk easily can keep track of billions of bits of information. If a tiny computer can track all that information, then God, the Creator of the universe, surely can keep track of and have knowledge of everything. To even begin to imagine this is to imagine an awesome God.

For me, I relate the awesomeness of God to the awesome sight I see when I look down on the Grand Canyon. The immensity is awesome and makes me feel very small. So when I stand before God and recite my prayers, one of the emotions that comes over me is the apprehension of God as awesome.

The Torah urges people to build relationships with God. At the beginning of one of the most popular sections of the Oral Torah, known as *The Saying of the Fathers,* the text says, "Be not like servants who serve their masters for the sake of receiving a reward, but be like servants who serve their master not upon the condition of receiving a reward; *and let the awe of Heaven be upon you.*" In other words, the Torah teaches Torah students to serve God without an ulterior motive and to feel awe as they serve. This kind of instruction motivates and molds students of the Torah as their relationships with God deepen.

Developing faith in and trusting God

The Hebrew word for "faith" is **emunah** (eh-*moo*-nah). The great sages of Jewish tradition teach that one of life's ongoing activities is a deepening of faith in God. Even if you believe that you receive faith as a gift from above, it's a common spiritual activity to work on one's faith through prayer, study, and deep contemplation. The goal is the belief in the following:

- ✔ That there is a God
- ✔ That God sustains the world
- ✔ That nothing happens without God allowing it to happen
- ✔ That God reveals Himself to His creation in many ways, including through His instruction book, the Torah

My teacher has taught me how important it is to recognize that even the most pious people have moments or periods of doubt. Given the abundance of bad news and tragedy in the world, it's easy to feel doubtful about the existence and nature of God. Does God exist? Is God a God of love and compassion? Does God take care of his creation? These kinds of questions can inspire doubt. The cultivation of faith in God is one of the important spiritual challenges of life.

It doesn't take much to shake your faith when you witness painful events around you or when you see bad things happening to good people or vice versa. It's easy to wonder if life makes any sense or if there's any justice in the world. The great Jewish sages teach the spiritual concept of **bitachon** (bit-ah-*khone*; trust), which has become traditional Jewish belief. As small specks in a vast universe, humans can barely expect to see everything or understand everything. The view is quite limited, making it easy to draw negative conclusions from the events around you. The spiritual attribute of bitachon expresses the feeling that despite your doubts, you know in the inner recesses of your heart that God knows what He is doing, so everything that happens is ultimately for the best.

Two of the major story lines in the Five Books of Moses are those of Abraham and of Moses. Both Abraham (the father of the Jewish people) and Moses (Judaism's greatest teacher, prophet, and leader) begin their journeys with calls from God to listen and to trust God. By studying the Torah and by learning how to listen to God, students of the Torah learn to trust that what happens in life has a divine purpose.

What's the purpose of bad news and suffering? Trust in God includes two seemingly paradoxical assumptions: It's important to improve and repair the world, and at the same time it's vital to trust that what God allows has a purpose. As one of my Torah teachers says, "Every descent is for the sake of ascension."

Dealing with the paradox of free will

When you cultivate a deeper relationship with God, you eventually arrive at the point that deals with the paradox of free will. On the one hand, Jewish tradition teaches that everything is foreseen by God and that God knows everything that will happen. On the other hand, Jewish tradition teaches that human beings have free will and can choose freely. Two concepts in relating to God can help students of the Torah handle this paradox: clinging to God and being supervised by God.

Clinging to God

The paradox of free will is resolved within the concept of **d'veykut** (dih-vay-*khoot*; clinging). D'veykut implies a clinging to God with such faith, devotion, dedication, and awareness that your will and God's will merge into one will. Sometimes d'veykut is described as a smashing of the ego and a merging into God. When a person arrives at a profound level of d'veykut, he almost stops being aware of his separateness from God and begins to glimpse the secret of the unity of all things.

In the book of Deuteronomy, Moses offers a long discourse on the ways of relating to God and getting closer to God. Moses said, "Oh Israel, what does God ask of you? Only to be in awe of God, to go in all His ways, and to love Him, and to serve Him, your God, with all your heart and all your soul, to observe the commandments of God, both those you can understand and those you cannot understand" (Deuteronomy 10:12–13).

Moses continues with many details of instruction and advice about relating to God. Finally, Moses summarizes and says that the commandment to develop a relationship with God is really an effort "to love God, to walk in God's ways through God's commandments, and to cleave to God" (Deuteronomy 11:22). The great Torah commentator the Ramban teaches that cleaving to God means always remembering God.

Being supervised by God

An important spiritual concept in traditional Jewish thought is **hashgakha pratit** (hahsh-*gah*-khah *prah*-teet; private supervision). This concept recognizes that every individual is under the private supervision of God. It's the awareness that the infinite God is constantly involved in every detail of existence, from the largest cataclysm to the tiniest movement of an insect.

The concept of hashgakha pratit also seems to challenge the belief in free will. While Jews recognize that the whole universe is under God's direct and individual supervision, they also recognize the divine human characteristic of free choice. The entire contents of the Five Books of Moses can be seen as stories of divine intervention, hashgakha pratit. Although there are hundreds of moments when the Torah tells of God's actions, students of the Torah don't assume that God is active in the world only when the Torah specifically indicates something that God has done. God ultimately allows *everything* to happen.

An interesting example is the book of Esther, found in the Holy Scriptures (the Bible). The book of Esther is the only book in the Scriptures where God isn't mentioned even once. The great Torah commentators point out that the book of Esther contains a great number of details about a complicated story and that God's name doesn't appear because God is present in every detail of the story, as in life. Jews live with the assumption of free will despite the fact that God foresees everything and knows everything that will happen.

Realizing you can never fully grasp God (and what to do about it)

My teacher taught me that if you ever think or feel that you fully understand God, one thing is sure: You're wrong. He also taught me that, in his words, "being Jewish is difficult: We have to establish a personal relationship with a God that we cannot conceive of." This reality often is a huge stumbling block for people because it's difficult to live with uncertainty. But although humans can't fully grasp God, the Torah teaches that we can be certain that there is a God, that God cares about and guides His creation, and that everything is ultimately for the best.

My bulletin board holds a quote from a book about physics that says, "In physics you never understand a new idea, you just get used to it." In some ways you can say the same thing about God: You can't really understand God, you simply get used to God. Jews who haven't grown up with a spiritual practice but who decide later in life to explore traditional Judaism often report an experience of God's presence unfolding and developing as a result of studying sacred texts regularly and praying daily. For the last 30 years, I've been studying the Torah, its commentaries, and related texts. I've been trying to follow the teachings of the Torah through proper behavior and the fulfillment of the commandments. I pray daily, and when I'm not praying, I'm often thinking about God. I can honestly say that I experience God as a constant presence in my life. But do I know God? Of course not. As my teacher says, "If you think you've arrived, you're lost."

But there came a point in my life when God's presence was constant for me and, in fact, God was more real than anything else I experienced. It's my experience that Torah study, prayer, the observance of the commandments, private meditation, and the performance of good deeds result in the awakening to God. At a certain point, as my teacher put it, you become aware of the fact that you're in the palace of the King. It becomes possible to establish a very close relationship with a God whom you can't conceive of.

Communicating Directly with God

It has been said that the Torah is God speaking to humans and that, in Jewish life, the Talmud (the Oral Torah) is humans speaking to God. The Talmud consists of over 60 volumes of discussions and debates covering just about every possible topic that exists. It's also an incredibly close reading of the Torah and is basically an effort to hear God's voice and to understand what it is that God wants of His people. In the following sections, I give you a quick rundown on how to communicate directly with God with the help of the Torah. For more about the Talmud, turn to Chapter 3.

Shhh . . . God is speaking! Hearing God's voice

In Jewish thought, the entire creation — all the details of everything that exists — is really the Voice of God. In fact, the Jewish sages describe creation as being constantly sustained by God's speaking.

In Jewish life, there are a number of ways to hear God's voice. The first and most primary is to study the Torah (see Chapter 15 for tips on Torah analysis) and the commentaries by the great sages (see Chapter 16 for details).

A student once asked my teacher how to hear God, and my teacher said, "Well, the first thing you must do is quiet down." He went on to say that people's thoughts are often the very thing that gets in the way of hearing God. In a tale from Buddhist tradition, a student asked a master to teach him wisdom. The teacher suggested that they first have some tea. When the teacher began to pour the tea into the student's cup, the student saw that the teacher kept pouring the tea without stopping. The student said, "Teacher, the cup is full." The teacher said, "This is your first lesson: Unless you make room for new teachings, you will not be able to receive them."

One of the most powerful phrases in the entire Five Books of Moses is **Lech l'chah** (lehkh le-*khah*; go): God tells Moses to go "from your land, from your relatives and from your house" (Genesis 12:1). When young Abraham left his home and essentially took the first steps of what would become the traditions of Judaism, Christianity, and Islam, he emptied himself of the ways of his former culture in order to hear God. Several times a day in the daily Jewish prayer book, Jews recite the Shema prayer. (I describe this prayer in more detail later in this chapter.) The divine command in this prayer is to listen.

Saying hello to God

In Judaism, prayer is basically a human effort to simply say hello to God. The Jewish sages instituted formal prayer three times a day as well as the hundreds of blessings to say throughout the day as a vehicle to keep a person on the right track and to constantly cultivate a close, deep, personal relationship with God.

Formally pray to God three times daily

The great sages of Jewish tradition established three daily prayer sessions: morning, afternoon, and evening. These three prayer sessions are said to derive from verses in the Torah regarding the three Patriarchs: Abraham, Isaac, and Jacob.

- ✔ **Abraham:** The rabbis in the Talmud teach that the morning prayers, known as **Shacharit** (shah-khah-*reet*), are based on the verse in the Torah, "And Abraham arose in the morning to the place where he had stood before God" (Genesis 19:27).

- ✔ **Isaac:** The rabbis teach that the afternoon prayers, known as **Mincha** (*mihn*-khah), are based on the verse in the Torah, "Isaac went out to converse in the field towards evening" (Genesis 24:63). The rabbis teach that the conversation was between Isaac and God. Because the Torah describes this as happening "before evening," they conclude that the time of Mincha is in the afternoon before sunset.

- ✔ **Jacob:** The rabbis teach that the evening prayer service, known as **Ma'ariv** (mah-ah-*reev*), is based on this Torah verse that speaks of Jacob: "He came to the place and slept there" (Genesis 28:11).

The centerpiece of all three prayer sessions is an ancient prayer called the **Amidah** (ah-mee-*dah*; standing). As the name implies, the prayer is recited while standing in silence and facing Jerusalem. The prayer consists of 19 parts. Here are the names of those parts and their content:

1. **Avot** (ancestors): Praising the God of the patriarchs Abraham, Isaac, and Jacob

2. **Gevurot** (powers): Praising God for God's power

3. **Kedushat ha-Shem** (the sanctification of the Name): Praising God's holiness

4. **Binah** (understanding): Petitioning God for wisdom and understanding

5. **Teshuvah** (return or repentance): Praising God for repentance

6. **Selichah** (forgiveness): Asking for forgiveness for all sins

7. **Geulah** (redemption): Praising God as a rescuer of the Children of Israel

8. **Refuah** (healing): Asking God to heal the sick

9. **Birkat HaShanim** (blessing for years): Asking God to bless the earth's produce

10. **Galuyot** (diasporas): Asking God for the Jews to return to the land of Israel

11. **Birkat HaDin** (justice): Asking God to restore righteous judges

12. **Birkat HaMinim** (the heretics): Asking God to destroy anti-Jewish heretical sects

13. **Tzadikim** (righteous): Asking God to have mercy on all who have divine trust

14. **Bo'ne Yerushalayim** (Builder of Jerusalem): Asking God to rebuild Jerusalem

15. **Birkat David** (Blessing of David): Asking God to bring the messiah

16. **Tefillah** (prayer): Asking God to accept our prayers and be compassionate

17. **Avodah** (service): Asking God to restore the Temple services

18. **Hoda'ah** (thanksgiving): Giving thanks for our lives, our souls, and miracles

19. **Shalom** (peace): Praying for peace, blessings, kindness, and compassion

Read the Shema twice daily

The oldest prayer in Judaism is the **Shema** (sheh-*mah*; hear or listen). Based on a few verses in the Torah, its core is as follows:

Hear, O Israel, God is our Lord, God is One.

Love God your Lord with all your heart, with all your soul, and with all your might.

These words which I am commanding you today must remain on your heart. Teach them to your children and speak of them when you are at home, when traveling on the road, when you lie down and when you get up.

Bind these words as a sign on your hand and let them be an emblem in the center of your head.

Also write them on your doorposts of your houses and gates.

Deuteronomy 6:4–9

Notice that the verses command you to speak of God "when you lie down and when you get up." This Torah commandment is fulfilled by reciting the Shema twice a day, in the morning and at night.

Express gratitude before and after you eat

Deuteronomy 8:10 says, "When you eat and are satisfied, you must therefore bless God your Lord for the good land that He has given you." In the Jewish tradition, this commandment is fulfilled by reciting the **Birkat HaMazon** (beer-*khaht* ha-mah-*zone*; blessing of the food) after each meal.

Here are the names of each of four blessings of the Birkat Ha-Mazon, along with their content:

- **Birkat Hazan** (beer-*khat* ha-*zahn*; the blessing for providing food): Thanks God for giving food to the world

- **Birkat Ha-Aretz** (beer-*khat* ha-*ah*-retz; the blessing for the land): Thanks God for bringing His children forth from the land of Egypt and for giving them the land of Israel

- **Birkat Yerushalayim** (beer-*khat* yeh-roo-shah-*la*-yeem; the blessing for Jerusalem): Asks God to rebuild Jerusalem and to bring the messiah

- **Birkat Ha-Tov v'Ha-Maytiv** (beer-*khat* ha-*towv* v'ha-*may*-teev; the blessing for being good and doing good): Stresses that God's work is good, that God is good, and that God does good

Chapter 3

Examining the Treasures of the Torah

T he Torah is filled with dazzling gems of all kinds. There are stories, spiritual ideas, laws, life lessons, and more. So when Jews say "Torah," the meaning goes beyond the text of the Five Books of Moses and includes all the teachings of the Oral Torah as well as the teachings and commentaries that grow out of both the Written and the Oral Torahs.

The Torah is like an onion, with layer upon layer of teachings. Understanding the structure of the Torah and its basic elements can help you uncover the gems, work through the layers, and be illuminated by the divine light embedded within it. I introduce you to the basics of the Torah's form and function in this chapter.

A Little History: Moses and the Torah

Knowing a little background about Moses's involvement with the Torah is important because aside from God, who is, in a sense, the main character of the Torah, Moses is the central figure throughout most of the Five Books of Moses; after all, the Torah isn't called the Five Books of Moses for nothing! In the following sections, I explain the role of Moses in bringing the Torah to the world. (If you want to get to know the man a little better, turn to Part II.)

There has been lots of speculation and so-called scholarship about the Torah. Some people have tried to prove through what's known as the Documentary Hypothesis that the Torah is really a bunch of ancient documents from different times and different places that were somehow thrown together to form what's now known as the Five Books of Moses. Others, including the greatest rabbis throughout history, insist that the Torah has always been one whole document and that the "evidence" to the contrary is based on ignorance of the Torah and the way the Torah communicates its teachings and ideas. While the debates about the Torah will surely rage for as long as there are people around to debate, the important thing to remember is that the Torah is a spiritual document containing eternal ideas, lessons, and instructions for living.

Who wrote the Five Books of Moses?

The Five Books of Moses was written . . . by Moses. Of course, not everyone believes that, and there appears to be some evidence to support these doubts about Moses being its author.

For example:

- There are references to Moses in the third person. For example, Deuteronomy 34:10 states, "There has never been another prophet like Moses. . . ."
- The names of the Edomite kings appearing in Genesis 36 apparently lived after Moses died.
- Different names for God appear in different places in the Torah.
- Deuteronomy 34:5–9 contains verses that describe the death, burial, age at death, physical condition at death, and mourning period for Moses.

Despite these provocative examples, every great sage throughout Jewish history has taught that Moses wrote the Torah as dictated by God. Jewish tradition also teaches that Moses was the greatest prophet who ever lived. If you accept the notion of prophecy, you should have no difficulty in accepting that elements of the Torah like those listed here are quite possibly true.

In all fairness, not all the groups within Judaism today believe that the Torah was written by Moses and dictated by God. Whereas traditional Judaism accepts the divinity of the Torah and accepts Moses as its sole author (except, perhaps, for the last eight verses, which describe the death of Moses), some representatives of the modern, liberal movements in Judaism teach otherwise.

- Many in the Conservative movement teach that the Torah is a human document written in response God's revelation of Himself to humans at Mount Sinai. One leading Conservative scholar suggests that God didn't reveal specific commandments but rather simply revealed His existence.
- The Reconstructionist movement often teaches that the Torah wasn't inspired by God but is the folklore of the Jewish people.

> ✔ The Reform movement often suggests that the Torah may be the product of divine inspiration but was written by people in the language and context of its time.

Despite these views, the great sages throughout the centuries and the leading traditional Torah scholars today teach that the Five Books of Moses was written by Moses himself.

Are the five books about Moses or by Moses?

The Five Books of Moses are both about Moses and by Moses. God dictated the Torah to Moses, so although it seems like the Torah was written *about* Moses, Moses was the scribe who wrote as God spoke.

It's important to stress that Moses is in no way considered a god or even a perfect person. The Torah describes the mistakes that Moses made and concludes by indicating that Moses didn't get his wish to enter the Promised Land. In fact, there's no marker for the grave of Moses, and tradition doesn't indicate its location. Jewish tradition resists all temptation to make Moses into a saint.

A great teacher named Reb Zusia put a well-known teaching from Jewish tradition into words. It's recorded that Reb Zusia said, "When I stand before the heavenly court, I am not afraid that they will ask me 'Zusia, why weren't you Moses?' But I am afraid they will ask, 'Zusia, why weren't you Zusia?'" Moses isn't represented as a complete role model for everyone to emulate. He certainly had many admirable qualities (such as humility), but Judaism teaches that each person, in a sense, must become himself or herself and not mimic others.

Understanding the Torah's Structure

In a nutshell, the Torah is a written document made up of five parts that are further divided into 54 sections; this document, while important on its own, is also the start of the Jewish Holy Scriptures. But the Torah doesn't end there! The Written Torah is also accompanied by the Oral Torah and additional commentaries that can help you improve your understanding of the divine wisdom it contains.

Introducing the Five Books of Moses

As you find out in Part II, the Written Torah has five distinct sections. This is why it's called the Five Books of Moses. The five sections are

- Genesis, or **Bereshit** (bur-aye-*sheet*; in the beginning)
- Exodus, or **Shemot** (sheh-*mote*; the names)
- Leviticus, or **Vayikra** (vah-*yik*-rah; and He called)
- Numbers, or **Bamidbar** (bah-*mid*-bar; in the wilderness)
- Deuteronomy, or **Devarim** (dih-*vah*-reem; words)

The Hebrew names of each of the five books are taken from the first words of each book. The English names for the books come from the Greek translation of the Torah from its original Hebrew.

Don't let the name "the Five Books of Moses" mislead you. A Torah scroll found in a synagogue consists of one long parchment made up of dozens of pieces of parchment that have been sewn together. (Chapter 14 has more about Torah scrolls.) In ancient times, there were no bound books with pages to turn. Ancient books were scrolls, so although there are five sections of the Torah, it's really one big book.

One of the names used to refer to the Five Books of Moses is **chumash** (khoo-*mahsh*; the five). The source for this word is another Hebrew term, **chumesh** (khoo-*maysh*; a fifth), which was used to refer to one of the Five Books of Moses. But "chumash" refers to a one-volume book (with pages and a binding) containing all five books.

Dividing the Five Books of Moses into 54 sections

The five sections of the Torah are divided into 54 sections known as **parshiot** (par-she-*oat*; portion). (The singular form is **parasha,** pronounced par-ah-*shah*.) Each parasha has a name that's usually taken from either the first word or one of the first words of the parasha. Sometimes it's a word of significance indicating some important aspect of that particular Torah portion.

For example, the second parasha of the Torah is called **Parashat Noach** (*par*-ah-shot no-akh). "Noach" is the Hebrew name for the biblical figure commonly known as Noah, the builder of the ark that survived the great biblical Flood. As you may have guessed, the central story in this parasha is the story of the Flood, but the word "Noach" is the fourth word in the parasha. The parasha begins **Zeh sefer Toledot Noach** (zeh *safe*-air *toll*-dote *no*-akh; This is the book of the generations of Noah).

One portion of the Torah is read during the weekly synagogue service that I describe in Chapter 13. Because 52 weeks are in a year, sometimes two portions of the 54 are doubled up so that the entire text can be completed in one annual cycle, which begins and ends on the Jewish holy day of Simchat Torah each fall (see Chapter 11). On that day, the last verses of the fifth book of the Five Books of Moses (Deuteronomy) are read publicly, followed by the first verses of the first book of the Five Books of Moses (Genesis.) Table 3-1 lists the 54 Weekly Torah Portions and their verses.

Table 3-1	The 54 Weekly Torah Portions	
Week	*Name of Torah Portion*	*Chapter and Verse*
Bereshit (Genesis)		
1	Bereshit	1:1–6:8
2	Noach	6:9–11:32
3	Lech-Lecha	12:1–17:27
4	Vayera	18:1–22:24
5	Chayei Sara	23:1–25:18
6	Toledot	25:19–28:9
7	Vayetzei	28:10–32:3
8	Vayishlakh	32:4–36:43
9	Vayeshev	37:1–40:23
10	Miketz	41:1–44:17
11	Vayigash	44:18–47:27
12	Vayekhi	47:28–50:26
Shemot (Exodus)		
13	Shemot	1:1–6:1
14	Vaera	6:2–9:35
15	Bo	10:1–13:16
16	Beshalach	13:17–17:16
17	Yitro	18:1–20:23
18	Mishpatim	21:1–24:18
19	Terumah	25:1–27:19

(continued)

Table 3-1 *(continued)*

Week	Name of Torah Portion	Chapter and Verse
20	Tetzaveh	27:20–30:10
21	Ki Tisa	30:11–34:35
22	Vayak'hel	35:1–38:20
23	Pekudei	38:21–40:38
Vayikra (Leviticus)		
24	Vayikra	1:1–5:26
25	Tzav	6:1–8:36
26	Shmini	9:1–11:47
27	Tazria	12:1–13:59
28	Metzora	14:1–15:33
29	Acharei Mote	16:1–18:30
30	Kedoshim	19:1–20:27
31	Emor	21:1–24:23
32	Behar	25:1–26:2
33	B'chukotai	26:3–27:34
Bamidbar (Numbers)		
34	Bamidbar	1:1–4:20
35	Nasso	4:21–7:89
36	B'ha'alotecha	8:1–12:16
37	Sh'lach L'cha	13:1–15:41
38	Korach	16:1–18:32
39	Chukat	19:1–22:1
40	Balak	22:2–25:9
41	Pinchas	25:10–30:1
42	Matot	30:2–32:42
43	Masei	33:1–36:13

Week	Name of Torah Portion	Chapter and Verse
Devarim (Deuteronomy)		
44	Devarim	1:1–3:22
45	Vaetkhanan	3:23–7:11
46	Eikev	7:12–11:25
47	Re'eh	11:26–16:17
48	Shoftim	16:18–21:9
49	Ki Teitzei	21:10–25:19
50	Ki Tavo	26:1–29:8
51	Nitzavim	29:9–30:20
52	Va'yeilech	31:1–31:30
53	Ha'azinu	32:1–32:52
54	V'zot Ha'beracha	33:1–34:12

Marking the start of the Jewish Holy Scriptures

The book that Christians know as the Old Testament is referred to as the **Tanakh** (tah-*nakh*) by Jews. In English, it's often called the Holy Scriptures, and the word "Tanach" is actually an acronym for three words that represent the three parts of the Jewish Holy Scriptures.

- ✔ T stands for "Torah" (the Hebrew letter "tav"). In this context, Torah means the Five Books of Moses.
- ✔ N stands for "Neviim" (the Hebrew letter "nun"). Neviim means the prophets. Eight books are in this part.
- ✔ Ch stands for "Ketuvim" (the Hebrew letter "kaf"). Ketuvim means the writings. Eleven books are in this part.

Building on the Written Torah

The term "Torah" has a number of meanings. In this book, my main focus is on the Torah as the Five Books of Moses. But the word also refers to the two Torahs received by Moses: the Written Torah and the Oral Torah. The Written

Torah is the text of the Five Books of Moses, whereas the Oral Torah consists of the explanations of the Written Torah as well as additional wisdom imparted to Moses by God. In addition, Midrash can help you read between the lines of the Written and Oral Torahs. I discuss the Oral Torah and Midrash in the following sections.

The Oral Torah

One of the oral traditions of the Jewish people is the prohibition against writing down the oral tradition. But at a certain point in Jewish history (about 2,000 years ago), the Oral Torah was cautiously put into writing because the leadership of the Jewish people knew that there was a great risk that the tradition would be lost. Hostility, murder, and repression of Jews put terrible strain on the transmission of the oral tradition. The Jewish leadership concluded that unless the oral teachings were recorded, there was a good chance they would be lost.

The leadership also understood the risks of writing down a tradition that was meant to remain oral. Once it's put into writing, it's apt to lose its flexibility. The act of writing it may mislead the reader into thinking that the written explanation of the verse is thorough and complete. But new situations are always presenting themselves, and the oral tradition must remain flexible enough to be applied to these new conditions.

You can see one simple example of this idea of flexibility in Exodus 21:28, which states, "And if an ox gore a man or a woman. . . ." This verse is the basis of the area of Jewish law known as *personal injury* or *damages*. Today, people rarely find themselves confronted by oxen. Therefore, the biblical law must be applied to contemporary situations. The biblical "ox" may be a dog or a bus or a bicycle today.

So how did the Oral Torah come to be written down? In the second century CE, the leader of the Jewish people at that time, Judah HaNasi (Judah the Prince), wrote down in a brief, sometimes cryptic outline the basic principles of the Oral Torah. The document, which is divided into six sections, is known as the **Mishnah** (mish-*nah*; repetition). The Mishnah codified the oral tradition and immediately became a part of the sacred literature of the Jewish people.

After the Mishnah was compiled, the next several generations of great rabbis and sages analyzed the Mishnah, explaining its principles and adding additional oral teachings that had been part of Jewish tradition since the revelation of the Torah at Mount Sinai. These additions became known as the **Gemara** (geh-mah-*rah*; completion). The Mishnah and the Gemara together are known as the Talmud. Check out a page from the Talmud in Figure 3-1.

The Talmud contains 63 sections within the six sections of the Mishnah. They are as follows:

1. Zeraim (Seeds)

- Berachot: Blessings and Prayers
- Peah: Corners of fields and gleanings left for the poor
- Demai: Produce bought from a person whose tithings are suspect
- Kilayim: Forbidden mixtures of plants, animals, and clothing
- Shevi'it: The Sabbatical Year
- Terumot: Produce set aside as gifts for the Priests
- Ma'aserot: Tithes given to the Levites
- Ma'aser Sheni: Tithes eaten in Jerusalem
- Challah: The portion of dough given to the Priests
- Orlah: Forbidden fruits of trees during the first four years after planting
- Bikkurim: First fruits brought to the Holy Temple

2. Moed (Festivals)

- Shabbat: Sabbath observance (the 39 forbidden labors of the Sabbath)
- Eruvin: Rabbinical decrees regarding Sabbath boundaries
- Pesachim: Observance of the Passover festival
- Shekalim: The annual half-shekel head tax paid to the Priests in the Holy Temple
- Yoma: Observance of Yom Kippur
- Succah: Observance of Sukkot
- Beitzah: The Rabbinical decrees regarding the Festivals
- Rosh Hashanah: Observance of Rosh Hashanah
- Ta'anit: Public Fast Days
- Megillah: Reading the book of Esther on Purim
- Moed Katan: The Intermediate days of Passover and Sukkot
- Chagigah: Sacrificial offerings during the three Pilgrimage Festivals: Passover, Shavuot, and Sukkot

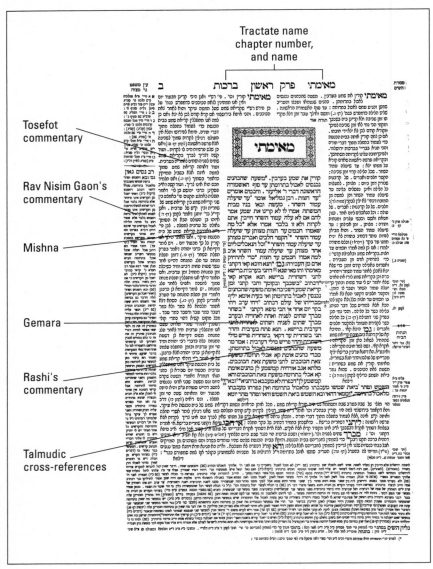

Tractate name
chapter number,
and name

Tosefot commentary

Rav Nisim Gaon's commentary

Mishna

Gemara

Rashi's commentary

Talmudic cross-references

Figure 3-1:
A sample
page from
the Talmud.

3. Nashim (Women)

- Yevamot: Marriage laws of particularly special cases

- Ketubot: Marriage contracts and the rights and duties of husbands and wives

- Nedarim: The making and annulment of vows and oaths

- Nazir: The Nazirite vows
- Sotah: The suspected adulteress
- Gittin: Laws of divorce and the annulment of marriage
- Kiddushin: Laws of marriage betrothals

4. Nezikin (Damages)

- Bava Kamma: Damage to person and property, loans and interest, and stolen goods
- Bava Metzia: Lost property, fraud, usury, and rights of hired laborers
- Bava Batra: Real estate, inheritance, evidence, and testimony
- Sanhedrin: Judicial procedure and capital punishment
- Makkot: False witnesses, cities of refuge, and corporal punishment
- Shevuot: Oaths
- Eidot: Testimonies
- Avodah Zarah: Idolatry
- Avot: Ethics of the Fathers
- Horayot: Erroneous judicial rulings

5. Kodashim (Holy Things)

- Zevachim: Animal and bird sacrifices in the Holy Temple
- Menachot: Flour offerings and wine libations
- Chullin: Laws of animal slaughter and dietary laws
- Bechorot: Firstborns
- Arachin: Consecration of personal worth to the Holy Temple
- Temurah: Exchange of sanctified things
- Keritot: Spiritual excision and sin-offerings
- Me'ila: Sacrilegious treatment of Holy Temple property
- Tamid: Daily morning and evening sacrifice
- Middot: Holy Temple architecture
- Kinnim: Birds' (nests) offerings

6. Tohorot (Purities)

- Kelim: Ritual uncleanliness of utensils and garments
- Oholot: The defilement caused by a corpse to a house
- Negaim: The complex laws of the skin disease known as **tzarat** (tzah-*raht*)

- Parah: Regulations concerning the red heifer

- Tohorot: Lesser degrees of uncleanliness lasting until sunset

- Mikva'ot: Ritual baths and immersion

- Niddah: The laws of family purity

- Machshirin: Liquids and foods that are susceptible to ritual uncleanliness

- Zavim: Secretions that render a person unclean

- Tevul Yom: Cleanliness acquired at sunset after daytime immersion

- Yadayim: The defilement of the hands and their purification

- Uktzin: Fruits and plants susceptible to uncleanliness

Midrash

Understanding the Five Books of Moses isn't limited to one meaning and certainly isn't limited to its literal meaning (see Chapter 15 for more about the different levels of meaning in the Torah). Although the Jewish approach to the Torah includes an inquiry into the plain meaning of the text, some say that there are countless ways of interpreting the many levels of the Torah.

Included within the many ways of approaching the Torah is one general method known as **Midrash** (*mid*-rahsh; explanation or interpretation). The word "midrash" has two meanings:

✔ It means analyzing the Torah.

✔ It's used to refer to the body of literature that contains the *midrashic* analysis of the Torah.

The Oral Torah includes precise ways in which the Written Torah is to be analyzed and understood. One set of rules for delving into the Torah text and its meaning is found in the traditional Jewish prayer book; the rules are known as Rabbi Ishmael's Measures. Rabbi Ishmael, who lived around the year 200 CE, presented a series of 13 principles that are applied to the Torah text. A review of these 13 principles is beyond the scope of this book, but I can offer a brief look at one principle — in fact, the first one — in order to help explain the approach. This principle forms the basis of Midrash.

The first principle is called **Kal v'chomer** (kahl v'*khow*-mare; all the more so). In modern logic, you may know it as "if . . . then." For example, *if* it's forbidden to work on the Shabbat, *then* "kal v'chomer" it's forbidden to work on Yom Kippur, which is known in Jewish tradition as the "Sabbath of Sabbaths."

Within the world of Midrash, there are two general subdivisions:

- **Midrash Halachah** (*mid*-rahsh ha-lah-*khah*; biblical interpretation to derive laws) is the way in which the great sages look at the Torah to identify divine laws. Although there are 613 laws in the Five Books of Moses (see Appendixes B and C for a full listing), in fact there are thousands of laws that can be derived from the teachings of the Five Books of Moses. These laws are derived through the method called Midrash Halachah.

- **Midrash Aggadah** (*mid*-rahsh ah-gah-*dah*; biblical interpretation to derive more details of biblical stories and moral lessons) is the way in which the great sages look at the Torah to fill in the blanks in the stories. For example, the Bible tells the famous story of Noah and his ark and the great Flood. But the Torah doesn't give any detail of what happened within the ark filled with animals during the Flood. The Midrash Aggadah tells the oral tradition, filling in the details.

There are many large, book-length collections containing midrashim (the plural of midrash). They provide a huge amount of details to supplement to text of the Five Books of Moses and to help to explain the meaning of the verses in the Torah. Several of the major midrashim are available in English translations from various publishers. Consult a good Jewish bookstore for available volumes. These collections are considered part of the Oral Torah and therefore part of the sacred texts of the Jewish people. The major ones include:

- Mekhilta (Midrash on the book of Exodus)
- Sifra (Midrash on the book of Leviticus)
- Sifre (Midrash on the books of Numbers and Deuteronomy)
- Sifre Zutta (legal Midrash on the book of Numbers)
- Tanna Devei Eliyahu (Midrash on many verses in the Torah)
- Midrash Rabbah (literally "the great Midrash"), which includes
  - Bereshit Rabbah, on Genesis
  - Shemot Rabbah, on Exodus
  - Vayikra Rabbah, on Leviticus
  - Bamidbar Rabbah, on Numbers
  - Devarim Rabbah, on Deuteronomy

The Zohar

The **Zohar** (*zoh*-har; splendor) is the major work of Kabbalah. It contains the most concentrated and extensive gathering of mystical teachings in Judaism. These teachings explore the nature of God, the structure and origins of the universe, the nature of the human soul, sin, good and evil, and many other subjects.

Originally, the Zohar consisted of many individual manuscripts, but it eventually was arranged parallel to many of the weekly Torah portions. The text, written mostly in Aramaic with some Hebrew, has been described as a mystical novel telling of a group of rabbis who wander about the Galilean countryside exchanging the secret teachings of the Torah. See the opening page of the Zohar in Figure 3-2.

Jewish lore relates that Rabbi Shimon bar Yochai, the author of the Zohar who lived during the later part of the second century, was pursued by the Romans. He and his son took refuge in a cave for 13 years, during which time they studied the Torah. The result of these years of hiding and studying was the writing of the Zohar.

The English-language reader doesn't have many options when it comes to studying the Zohar. For many years, the only English-language translation of a significant piece of the Zohar was a literal translation available from Soncino Press. But it's not useful for the beginner. More recently, a new translation has appeared known as the Pritzker Edition (Stanford University Press). It's a highly scholarly edition and also isn't terribly useful for the beginner. A number of single-volume anthologies quoting from portions of the Zohar are also widely available in both Jewish and major general bookstores. While the English-language material isn't very useful, insights from the Zohar do appear in small doses in many books on the Torah.

Figure 3-2:
The opening
page of the
Zohar.

Getting a Grip on What the Torah Isn't

Sometimes an effective way of understanding what something *is* is knowing what it *isn't*. This is certainly true of the Torah. Many misconceptions about the Torah are floating around, so in the following sections, I clarify what the Torah is by making sure you know what it isn't. It all boils down to this fact: At its core, the Torah is a set of instructions from God meant to provide divine wisdom; it simply uses several methods, such as stories, commandments, and history, to impart those instructions.

The Torah isn't a storybook

The Torah begins with the phrase "In the beginning," but this doesn't simply mean "Once upon a time." The Torah contains many stories, but they're far more than casual narrations. It's a fundamental principle that every letter of the Torah is rich with meaning.

Here's an example: The Hebrew letter "bet" that begins the Torah is the first letter of the Hebrew word **bereshit** (buh-ray-*sheet*; in the beginning). Often you'll see the first sentence of the Torah translated as "In the beginning God created the heaven and the earth." But the great Torah commentator Rashi (see Chapter 16 for more about him) says that the phrase should be read as, "In the beginning *of* God's creation of heaven and earth. . . ." In other words, God *created* the beginning and therefore existed before the beginning. The great sages of Jewish tradition teach that God is, was, and will be. God is beyond space and beyond time. The Torah begins with the second letter of the Hebrew alphabet, not the first, signifying that the Torah doesn't begin at the beginning; it begins when God created existence and time.

I offer this example to show you that the very first letter of the Torah is more than just the start of the first word of a story. The letter itself contains a profound teaching. Divine insight and wisdom lie within every letter and every word and every so-called story in the Torah.

This doesn't mean that the Torah is devoid of stories. There are lots of stories in the Torah. But they're more than just stories. The Torah is a message written by God to the world.

The Torah isn't a law book

One of the greatest misconceptions about the Torah comes from the mistranslation of the word "Torah." Too often throughout history the word has been translated as "law," when it should actually be translated as "instruction." The Torah is God's instructions to the world.

If you want to learn about the details of how to observe Jewish law, by the way, don't go to the Torah. The Five Books of Moses don't give the details of how a law is to be clearly understood and observed. And don't go to the Talmud, which is often thought to be the repository of Jewish law. Neither the Torah nor the Talmud contains the specifics of how Jewish laws are to be followed. Both the Five Books of Moses and the Talmud form the basis of Jewish law, but Jewish law is to be found in the various codes of law compiled throughout Jewish history. One such compilation (in fact the most authoritative one) is called the **Shulchan Aruch** (shool-*khan* ah-*rookh*; the prepared table). It was compiled by Rabbi Joseph Karo in the 16th century. The Shulchan Aruch has not been translated into English.

It may not contain Jewish laws, but the Torah certainly does contain lots of commandments. And the Talmud certainly contains lots of discussions, debates, and explanations on the commandments. But the Written Torah and the Talmud (the record of the Oral Torah) contain the raw material from which Jewish law is derived. Only a rabbi who's highly trained in the correct methodology of reading the Torah and Talmud is qualified to determine Jewish law.

The Torah isn't a history book

A fundamental principle regarding the Five Books of Moses is expressed in this well-known saying among Torah scholars: "There is no earlier or later in the Torah." It means that the Torah isn't a historical narration and isn't in chronological order.

This expression doesn't mean, of course, that it's impossible to find facts of history within the Torah. After all, the story of the exodus of the Children of Israel, for example, is a major part of the Torah and is basically the history of the birth of the Jewish people as a growing family. The Torah contains the earliest recorded history of the family history of the Jews. But the Torah is not primarily a source for history; rather, it's a spiritual document with the purpose of communicating divine eternal wisdom.

The Torah isn't literal (even though it's essentially true)

An important principle repeated often in books of Jewish wisdom and Torah commentaries can be found in many places in the Talmud: "The Torah speaks in the language of man." What this means is that when you read the Torah, you need to be aware of the fact that just as in conversation and literature and poetry, the literal meaning often limits your understanding of what's being said.

For example, the saying "a bird in the hand is worth two in the bush" has little practical meaning when taken literally. But as an expression taken as a metaphor or an analogy, the statement has wisdom. It means that it's better to be satisfied with what you have than to risk losing it by trying (perhaps unsuccessfully) to get something better. There's truth to the expression, but only when you break it open and discover its true meaning.

The Written Torah works in a similar way. By speaking in the language of man, the Torah often makes a point, but taking it at face value misses the point. However, when you understand how to read the text based on traditional teachings and the Oral Torah, the literal meaning falls away and you're left with the true meaning of the text.

The best example of the fact that Jews don't read the Torah literally is the famous quote, "An eye for an eye, a tooth for a tooth" (Leviticus 24:20). According the Jewish tradition, taking this biblical phrase literally is totally against Torah law! Jewish tradition interprets the Torah by using ancient principles that go beyond the literal meanings of the words.

According to Jewish law, if I knock your tooth out, you don't get to return the favor. Rather, I have to compensate you monetarily for the injury I caused. The rabbis suggest that "an eye for an eye" really refers to a system of monetary compensation; payment is required for the injury, the pain, the cost of medical care, and lost wages as well as the shame of it all.

Considering the Torah's Commandments

The Written Torah is the cornerstone of Jewish life and law. The basic commandments, principles, ideas, and teachings of Judaism are found in the Written Torah (also known as the Five Books of Moses). In the following sections, I introduce the commandments found in the Written Torah; I discuss these commandments throughout this book, but if you would like a full listing of the commandments on their own, see Appendixes B and C.

Halachah: The way to walk

The term for "Jewish law" in Hebrew is **Halachah** (ha-lah-*khah*; the way to walk). Throughout the centuries, the great sages of Jewish tradition have consulted both the Written and Oral Torahs in order to determine how God wants the Children of Israel to act and behave. But it's never enough to simply look into the text and decide what God wants. The development of Jewish law is a combination of both an understanding of the text as well as an understanding of how to apply it to real life. For example, there's only one appropriate and acceptable answer to the question, "What is the Jewish view of abortion?" And that answer is, "Tell me the case!"

Jewish law isn't a static list of do's and don'ts. The Torah provides both general principles and details, but all the details in the world can't easily fit into each unique case of life. By understanding the Torah and how it communicates, trained rabbis throughout the centuries have been able to determine the Jewish way to walk, the halachah.

The three types of commandments: Rituals, morals, and the mysterious

A key verse in the Torah lists the three basic types of commandments that appear in the Torah. Deuteronomy 4:45 states, "These are the testimonies, decrees and ordinances that Moses discussed with the Israelites when they left Egypt." The important words here are

- ✔ Testimonies or **eidot** (aye-*dote*): The testimonies referred to are religious rituals. Jewish rituals are commandments from God that remind people of important events in the life of the Jewish people or important spiritual truths. The reasons for eidot are always indicated in the Torah. For example, the wearing of tefillin (see Chapter 12) is a ritual that serves as a reminder of the presence of God as well as a reminder to keep God, God's Torah, and God's commandments in one's mind and heart at all times.

- ✔ Decrees or **chukim** (khoo-*keem*): Decrees are the tough commandments of the Torah. They're the ones that don't seem to have any rational reason behind them. They aren't commemorative of events or ideas like eidot, and they aren't obvious ethical teachings like mishpatim. An example of one of the Torah's chukim is the prohibition against combining wool and linen in a garment. This commandment, known as **shatnez** (*shot*-nez), is stated in the Torah: "Do not wear shatnez, wool and linen together" (Deuteronomy 22:11).

  It's important to note that the great sages urge students of the Torah to try to grasp the inner meaning of the many commandments that are actually beyond human understanding. See Chapter 15 for details on Torah analysis.

- ✔ Ordinances or **mishpatim** (mish-pah-*teem*): Ordinances (sometimes referred to as "rules") are the ethical commandments in the Torah. These are the commandments that are self-evident, good ideas, and moral or ethical acts. Mishpatim don't really need justification because they're obvious to reasonable people. "Thou shall not murder" is an example of one of the mishpatim.

Breaking down the 613 commandments

In the Talmud, the Jewish sages teach that there are 613 commandments in the Torah (see Appendixes B and C for a list of these commandments). In a sense, the idea of 613 commandments is misleading because there are actually thousands of correct and incorrect actions as taught by Jewish tradition. But all the thousands of commandments grow out of the basic 613 commandments in the Five Books of Moses. A number of sages throughout Jewish history have made lists of these 613 commandments, and they sometimes differ slightly. The list in this book is based on the teachings of Maimonides.

The term used to refer to these 613 commandments is **Taryag** (tar-*yahg*). It's an acronym made up of four Hebrew letters:

- Tav (T)
- Resh (R)
- Yud (Y)
- Gimmel (G)

Each letter in the Hebrew alphabet corresponds to a number (see Chapter 15), so taf is 400, resh is 200, yud is 10, and gimmel is 3. The four numbers add up to 613.

The 613 commandments are the do's and don'ts of the Torah. Here are some of the many categories of commandments that have been identified:

- Positive commandments
- Negative commandments
- Time bound commandments (for specific times)
- Non–time bound commandments (for any time)
- Simple commandments (known as mitzvoth kallah)
- Complex commandments (known as mitzvoth chamurah)
- Rational commandments (mishpatim)
- Non-rational commandments (chukim)
- Ritual commandments (eidot)
- Commandments between humans and God
- Commandments for all Jews at all times
- Commandments for the priesthood only

- Commandments for women only
- Commandments for all humankind
- Commandments for the King of Israel only
- Commandments in the Holy Temple
- Commandments for specific times and places
- Commandments that are constant

Another way to classify commandments (and the way in which I break them down in Appendixes B and C) is by negative and positive:

- There are 365 negative commandments called **mitzvoth lo ta'aseh** (mitz-*vote* low tah-ah-*seh*) in the Torah. By negative, I mean commandments that tell you what *not* to do. They're said to correspond to the 365 days of the year. The symbolism of these commandments lies in the idea that, according to the Torah, these prohibitions must be observed every day.

- There are 248 positive commandments called **mitzvoth aseh** (mitz-*vote* *ah*-seh) in the Torah. By positive, I mean commandments that tell you specific actions or beliefs that you must do. These commandments correspond to the 248 parts of the body (as counted by the Talmudic rabbis). The symbolism of these commandments lies in the idea that the Torah is saying that the positive commandments must performed with a wholeness of being. The Torah must be integrated into your life every day and with your whole body.

One Jewish teaching says that all 248 positive commandments are contained within the first of the Ten Commandments: "I am the Lord thy God," and all 365 negative commandments are contained within the second of the Ten Commandments: "Thou shall have no other gods before me."

Part II
One by One: The Books of the Torah

The 5th Wave   By Rich Tennant

In this part . . .

The term "Torah" has a number of different meanings, each of which I explain in this book. But the primary meaning is the Five Books of Moses: Genesis, Exodus, Leviticus, Numbers, and Deuteronomy. In this part, I go through each of the five books, almost page by page and topic by topic, and provide you with a detailed overview of each one. The Torah begins with the creation of the world and ends with the Children of Israel about to enter the Promised Land. The five chapters in this part take you on the journey from pre-history to the death of Moses, just before his people arrived in the Land of Israel.

Chapter 4

"In the Beginning": The Book of Genesis

In This Chapter

▶ Witnessing the creation of the universe

▶ Meeting Adam and Eve

▶ Telling the story of Noah and the Flood

▶ Understanding the story of the Tower of Babel

▶ Getting to know Abraham, Isaac, Jacob, Sarah, Rebecca, Rachel, and Leah

▶ Becoming familiar with Joseph, the Jewish leader of Egypt

T he first book of the Torah (which is also the first book of the Bible) is commonly known as the book of Genesis. The word "Genesis," which means "creation or birth," is Greek and comes from the ancient Greek translation of the Torah from its original Hebrew; that Greek work is known as the Septuagint. Among the Jewish people, the book of Genesis is called **Bereshit** (buh-ray-*sheet*; in the beginning), which is the very first word of the Torah.

The book of Genesis is the story of the birth of the universe and also the birth of the Jewish people, originally known as the Children of Israel. As you find out in this chapter, the patriarch Jacob was ultimately renamed Israel, and Jews are the descendants of his children and his children's children, down to the present. This is why all Jews today are the Children of Israel.

In this overview of the book of Genesis, I focus on the main characters, the most important ones being the three patriarchs of Judaism: Abraham, Isaac, and Jacob. It's crucial to be aware of the fact that the three patriarchs had wives (and concubines) and that these women are also significant personalities not only in the Torah text but also in the commentaries. For example, Abraham's wife, Sarah, is considered the mother of the Jewish people; when a woman converts to Judaism, her name is changed and she becomes the "daughter of our mother Sarah." Isaac's wife, Rebecca, and Jacob's wives, Leah and Rachel, join Sarah, and as a group, these four women are known as the four matriarchs of Judaism. These four women were strong and wise and became spiritual leaders of the Jewish people along with their husbands.

The book of Genesis is filled with episodes and stories and is rich with detail. It's impossible to summarize the entire book in just one chapter of *The Torah For Dummies*. In fact, because the Torah often uses multiple words to mean so much more than is literally written, a summary of every story would use far more words than this book itself! In this chapter, I explain a selection of some of the key characters, episodes, and stories found in the book of Genesis. Some who are very familiar with Genesis may wonder why I choose some incidents, descriptions, and stories and leave others out, or why I omit key details from my selections. The answer is that I include some of the more well-known events and stories in Genesis as well as some of my favorites to give you a taste of the kinds of timeless and prophetic tales that appear in the first book of the Torah.

Before You Begin: Approaching the Story of Creation

A friend of mine once asked me, "Does Judaism have a creation myth?" Being one of those people who often answers a question with another question, I said, "What do you mean by the word 'myth'?" My friend responded, "You know, a made-up story that foolish people claim to be true."

Well, the Torah does have an account of the creation of existence and the creation of the world, but many contend that a "made-up" story can be more true than a so-called true story. The story of Creation as it appears in the Torah may be of interest to fools, but it has also been contemplated by geniuses, including some of the greatest minds in Jewish history.

Anyone who reads novels or watches movies quickly finds out that a work of the imagination often captures reality — inner reality, that is — more accurately than the daily newspaper, for example. What happens in a person's life has much more to do with what's occurring beneath the surface — in emotions, memories, experiences, and dreams. A story or tale can capture the unseen reality of lives with far more accuracy than the most-objective reporter or the highest-quality camera.

It's in this light that I approach the account of Creation in the Torah — and the entire Torah, for that matter. Moses, the "author" of the Five Books of Moses, is considered by Jewish tradition to be the greatest prophet who ever lived. And a prophet is someone who experiences a profound level of consciousness that makes it possible to receive images and communications from God; God communicates to a prophet in ways that humans can grasp. The story of Creation and the entire Torah is the result of a prophetic experience by the greatest of prophets. You don't look to the Torah for scientific information or objective history. Rather, the Torah communicates deeper and more profound messages from the Creator.

You can spend a lifetime studying the amazing books that brilliant Torah scholars have written over the centuries on just on the first few lines in the Torah. In Jewish tradition, this field of study is called **Ma'aseh Bereshit** (mah-ah-*she* buh-ray-*sheet*; the Work of Creation). Jewish law actually urges the study of Creation (as found in the Torah) to be done one-on-one, with a teacher of the Work of Creation teaching only one student at a time. The words, their meanings, and their relationships to each other give expression to an abstract vision of the elements of Creation itself, and an understanding of this process leads to an understanding of oneself. Jewish theology sees the human as a microcosm of the whole of Creation, so by addressing the elements that God used to create the world, the Torah provides students with information on the same elements that comprise humankind.

The book of Genesis begins, "In the beginning God created heaven and earth. The earth was without form and empty, with darkness on the face of the deep, but God's spirit moved on the water's surface" (Genesis 1:1–2). This is only the first sentence, and when combined with the traditions in the Oral Torah (see Chapter 3), deep concentration, analysis, and scholarship, each word is revealed as being rich with meaning and containing profound insight. For general information on studying the Torah and using helpful commentaries, see Chapters 15 and 16.

Get Going: God Creates the World

As I mention in the previous section, the book of Genesis starts with these words: "In the beginning God created heaven and earth. The earth was without form and empty, with darkness on the face of the deep, but God's spirit moved on the water's surface" (Genesis 1:1–2). What happened next? Keep reading to find out.

Setting up took six days

The Torah teaches that it took God six days to complete Creation (Genesis 1:1–31). Please don't get hung up on evolution and whether the whole thing really took less than a week. By definition God can do anything, so God certainly could complete Creation in any amount of time.

The Torah's concerns are more spiritual than scientific. The Torah is deeply practical and offers teachings on every aspect of physical life. But the Torah is both physical and metaphysical in that it explores spiritual questions and concerns such as: Who am I? Where did I come from? Where am I going? What for? Why? For centuries, Torah students have been captivated by the study of the six stages of creation as found in the Torah, and the commentaries are rich with meaning.

Here's how Creation unfolds in the book of Genesis:

- **First day:** Light, Day, Night
- **Second day:** Sky, Water Below the Sky, Water Above the Sky, Heaven
- **Third day:** Earth, Seas, Vegetation, Seed-bearing Plants, Fruit Trees
- **Fourth day:** Sun, Moon, Stars
- **Fifth day:** Living creatures of all kinds (except humans)
- **Sixth day:** Adam, an androgynous being (I talk about Adam later in this chapter)

The important commentaries all connect each day of the week with one of the seven "lower attributes," as they're sometimes called in the books of Kabbalah, the Jewish traditional teachings on God. The seven lower attributes combine to form the constant downpour of divine light as it creates and sustains the world. For example, the seventh day of the week, known in the Torah as **Shabbat** (shah-*baht*; the Sabbath), corresponds to the seventh of the lower divine attributes, known as **malchut** (mahl-*khoot*; kingdom). The more you understand the significance of malchut and its relationship to the other divine attributes, the more you pierce the surface of the Torah text to explore the secrets of Creation.

God rested on the seventh day

The Torah says that after the six stages of Creation, God stopped, looked at Creation, and said that it was "very good" (Genesis: 1:31). The seventh day, the day God stopped the initial Creation, is known as Shabbat. The Torah says, "God rested on the seventh day from all the work that He had been doing" (Genesis 2:2).

The great Torah commentaries say that before Creation, there was no existence. The original pattern of Creation, with God actively constructing existence, consisted of six stages of activity followed by one stage of stillness. This pattern ultimately became the basis of the Jewish view of time. Traditional Jewish life based in the Torah is a life in which time centers around Shabbat, the echo of the stillness that followed God's work with the Creation.

The human calendar is based on this pattern of seven, with seven days making up the week. In Jewish thought, there are six days and then there's Shabbat, which corresponds with Saturday on the calendar but actually begins Friday night and ends Saturday night. More importantly, Shabbat isn't even really considered a day; rather, it's a different level of time that's more unlike the other days than similar to them. Shabbat may feel like a day, but in Jewish tradition, it's an oasis from time when stillness reigns and Jews celebrate as though they were royalty in the Palace of the King of King of Kings. See Chapter 11 for more on Shabbat and the general concept of time in the Torah.

It Takes Two: Adam and Eve

Before there was Adam and Eve, there was one being, Adam, who the Torah says was created by God. The Hebrew word **Adam** (ah-*dahm*) shares the same linguistic root as the Hebrew word **adama** (ah-dah-*mah*; earth). The Torah says that unlike the other living creatures, each of which God created out of nothing, "God formed man out of the dust of the ground" (Genesis 2:7). The creation of woman followed shortly thereafter. The Torah calls Eve by the Hebrew word **Chava** (*khah*-vah; life).

Turning dust and breath into body and soul

God made Adam by forming him out of the dust of the earth and by breathing what the Torah calls **nishmat chaim** (*nish*-maht khah-*yeem*; the spirit of life) into the body (Genesis 2:7). Torah scholars point out that the Oral Torah explains that this spirit is actually the soul. Humans, according to the Torah's view, are made of body and soul.

- ✔ The body comes from the earth and ultimately returns to the earth after death.
- ✔ The soul comes directly from God, and it lives on after the death of the body.

People aren't bodies with souls but rather are souls with bodies. The soul existed before the body, it uses the body as an instrument, and then the soul drops the body and continues on.

Splitting male and female

If you were to ask most people how females were created according to the Bible, they would probably say that Eve was made from Adam's rib. But the actual text doesn't explain it that way. Rather, the Torah says that first the human was made androgynous, meaning both male and female. One of the most mysterious verses in the Torah states, "In the image of God, He created him, male and female He created them" (Genesis 1:27).

Several verses later, the Torah says, "God then made man fall into a deep state of unconsciousness and he slept. He took one of his sides and closed the flesh in its place. God built the side that he took from the man into a woman and He brought her to the man" (Genesis 2:21–22). The authoritative Torah commentator Rashi establishes that the traditional understanding of "side" refers not to a body part but rather to the idea that the original "man" was split into two sides. This verse establishes one of the pillars of thought in the Jewish concept of marriage: Each person is really half and in coupling becomes, in a sense, whole.

Avoiding the Tree of Knowledge of Good and Evil

The Torah tells that Adam and Eve lived in **Gan Eden** (gahn *aye*-den; the Garden of Eden), a perfect environment. Jewish thought represents the view that the Garden of Eden exists at both the beginning and the end of time: Humans began in a perfect environment, and man's goal is to rebuild the imperfect world and return it to its pristine state. Jewish thought sees the world as incomplete and in need of human participation to repair the world and make it whole again.

One of the deep and profound riddles of the book of Genesis surrounds God's statement, "You may definitely eat from every tree of the garden, but from the Tree of Knowledge of Good and Evil do not eat, for on the day you eat from it you will die" (Genesis 2:17). Jewish scholars and students of the Torah understand this image in many ways.

One profound interpretation of this verse explains that humans don't always know good from bad. What often seems like a good event in fact may be the beginning of a bad event, and vice versa. One example is lottery winners; many lottery winners who suddenly become wealthy ultimately tell sad stories of misfortunes resulting from the sudden windfall. Others see this verse as referring to God's desire that humans work at the struggle to know how to choose freely and correctly rather than just "eat" of that knowledge without doing the necessary work.

Only God knows true good and true evil. Only God has the infinite vantage point to be able to see the results of things clearly. Despite the free will given to people by God, God sees what will be. As the great Talmudic sage teaches, "All is foreseen and free will is given." But when humans think they have quickly eaten (by which I mean that they think they understand) what's good and evil, the arrogance of such a posture often spells trouble.

Falling to the temptation of the serpent

The story of Adam and Eve includes the serpent or snake, which is a symbol of temptation and evil. The Torah says, "Now the snake was cunning beyond every beast of the field that God had made" (Genesis 3:1). The snake cunningly involves Eve and then Adam in the eating of the forbidden Tree of Knowledge of Good and Evil. When Eve encountered the snake, she said of the Tree, "You shall neither eat it nor touch it" (Genesis 3:3). Drawing from this story, Jewish thought understands the human situation as a constant struggle between two urges found in each person's being — a good urge and an evil urge.

An exploration of the *primal sin,* the function of the serpent and the result of the whole episode, forms the basis of Judaism's understanding of human inner struggle. This seemingly fanciful tale is really the basis of the subtle and complex Jewish understanding of human psychology and the human predicament. Also, it's important to keep in mind that Jewish commentaries on the Torah don't view the sin of the Garden of Eden as a sexual sin.

The result of Adam's and Eve's failure to follow God's command not to be tempted by things that are inappropriate or forbidden is that God tossed Adam and Eve out of the Garden of Eden. The Torah says, "God banished him from the Garden of Eden, to work the soil from which he was taken" (Genesis 3:23).

Sibling Rivalry: Cain and Abel

Adam and Eve's first two children were Cain and Abel. The Torah says that "Abel became a shepherd and Cain became a tiller of the ground" (Genesis 4:2). When it came time for each of them to present an offering to God, Cain offered fruit from the ground, and Abel offered the firstborn of his flocks. Then the Torah offers a mysterious line: "God turned to Abel and to his offering, but to Cain and his offering He did not turn" (Genesis 4:4–5).

God told Cain, who was disappointed in God's rebuff, that he needed to improve himself. Cain then confronted Abel and murdered him. When God asked Cain where his brother was, Cain spoke one of the most well-known lines in the Torah, "Am I my brother's keeper?"

Cain and Abel are the first human beings to be born of human parents, and they're the first pair of siblings, the first brothers. They're also involved in the first murder. (That's a lot of firsts!) But there's great spiritual significance in the very first fully human episode in the Torah. The Torah teaches that the greatest human pleasure is nearness to God, and the proper perspective on life has God at the center. Viewed in this light, there's a vast difference between the symbolic offering of Cain with his rather lowly "fruit from the ground" and Abel's offering of "firstborn of his flocks." Torah commentators also explain that the occupation of shepherd symbolically represents a profession that allows for contemplation of God, whereas a tiller of land often becomes a worshipper of the earth and not God.

When It Rains, It Pours: Noah and the Flood

There's an old joke about a rabbi who was in a hospital bed next to an atheist. The atheist said to the rabbi, "Oh rabbi with your silly beliefs. Don't you know that there are dozens of cultures that have an ancient flood myth!?" The rabbi replied, "That makes me feel so much better. I've often wondered how nobody heard of the Flood except we Jews. Now that I know others have also heard about it, I'm sure it happened."

Whether the Flood actually happened or not, it's a story that has captivated the imaginations of countless children and adults for many centuries. I give you an overview of the story in the following sections.

A 40-day trip on the high seas

Basically, the story of Noah and the Flood says that the world was filled with wicked people and God saw that Noah was the most righteous. As the Torah says, "God saw that the wickedness was great . . . but Noah found grace in the eyes of God" (Genesis 6:5–8). God decided to send a Flood that essentially wiped away the first experiment and allowed the human family to begin again. God commanded Noah to build a huge boat, an ark, in preparation for the Flood. Noah, his wife, his sons, and their wives joined a sampling of every animal for 40 days while the rains turned to floods and wiped out the rest of the humans and animals in the world.

You may be wondering: Did Noah really take two of each kind of animal with him on the ark? When I was a librarian working at the reference desk of a public library, I occasionally got phone calls that librarians call "bar bets." The assumption is that two people are sitting at a bar (or elsewhere) and get into a debate over some fact, which prompts them to call the library to get the answer. Well, here's a good bar bet: Bet someone that Noah didn't take two of each kind of animal into the ark but instead took two of each "unclean" animal and seven of each "clean" animal. (A clean animal can be used in the Holy Temple as a sacrifice. See Chapter 6 for more about Temple sacrifices.)

Common knowledge of the story of Noah and the Flood says that Noah took two of each species with him. But if you check the Torah, you find that it says, "God said to Noah, 'Come into the ark, you and your family . . . Take seven pair of every clean animal, and of the animal that is not clean, two, a male and its mate . . .'" (Genesis 7:1–2).

The rainbow covenant

As a result of the Flood, "All flesh that walked the earth perished" (Genesis 7:21). When the rains stopped and the water subsided, God spoke to Noah, saying, "Leave the ark, you along with your wife, your sons, and your sons' wives. Take out with you every living creature . . ." (Genesis 8:15–16).

The human race began again but this time with a promise from God. The Torah says that God said to Noah and his sons, "I am making a covenant with you and with your offspring after you. It will include every living creature that is with you among the birds, the livestock, and all the beasts of the earth . . . all life will never be cut short by the waters of a flood. There will never again be a flood to destroy the earth" (Genesis 9:9–11).

The statement and promise from God has become known as the *rainbow covenant* because, in reference to that promise, God said, "I have placed My rainbow in the clouds and it shall be a sign of the covenant between Me and the earth."

The sons of Noah

Throughout this book, I explain that the Torah is filled with commandments and that the Jewish people are obligated to observe them by doing the positive commandments and avoiding the negative commandments. (See Appendixes B and C for more about these commandments.) The idea that the Jews are the chosen people has nothing to do with any belief in superiority. In the Torah, the Jewish people are chosen by God for more burdens and responsibilities, not for privileges.

Through a careful analysis of the Torah text along with the oral tradition, Jewish tradition teaches that there are seven universal laws, commonly known as the *Noahide Laws,* that were commanded of the sons of Noah and are now incumbent on all humankind. These seven laws aren't listed in the Written Torah; they're named and elucidated in the Talmud. They are as follows:

- ✔ Idolatry is forbidden.
- ✔ Incestuous and adulterous relations are forbidden.
- ✔ Murder is forbidden.
- ✔ Cursing the name of God is forbidden.
- ✔ Theft is forbidden.
- ✔ Eating the flesh of a living animal is forbidden.
- ✔ Mankind is commanded to establish courts of justice.

The story of Noah's sons in Genesis doesn't stop there. The entire tenth chapter of the book of Genesis (10:1–32) is sometimes referred to as the *Table of Nations* because it gives the genealogies of two of Noah's three sons, Ham and Japheth. These families' trees, consisting of dozens of names, form the basis of the view that after the Flood, the descendants of Noah spread throughout the world and established families and ultimately nations. Ham's family settled in northern Africa, and Japheth's family settled in Europe.

Noah's third son was Shem, and it's from Shem that Jews, Arabs, and others, descend. The term "Semite" comes from the Greek translation of Shem, which is Sem.

Reach for the Sky: The Tower of Babel

The English word "babble," meaning incomprehensible sounds coming from a person's mouth, comes from the story in the book of Genesis about the Tower of Babel. The Torah explains that at one time everyone in the world spoke the same language. A unity existed among the people of the world, but unity turned to arrogance when some people got the idea that they could conquer God.

The Torah says, "They said to each other, 'Come let us mold bricks and fire them.' They then had bricks to use as stone, and asphalt for mortar. They said, 'Come, let us build ourselves a city, and a tower whose top shall reach the sky. Let us make ourselves a name . . .'" (Genesis 11:3–4).

Torah commentaries point out that by trying to build a tower to God, human arrogance destroyed the peace and unity in the world. Before the tower, God and humans maintained their proportions. But because of the attempt to disrupt this original combination, God punished the people by scattering them both geographically and through the development of many languages. The Torah says, "Come, let us descend and confuse their speech" (Genesis 11:7). (The commentators say that the "us" in this verse are the angels.)

The story of Babel helps explain why the humble position is honored in Jewish thought. One way this translates into daily experience is that people are supposed to teach themselves that they're just a small piece of a vast universe and simply can't understand God's ways. God's thoughts aren't human thoughts; God's logic isn't human logic. There's no way for humans to grasp the universe as God does. By cultivating a humble view, humanity ultimately looks more realistically at its capacities and limitations. By trying to reach the sky with the Tower of Babel, human arrogance took over and attempted to fool itself.

Father Figure: The Story of Abraham

The book of Genesis contains many genealogies. Even people who aren't that familiar with the Bible are vaguely aware of all the "begats" in the text. One of the most striking family trees appearing in the Torah is the continuous line traced from Adam and Eve to one of the three patriarchs of Judaism, Abraham.

Before I delve into the story of Abraham, it's important to clear up a common misconception about Abraham. It's often said that Abraham was the inventor of *monotheism,* the belief in one God, and that before Abraham there were pagans, and then Abraham came and introduced the idea of God to the world.

As my teacher points out, Abraham was surely not the inventor of an idea called monotheism. God isn't an idea that someone invented; God is the Creator and Ruler of the universe, and God was known long before Abraham, by Adam and Eve, Noah, and others. It seems that in Abraham's birthplace of Ur and in many other places in the world, knowledge of God was forgotten and idolatry blossomed. So Abraham didn't invent God; he simply reminded the world that there's one nameless, formless, all knowing, all powerful, omnipresent God, and that although generally hidden from the world, God is nevertheless always present and the mover of everything. (As for pagans, they aren't people who lived a long time ago. Pagans, as one common definition suggests, are people who deny God's existence.)

Abraham (whose original name was Abram — more on that later in this chapter) was born in the city of Ur, whose remnants can be found today in Iraq. The son of Terach, he lived in a community of idolaters. The Torah records a pivotal moment in Abraham's life, and this episode ultimately became a pivotal moment in the history of humankind.

Abram gets a call and leaves town

In Genesis 12, this previously unknown man named Abram heard the voice of God saying, "Go for yourself away from your land, from your birthplace, and from your father's house, to the land that I will show you. I will make you into a great nation. I will bless you and make you great. You shall become a blessing. I will bless those who bless you, and he who curses you I will curse. All the families of the earth will be blessed through you" (Genesis 12:1–3).

The call from God begins with the Hebrew words **lech l'cha** (*lekh* leh-*khah*; go for yourself). Torah commentators point out that this unusual phrase, which could easily have just been "Go" rather than "Go for yourself," teaches that this call from God was for Abram's own benefit. He needed to leave the pagan environment of his family, but he needed to take a great risk. Of course, when God speaks directly to you, it's more of a risk to disobey God's charge than to do what He says.

In any event, the call from God to Abram urged him to leave his home and become the father of a great nation, the Children of Israel, the Jewish people. Abram left his home and began his journey, which begins in the Torah with Genesis 12:1. He went

- From Ur to Haran (near the border of today's Turkey and Syria): Haran was Abram's first stop. It was already a well-settled area, so Abram moved on in search of a better place to settle.

- From Haran to Shechem (a few miles from Nablus in modern Israel's West Bank): Shechem was Abram's first stop in the Holy Land, and the Torah says that he built an altar there but then moved on in search of the right place to settle.

- From Shechem to Bethel (also in modern Israel's West Bank): Bethel is 10 miles north of Jerusalem and 20 miles south of Shechem and was one of the highest points in the region. Abram built an altar there (as he did in Shechem) and left the place, although he would eventually return.

- From Bethel to Egypt: Abram was prompted to go to Egypt because of a famine, and he planned to stay there until the famine ended. In Egypt, Abram and Sarah got entangled in a little difficulty. Because Sarah was beautiful, the Pharaoh's assistants brought her to the Pharaoh. Fortunately, Abram and Sarah miraculously managed to escape the Pharaoh's advances (Genesis 12:10–20).

- From Egypt to Bethel: Lot, Abram's nephew, went with Abram and his family to Egypt. Then God commanded Abram to go back to the Holy Land, so they returned to Bethel. At a certain point, it became clear that Abram and Lot could no longer live together because they both had sizable flocks and their shepherds argued. Abram gave Lot the choice of where to live. Lot headed to the southeast, near the cities of Sodom and Gomorrah (Genesis 13:10–12).

- From Bethel to Hebron (in modern Israel's West Bank): Abram settled in Hebron, and that's where you can visit his tomb.

Abram and Sarai become Abraham and Sarah

Abram's original name was a contraction of **av Aram,** meaning "the father of Aram," which was his native country. In Genesis 17:5, the Torah explains that God changed Avram's name to Avraham, a contraction of **av hamon,** or "the father of a multitude," because Abraham ultimately became the direct ancestor of millions of Jews, Arabs, and others.

Sarah, Avraham's wife and the first matriarch of the Jewish people, was originally named **Sarai,** which means "my princess." In Genesis 17:15, the Torah explains that God changed her name to Sarah, a change in spelling and pronunciation that changes the meaning of the name to "princess to all the nations of the world." In both cases, the name changes were the result of adding the fifth letter "hey," which traditionally represents the name of God. Much of the heart of the book of Genesis is the story of Abraham and Sarah, their off-spring, and their fate.

God's covenant with Abraham

The Hebrew word **brit** (brit; covenant) is also the term used for ritual circumcision in Jewish life. The Torah explains the connection between the two meanings in Genesis 17:9–14. God promises Abraham that

- ✔ Abraham will be the father of a great nation.
- ✔ Abraham shall be a blessing.
- ✔ Abraham will be given, for eternity, the land of Canaan (also known as the Holy Land, the Land of Israel, and the Promised Land) for his descendants.
- ✔ Abraham's descendants will be as numerous as the stars in the sky.
- ✔ Abraham's descendants will be in a foreign land for 400 years (foreshadowing of the slavery of the Children of Israel in Egypt; see Chapter 5).
- ✔ Abraham and God will have a covenant that will last for eternity.

And what will Abraham do in exchange? God commands that, in return, Abraham will circumcise himself and all his male descendants shall be circumcised, and he and his descendants will walk with God — meaning that they will promote knowledge of God in the world, will have faith in God, will believe in God, will trust in God, and will work to better know God. Abraham agreed and circumcised himself (he was 99 years old). The sign of this covenant, this promise between God and Abraham, was the circumcision, and to this day it's a strict requirement both for Jews at the age of eight days and for all males who convert to Judaism to be circumcised. (Turn to Chapter 12 for more about the subject of circumcision.)

The destruction of Sodom and Gomorrah

In Genesis 18, the Torah describes the sins of the cities Sodom (where Abraham's nephew Lot settled) and nearby Gomorrah. The Torah tells of three angels who were sent to inflict divine vengeance on the residents of the cities. Abraham accompanied them in the direction of Sodom; two of the angels went to the city of Sodom, and the third stayed with Abraham and told Abraham of the coming destruction of Sodom and Gomorrah. Abraham prayed (Genesis 18:23–26) that if 50 righteous persons were found in the city, it should be spared. Gradually, he reduced the number to ten, but not even ten righteous men could be found (or God, in answer to his prayers, would have averted his design). Lot, the only man deserving, was spared.

The modern word "sodomy," referring to a variety of "unnatural" or non-procreation-oriented sexual acts, unfortunately perpetuates the popular false notion that the sin of the wicked ancient city of Sodom described in the Torah was a sexual sin. Both cities of Sodom and Gomorrah are described as sinful cities, but the Torah text in combination with the Oral Torah provides a clear vision of Sodom and, by association, Gomorrah as well. What emerges from careful analysis of the holy texts is surely a picture of a sinful city, but the sins of the city of Sodom and Gomorrah were insensitivity to others, perversions of justice, excessive wealth, conformity, and cruelty.

The Birth and Binding of Isaac

The Torah says that Sarah was childless, so she offered Hagar, a concubine, to be the mother of Abraham's child, and Hagar gave birth to Ishmael. In her old age, Sarah finally gave birth to Isaac. Abraham was 100 years old when Isaac was born, and Sarah was 90. In response to giving birth at such an old age, the Torah says that Sarah declared, "God has given me laughter" (Genesis 21:6). Isaac, or **Yitzchak** (*yihtz*-khak) in Hebrew, means "he will laugh."

Abraham's son Isaac is the second of the three patriarchs in Jewish tradition. The book of Genesis includes many stories about the patriarchs, and perhaps the most challenging one deals with Abraham and Isaac. Known in Jewish tradition as the **Akedah** (ah-kay-*dah*; binding), the Torah story of the binding of Isaac is a pivotal one in Jewish life, Jewish liturgy, and Jewish scholarship.

In a nutshell, Genesis 22:1–19 says that God commanded Abraham to sacrifice (and therefore kill) his son Isaac on an altar. Abraham and Isaac were prepared to go through with it when God stopped Abraham and an animal took the place of the sacrifice; Isaac was spared, and Abraham was spared from having to slaughter and sacrifice his son.

A myth that I'm happy to correct is that the meaning of this story is *not* an indication of a historical moment when human sacrifice was eliminated from the rituals of ancient people. According to the great Torah commentaries, the story is about the boundaries of faith, belief, trust in God. The Oral Torah teaches that "With Ten Trials was our father Abraham tried, and he stood firm through all of them" (Mishnah, Ethics of the Fathers 5:4). Ten different events described in the Torah are singled out by the sages as Abraham's ten tests.

- ✔ The first test was God's call to Abraham to leave his home (which I cover earlier in this chapter in the section "Abram gets a call and leaves town").

- ✔ The last test was God instructing Abraham to sacrifice his son Isaac in perhaps the ultimate test of faith. Many commentators have taught that

Abraham knew two things at once: That God wouldn't allow Abraham to go through with the sacrifice; and that Abraham still had to go through the process, listen to God, be prepared to do what God commanded, and show his absolute faith and obedience to God.

Based on the Torah, Judaism takes the fundamental position that, as with Abraham, life for each human is a series of tests of trials given by God for their benefit. All trials, from the smallest frustration to the greatest tragedy, are really for the best even though you can't always see them that way. A basic tenant of Jewish faith is the principle that God knows what He is both doing and allowing and that the tests you face are for the benefit of your soul.

The Story of Jacob

Isaac's son Jacob is the third of the three patriarchs of Judaism, but he holds a particularly special place in the history of the Jewish people, spiritually and otherwise, because he fathered 12 sons whose descendants eventually became the nation of Israel.

Jacob and his twin brother Esau, born to Isaac and his wife Rebecca, were at odds with each other even before they were born ("the children struggled together within her" [Genesis 25:22]). Before their birth, God spoke to Rebecca and told her that she would have twins and that the older would serve the younger (Genesis 25:23).

Jacob and Esau had very different personalities. Jacob valued the tradition of his ancestors, but Esau did not. Jacob was gentle and studious, whereas Esau was a harsh man and a hunter. Although Esau was the older twin, he sold his birthright to Jacob in exchange for some food following an unsuccessful hunting trip (Genesis 25:29–34).

When Isaac was old and blind, he sent for his oldest son Esau in order to offer his son a blessing, but Isaac's younger son, Jacob, at the encouragement of Rebecca (his mother and the wife of Isaac), fooled his blind father into thinking that he was Esau and received the blessing. As the Torah says, "Rebecca then took her older son Esau's best clothing and put them on her younger son Jacob" (Genesis 27:15). This episode is of great interest to commentators as they explain what this apparent moment of deception by Jacob actually means. This story, like so many from the Torah, contains explorations of deep mysteries about the human condition, the nature of good and evil, and the path of God. The deception in this story isn't a legal detail in the Torah; what I mean is that it doesn't give permission to be deceptive or to lie. Both the Written Torah and the Oral Torah contain strict laws on the requirement of honesty in one's life and dealings.

Many verses before the story of this great deception, the Torah tells of the birth of these twins and says, "God's word to her was, 'Two nations are in your womb . . . the greater one will serve the younger'" (Genesis 25:23). The commentators point out that, in helping Jacob deceive Isaac, Rebecca was merely doing what was necessary to help Jacob fulfill the message that she received from God.

But the central message in the story comes from an understanding of the differences between the nature of Jacob and the nature of Esau. The Torah quotes Jacob as saying, "But my brother, Esau is a hairy man and I am a smooth skinned man" (Genesis 27:11). The vast differences between the twins are what occupies the Oral Torah's discussions of Esau. Jacob is the refined, educated scholar who's faithful to God. The Oral Torah describes Esau as an evil man who attacked Jacob while they were in the womb. The sages speak of his insults to women as well as his murderous, bloodthirsty nature.

A well-known story in the book of Genesis is Jacob's dream. According to Jewish tradition a dream in the Torah is considered prophecy. The Torah says of Jacob, "He dreamed that . . . a ladder was standing on the ground and its top reached toward heaven . . . and angels of God were ascending and descending on it" (Genesis 28:12). The great Torah sages suggest that the ladder is a symbol of Mount Sinai, indicating that the Torah is the connection between heaven and earth, God and people.

Jacob also is involved with the great love story of the Torah. He wanted to marry a girl named Rachel and worked seven years to earn the right, but at the wedding her older sister Leah was secretly put in her place by their father. Jacob then worked another seven years to marry Rachel. Jacob also had two concubines, Bilhah and Zilpah. These four women bore him 12 sons and one daughter, Dina (Genesis 35:22–26). With the exception of Levi, whose descendants served a sacred function in the Holy Temple (see Chapter 6), and Josef, each of Jacob's sons became the head of one of the Twelve Tribes of Israel (see Chapter 7): Reuven, Shimon, Yehuda, Issachar, Zebulun, Dan, Naphtali, Gad, Asher, and Benjamin. The sons of Josef (also spelled Joseph), Manasseh and Ephraim, each became the head of a tribe of their own, while the descendants of Levi were not a separate tribe, totaling 12 tribes in all.

Losing track of all these people is easy, but rest easy; Figure 4-1 shows the family tree of Abraham, Isaac, Jacob, and Jacob's many sons.

In the last part of his story, Jacob wrestled with an angel, and in the process, God changed his name to Israel. The Torah says that "Jacob was alone and a strange man wrestled with him until just before dawn. When the man saw that he could not defeat him, he touched the upper joint of Jacob's thigh.

Jacob's hip joint became dislocated as he wrestled with the man" (Genesis 32:25–26). The man wanted to leave, but Jacob held him. Before Jacob let the man go, Jacob asked for a blessing. When asked for his name, Jacob told him, and the man said, "Your name will no longer be Jacob, but **Yisra'el**" (yis-rah-*ail*; one who wrestles with God) (Genesis 32:29). The great Torah commentators teach that the man was an angel and that just as Jacob was hurt but only temporarily, the Jewish people suffer loses but always emerge with great strength and blessings.

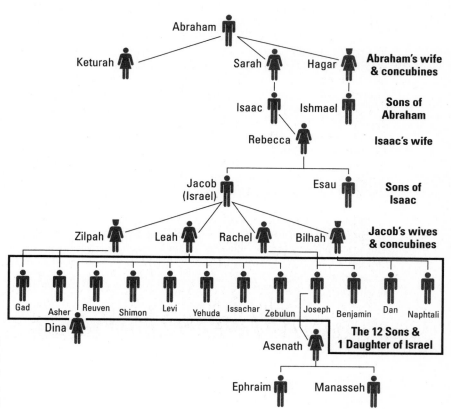

Figure 4-1: Abraham's family tree.

Introducing Joseph, Jacob's Favorite Son

The book of Genesis ends with the story of Jacob's favorite son, Joseph (Genesis 37:1–50:26). Joseph's brothers sold him into slavery as a boy because they were jealous of Joseph's status in the family and of Joseph's dreams about his brothers bowing down to him. They were also jealous of the coat of many colors that Jacob gave him.

The person who bought Joseph sold him again to Potiphar, a leader of Egypt. In Egypt, Joseph gained a position of authority in the household of Potiphar by the will of God. The Torah says, "God was with Joseph, and God made him very successful" (Genesis 39:2); he was later imprisoned when Potiphar's wife wanted to have sexual relations with Joseph and Joseph refused. She falsely accused him of attempted rape. Of her account, the Torah says, "He came to rape me but I screamed as loud as I could" (Genesis 39:14).

Joseph earned a reputation as an interpreter of dreams and was released from prison after wisely and correctly interpreting the Pharaoh's dream. The Pharaoh renamed him Zaphnath-paaneah (Genesis 41:45) and ultimately appointed Joseph in charge of all Egypt. Some Torah commentators say the name Zaphnath-paaneah means "revealer of secrets," whereas others suggest different meanings including "Lord of life."

According to the Torah, Joseph recognized his brothers when they came to Egypt looking for food during a famine. After some tense moments, he invited them to settle in Egypt. The rest of their family, including Jacob, joined them in Egypt, and the story continues in the book of Exodus, which I cover in Chapter 5.

Chapter 5

"These Are the Names": The Book of Exodus

Despite the popular view that the Jewish people are a religion, the Jewish people are essentially a family. To be Jewish has nothing to do with subscribing to a religion, which makes it different from other religions. For example, a person who's born into a Buddhist or Christian family and who decides to leave his faith is no longer considered a member of that religion. But a person who's born into a Jewish family can abandon all Jewish beliefs and even convert to another religion and still be considered Jewish — that is, a part of the Jewish family.

The Jewish people also aren't a race. Anyone who visits Israel quickly sees that there are European Jews, Ethiopian Jews, North African Jews, and Middle Eastern Jews. They come in different colors with different racial features, but they all belong to the Jewish family.

The Jewish family is centered upon a belief in God, but essentially the Jewish people are one big family. This family grew in size and ultimately became a nation. But Judaism never lost sight of the fact that Jews are all part of one family.

In this chapter, I introduce the book of Exodus, which is the second of the Five Books of Moses, and its story of the Jewish family growing into a nation. It tells of the transformation of a group of 70 descendants of Jacob the patriarch, the son of Isaac and the grandson of Abraham (see Chapter 4), and their departure from Egypt under the leadership of Moses. Moses led the Children of Israel to Mount Sinai, where they (all 2 to 3 million of them) encountered God and received God's teachings.

The Rise of a New Pharaoh and the Early Life of Moses

Jacob's favorite son Joseph arrived in Egypt and ultimately was promoted to high office. Joseph's position and reputation protected his relatives, the Children of Israel. But when a new regime took over in Egypt, problems began for Jacob's descendants. In this section, I describe how the new Pharaoh forced them to do backbreaking work and surrender their baby boys to be killed.

Moses was an Israelite child whose parents put him (as an infant) into a floating box and put the box in the river with the hope that the baby would survive rather than be killed. As fate had it, Moses ended up as a prince in the Pharaoh's palace. One day, Moses ventured out of the palace and witnessed an Egyptian guard beating an Israelite. In this section, I explain that Moses killed the guard, realized he was in trouble for it, and then fled to a place called Midian. It was in Midian that Moses met his wife.

The peaceful life of Jacob's descendants

The book of Exodus begins, "These are the names of Israel's sons who came to Egypt with Jacob" (Exodus 1:1). As I explain in Chapter 4, Jacob and Israel are the same person, so the descendants of Jacob are often called *Israelites* or the *Children of Israel*.

The Torah indicates that "The original number of Jacob's direct descendants . . . was seventy" (Exodus 1:5). But it also states, "The Israelites were fertile and prolific, and their population increased. They became so numerous that the land (of Egypt) was filled with them" (Exodus 1:7).

An ancient Jewish commentary on the book of Exodus, called the **Mechilta** (meh-*khil*-tah), teaches that while the Jewish family in Egypt grew, it retained its family identity and didn't assimilate. The Children of Israel, says the commentary, did four things that resulted in their being able to maintain their identity:

- ✔ They were sexually moral.
- ✔ They did not gossip.
- ✔ They did not change their names.
- ✔ They did not change their language.

As vast as the group had become, the descendants of Jacob knew who they were and from whom they descended. They also knew that they were related to Jacob's son Joseph, who had attained the highest status in the palace of the Egyptian Pharaoh, that of viceroy. And as long as the Israelites' connection to Joseph was known, they lived peacefully in the land of Egypt.

The new Pharaoh's plan to deal with the Israelites

A line appears in the beginning of the book of Exodus that indicates when things changed for the Jewish family in Egypt: "A new king arose over Egypt who knew not Joseph" (Exodus 1:8). With the event reflected in that one line, the situation changed radically. The new king (or Pharaoh) in Egypt said, "The Israelites are becoming too numerous and strong for us. Let us deal wisely with them. Otherwise they might increase so much that if there is a war they will join our enemies and fight against us" (Exodus 1:9–10).

The Torah explains that the Pharaoh wanted to crush the spirit of the Jews and tried to do so by forcing them into hard labor, requiring them to build up the cities of Pithom and Raamses. But the Egyptians soon discovered something seen many times in Jewish history: Instead of crushing the spirit of the Jewish people, oppression had the opposite effect as the Jews proliferated and spread out.

The expression of the events of this period is an excellent example of the Torah as an eternal document and not just an ancient history. Jewish commentators throughout the centuries observe that the Jewish people function as a plant does in that, when it's cut back, the result is growth. So it is with the Jewish people: After many periods of oppression against Jews, the result has been unprecedented growth.

The Egyptians saw this continued growth among the Children of Israel and put even more pressure on them. Jews were forced to do even more hard labor to break not only their spirits but their bodies as well. As the Torah says, the Egyptians "made their lives bitter with harsh labor involving mortar and bricks" (Exodus 1:14).

The Pharaoh's plan to break the Children of Israel involved more than hard labor. He spoke with two midwives who were apparently in charge of helping in the delivery of Jewish children. Jewish tradition teaches that the two midwives were Yocheved and Miriam (see the next section for more about these women).

The Pharaoh declared, "When you deliver Hebrew women . . . if the child is a boy, kill it" (Exodus 1:16). The midwives disobeyed this order, explaining that the Hebrew women were unlike the Egyptian women who needed midwives to help in their births. The midwives said, "They know how to deliver. They can give birth before a midwife even gets to them" (Exodus 1:19). So the Pharaoh instructed that every Hebrew boy must be thrown into the Nile River.

An Israelite baby floats up the Nile River

One of the sons of Jacob was Levi. Jewish tradition teaches that Levi had a son named Kehoth, who had a son named Amram. Amram married **Yocheved** (yoh-*kheh*-vehd), a daughter of Levi. She was the mother of the baby who was eventually named Moses.

Yocheved hid Moses successfully for three months to avoid being forced to surrender him to the Pharaoh's decree. But when she realized that hiding the baby was no longer practical, she built a little box out of the same materials used by Egyptian boat builders. She placed the baby in the box and put the box into the Nile River, among the uncut papyrus shoots. The baby's sister Miriam stood by and watched the floating box to see what would happen to it.

The Pharaoh's daughter finds the Israelite baby and names him Moses

The Torah explains that the Egyptian Pharaoh's daughter went to the Nile River to bathe and discovered the box with the baby inside. The Talmud (also known as the Oral Torah; see Chapter 3) teaches that she either sent one of her slaves or reached out herself and took the box from the river. When she opened the box, she discovered the baby boy inside. Suddenly the baby boy began to cry, inspiring pity from the Pharaoh's daughter, who knew it was a Hebrew boy.

Miriam, the baby's sister, was watching this discovery; she approached the Pharaoh's daughter and asked her if she would like her (Miriam) to find a Hebrew wet nurse to suckle to baby. The Pharaoh's daughter agreed, and Miriam went to get her own mother — the mother of the baby himself! The Pharaoh's daughter offered Yocheved a job to care for the baby until he grew up, at which point Yocheved would return him to the Pharaoh's daughter. That's just what Yocheved did. The Pharaoh's daughter adopted the boy "and named him Moshe" (Exodus 2:10). **Moshe** (mow-*sheh*), the Hebrew name as it appears in the Torah, is translated into English as "Moses."

Moses grows up in the Pharaoh's palace

The Torah gives no details about Moses's experience growing up in the palace of the Pharaoh. But the Oral Torah teaches one of the most famous stories about Moses's childhood.

When Moses was 3 years old, he was sitting on the Pharaoh's lap. Suddenly he reached for the gems on the royal crown and knocked it off the Pharaoh's head. An evil advisor to the Pharaoh said that this was a bad omen that predicted that one day Moses would try to overthrow the Pharaoh.

Tradition teaches that God assigned the angel Gabriel to watch over Moses's safety. Gabriel transformed himself into one of the Pharaoh's advisors and suggested that 3-year-old Moses be put to a test. Two bowls were placed in front of Moses — one containing gems and the other containing red-hot coals. The test was this: If Moses reached for the coals, he would be seen as a normal child because he wanted the coals that burned brighter than the gems. But if Moses reached for the gems, it would be a sign that he was out to usurp the Pharaoh's power.

Moses, of course, was a highly intelligent child and knew the difference between hot coals and gems. He began to reach for the gems when the angel Gabriel moved his hand in the direction of the hot coals. Moses grabbed a hot coal and brought it to his mouth, burning his tongue. The Pharaoh concluded that Moses was only an innocent child.

This ancient tale is one of the traditional Jewish explanations for the view that Moses had a stutter or some speech impediment. As the Torah says, "Moses said to the Lord: 'Oh Lord, I am not a man of words, neither yesterday and not the day before and not from the very first time You spoke to me, for I am slow of speech, and of a slow tongue'" (Exodus 4:10).

Moses kills an Egyptian guard and flees

When Moses, who knew he was one of the Children of Israel, was old enough, he began leaving the palace of the Pharaoh where he grew up; the Torah says, "He began to go out to his own people" (Exodus 2:11). Moses saw the oppression that the Children of Israel were subjected to. One fateful day, he saw an Egyptian beating one of the Hebrews. Moses looked around, and when he saw that nobody was watching, Moses killed the Egyptian and hid the man's body in the sand.

The next day Moses went out of the palace again and saw two Hebrews fighting. Moses said to the man who was in the wrong, "Why are you beating your brother?" (Exodus 2:13). But the other one said, "Who made you our prince and judge? Do you intend to kill me the way you killed the Egyptian?" (Exodus 2:14). At that moment, Moses knew that the incident was no longer his secret. In fact, the Pharaoh learned that Moses had killed an Egyptian and gave directions that Moses be put to death. Moses fled and ended up in the land of Midian, where he met and married his wife, Tzipporah, and fathered a son, Gershom.

Get Moving! The Exodus from Egypt

In the book of Genesis, when God calls Abraham to take his son Isaac to be a sacrifice, Abraham responds to God's call by saying **Heneni** (hee-*nay*-knee; Here I am). And in the book of Exodus, when God calls Moses to lead the Children of Israel out of the bonds of slavery in Egypt, Moses also responds to God's call by saying, "Heneni."

In this section, I describe how God convinced a reluctant Moses to lead the Hebrew slaves to freedom. With his brother Aaron, Moses repeatedly tried to convince the Pharaoh to let the Children of Israel go, but the Pharaoh dug in his heels, and things went from bad to worse as conditions for the Israelites worsened. Finally, God created ten terrible plagues that ultimately forced the Pharaoh to grant freedom to the Children of Israel. In this section, I discuss the first Jewish family holy day of Passover ever celebrated; it took place in Egypt the night before the former slaves fled to freedom.

The burning bush

The Torah explains that, despite the death of the Egyptian Pharaoh under whom Moses had grown up, the subjugation of the Children of Israel continued. They cried out to God, and "God heard their cries, and he remembered His covenant with Abraham, Isaac and Jacob" (Exodus 2:24). God then took action by appearing to Moses in a burning bush.

Receiving a directive from God

Moses worked for his father-in-law, **Yitro** (*yit*-row; Jethro), as a shepherd. One day, Moses took his sheep to the edge of the desert to a mountain known as Horeb, eventually to be known as the mountain of God. It's also the location of Mount Sinai. Moses then noticed a fire in the middle of a thorn bush and saw that the flame was not damaging the bush. Intrigued by the phenomenon, he decided to investigate.

It was at that moment that Moses had his first encounter with God. As Moses approached the burning bush, God called out to him, "Moses, Moses" (Exodus 3:4). Moses said, "Here I am," and God told Moses not to come any closer. God instructed Moses to take his shoes off, explaining that he was standing on holy ground.

God said, "I am the God of your fathers, the God of Abraham, the God of Isaac, the God of Jacob" (Exodus 3:6). Moses hid his face, fearful of looking at the Divine. God then said, "I have seen the suffering of My people in Egypt. I have heard how they cry out because of what their slave drivers do, and I am aware of their pain. I have come down to rescue them from Egypt's power. I will bring them out of that land, to a good, spacious land, to a land flowing with milk and honey" (Exodus 3:7–8).

God then gave Moses a directive to go to the Egyptian Pharaoh. God said to Moses, "Bring My people, the Israelites, out of Egypt" (Exodus 3:10).

Objecting to God's directive

Moses objected to God's directive. He said to God, "Who am I that I should go to Pharaoh and that I should take the Children of Israel out of Egypt?" (Exodus 3:11). God assured Moses that He would be with Moses. Moses said that when he got to Egypt, the people would ask him who sent him; they would ask Moses to tell them God's name. He asked God, "What shall I say to them?" (Exodus 3:13). God's response was, "Ehyeh Asher Ehyeh" (*eh*-yeh *ah*-share *eh*-yeh; I will be Who I will be). God said, "This is what you must say to the Israelites: 'I will be' sent me to you" (Exodus 3:14).

God instructed Moses to go to Egypt and gather the elders of the Israelites, describing to the elders that God had appeared to Moses and would bring them out of their wretched oppression. God told Moses that he and the elders should request that the Pharaoh allow the Israelites to leave.

Moses was skeptical and insisted that the people wouldn't believe him. God asked Moses to throw his staff on the ground. When Moses did as God asked, the staff suddenly turned into a snake. God told Moses to grab the snake's tail, upon which the snake turned back into a staff. God then told Moses to put his hand on his chest inside his robe. When Moses did this, his skin suddenly turned white like a leper. Moses touched his chest again, and his skin returned to normal. God assured Moses that when the Egyptians saw these things, they would see God's power. God suggested that if they weren't impressed, Moses should take some water from the Nile River and throw it on the ground, upon which it would turn to blood.

Moses didn't want the job, and he explained to God that he was "heavy of mouth and heavy of speech" (Exodus 4:10). God told Moses that his slow speech and everything else in the world was the result of what God created. God insisted again that He would be with Moses.

Moses still wasn't convinced. He pleaded with God to send someone else to do the job. God told Moses that He would send Moses's brother Aaron with him and explained that Aaron would be the spokesperson. But God also suggested that Moses take the staff and do the "staff into snake" trick to really drive the message home with the Israelites.

Preparing for the trip to Egypt

Moses asked his father-in-law for permission to go to Egypt to see his people, and Yitro agreed. Moses packed up his wife and two sons and headed to Egypt. Before they left, God offered Moses this additional reassurance: "Return to Egypt. All those who want to kill you are now dead" (Exodus 4:19). That must have sounded pretty reassuring, but then God told Moses some seemingly bad news: Even though you know that I (God) have amazing powers and that I have given some of those powers to you (the magical staff), "I will harden Pharaoh's heart and Pharaoh will not allow the people to leave" (Exodus 4:21).

Arriving in Egypt to deliver God's message

Moses's brother, Aaron, was in Egypt, and God instructed him to meet Moses in the desert. Moses told Aaron about his encounter with God and the instructions that Moses received. The two brothers then proceeded with their important task.

Meeting with the Children of Israel and the Pharaoh

Together, Moses and Aaron went to the elders of the Children of Israel in Egypt, told them what God had instructed, and gave the elders a little demonstration of the amazing staff. The elders were convinced (I would be too if I saw a wooden staff turn into a snake and then back again!). They also now knew that God understood their misery.

Moses and Aaron then went to see the Pharaoh and said to him, "God told us to tell you: Let My people go." The Pharaoh understandably said, "Who is your God that I should obey him? I don't believe in your God and I won't let the Children of Israel leave."

Protesting to God

Just as God promised, the Pharaoh's heart was hardened, and things got worse for the Children of Israel. The Pharaoh's new, harsher orders included denying Jewish slaves straw, a key ingredient for making the bricks for the Pharaoh's cities. But the Pharaoh insisted that their daily brick quota remain the same, and he also added additional tasks, making their work even more difficult. The Pharaoh said, "Make the work more difficult for the people and make sure they do it. Then they will stop believing in false ideas" (Exodus 5:9).

The Pharaoh's supervisors whipped the Jewish slaves, and the slaves protested to Moses and Aaron, claiming that they had only made things worse. So Moses spoke to God and said, "Why did you send me? You have done nothing to help Your people." God urged Moses to believe that the Pharaoh would let the Jews go, reminded Moses that He promised Abraham that He would give them the Holy Land, and asked Moses to reassure the people that they would be free and would get a chance to see the might of God firsthand. Moses conveyed God's message to the Children of Israel, but they didn't believe him.

The Egyptian cobra's magic trick

A species of snake known in Egypt as a *naja haje* is commonly called an *Egyptian cobra*. (It's the kind of snake that killed Cleopatra.) It's said that applying pressure to this snake just below its head makes it temporarily paralyzed and quite rigid, so that it looks like a stick. When the rigid snake is then thrown to the ground, the temporary paralysis breaks and the snake becomes active again. Many have speculated that this snake is the explanation of the illusion performed by the Pharaoh's magicians. But there's no similar explanation of how a staff can swallow other staffs, as Aaron's staff did!

God instructed Moses to go back to the Pharaoh and reminded him that the Pharaoh's heart would be hardened once again. But God explained that hardening the Pharaoh's heart ultimately would be a good thing because it would result in a major display of God's power. In other words, if the Pharaoh were to simply let the Children of Israel go, there would be no reason to show Egypt and the world God's absolute might. But when they saw God's might, they would know that God is, well, God!

Performing magic (but to no avail)

Moses and Aaron returned to the Pharaoh (the Torah says that at the time Moses was 80 years old and Aaron was 83). God had warned them that the Pharaoh would want proof of their God's powers. God suggested that Aaron throw his staff on the ground in front of the Pharaoh, which is just what he did. Aaron threw down the staff, and it turned into a snake.

The Pharaoh summoned his scholars and magicians, who were able to duplicate the demonstration with their magic tricks. Several Egyptian magicians threw down their staffs, and they all turned into snakes. Suddenly, Aaron's staff swallowed all the other staffs. It was a very cool demonstration, but the Torah says, "Pharaoh remained obstinate and did not pay attention — just as God predicted" (Exodus 7:13).

The Ten Plagues

After the demonstration with the staffs for the Pharaoh and his magicians, God instructed Moses to go to the Pharaoh again the next morning with his staff and to tell the Pharaoh that God wanted His people to be free. Moses found the Pharaoh by the Nile River and, as instructed by God, said to him, "So far, you have not paid attention. God now says, 'Through this you will know that I am God. I will strike the water of the Nile and it will turn to blood. The fish will die and it will stink'" (Exodus 7:17–18).

As promised, all the water in Egypt turned to blood, but once again, the Pharaoh's magicians claimed to be able to duplicate the "trick." And the Pharaoh just continued to be obstinate.

God then produced additional plagues adding up to ten in all. With each plague, life became worse for Egyptians, but miraculously the plagues had no ill effect for the Children of Israel. And with each plague, the Pharaoh just dug in his heels and remained stubborn.

Following are the plagues and the verses where you can find them described in the Torah:

- **Dam** (*dahm*; blood): Exodus 7:14–25

- **Tzefardaya** (tzeh-fahr-*day*-ah; frogs): Exodus 7:26–8:11

- **Kinim** (*kee*-neem; lice): Exodus 8:12–15

- **Arov** (*ah*-rove; wild animals): Exodus 8:16–28

- **Dever** (*deh*-vehr; livestock disease): Exodus 9:1–7

- **Sheckin** (sh-*kheen*; boils): Exodus 9:8–12

- **Barad** (*bah*-rahd; hail): Exodus 9:13–35

- **Arbeh** (*are*-beh; locusts): Exodus 10:1–20

- **Choshech** (*khoh*-shekh; darkness): Exodus 10:21–29

- **Makat b'Chorot** (*mah*-khat beh-*khor*-oat; death of Egypt's firstborn): Exodus 12:29 (see the next section for more about this plague)

Celebrating the first Passover before leaving Egypt

Egyptians experienced great suffering during the Ten Plagues, but as God had predicted (and caused), the Pharaoh remained obstinate and refused to release the Israelites. Before the final plague, the death of the firstborn of Egypt, God told Moses that the Pharaoh would finally let the Children of Israel leave Egypt after one more plague. God instructed Moses to discreetly tell the people to gather their things and prepare to leave.

Moses said to the Pharaoh, "Around midnight, every firstborn in Egypt will die" (Exodus 11:5). The plague would include every firstborn male, female, and animal but wouldn't touch the Children of Israel. As the Torah states, ". . . among the Israelites, not even a dog will whimper" (Exodus 11: 7).

Under God's instruction, Moses told the Israelites that each family must slaughter a perfect 1-year-old lamb, sheep, or goat as a sacrifice. They were to rub blood from the sacrifices on their doorposts and on the beams above their doors before roasting and eating the meat.

God told Moses that during that night He would kill each firstborn of Egypt and would pass over the homes with blood on them. God instructed the Israelites to remember this day forever and to eat matzah for seven days. These events resulted in the Jewish holy days of **Pesach** (pah-*sakh*; to pass over), or Passover (see Chapter 11 for more about this holiday).

The final plague happened, and God killed every firstborn in Egypt (Exodus 12:29). There was terrible suffering on that night, and the Pharaoh sent for Moses and Aaron, saying to them, "Get out." The Israelites took their belongings and rushed out of Egypt. They were in such a rush that their bread didn't have time to rise, resulting in **matzah** (*mah*-tzah; unleavened bread).

What a Trip: Journeying through the Wilderness

The Torah states that God showed the Children of Israel the way out of Egypt by means of a cloud and a pillar of fire: "God went before them by day in a pillar of cloud to lead them on the way, and at night in a pillar of fire to provide them with light, so that they could travel by day and by night" (Exodus 13:21). In the following sections, I describe the Israelites' adventures as they journey through the wilderness, including crossing the Red Sea, finding food and water, and fighting battles.

Crossing the Sea of Reeds (also known as the Red Sea)

The Torah explains that 2 to 3 million Israelites, 600,000 of whom were men, left Egypt. And so ended 430 years of bitter servitude by the Children of Israel in Egypt. But trouble from the Pharaoh wasn't completely behind them. God directed the Israelites as they fled but took them on a circuitous route. The Pharaoh learned of their path, and one last time God hardened the Pharaoh's heart, causing him to change his mind about letting the Israelites go. The Pharaoh realized that he had released millions of people who provided free labor to Egypt — what a mistake! About 2,000 years ago, the historian Josephus wrote that Pharaoh gathered 600 chariots, 50,000 horsemen, and 200,000 foot soldiers and went after the Israelites.

The Israelites wound up caught between the Egyptian army on one side and the Red Sea on the other. The Torah calls the sea the **yam suf** (yahm soof; Sea of Reeds); it's better known as the Red Sea, which is the erroneous Greek translation. They protested to Moses, saying "How could you do this to us?" (Exodus 14:11). Moses reassured the people and told them that they were about to see something amazing.

God instructed Moses to raise his staff and arms. The sea split, dividing the waters. The Israelites entered the dry sea bed and the water formed as two walls, one on each side of them. The Egyptian army followed them into the sea bed, where the wheels of their chariots got stuck and they all drowned. As the Torah says, "Not a single one was left" (Exodus 14: 28).

Singing a Song at the Sea

According to the Torah, "On that day God rescued the Israelites from Egypt . . . the Israelites saw the hand of God and the power He unleashed on Egypt, and the people were in a state of awe. They believed in God and in Moses" (Exodus 14:31).

As the Pharaoh's horse came into the Red Sea and the Egyptians drowned, Moses and the Israelites sang a song together known as **Shirat Ha Yam** (sheer-*aht* ha yahm; the Song at the Sea). The song commemorates the miracle of the Israelites' escape from Egypt's armies through the divided sea. The song appears in the standard Jewish prayer book and has become a part of the daily liturgy. Some of the key verses are:

> *I will sing to God a song for His great victory . . . Horse and rider He threw in the sea . . . The Lord is my strength and song, and He has become my salvation; He is my God, and I will praise Him; my father's God, and I will exalt Him . . . Pharaoh's chariots and his army has he thrown into the sea; his chosen captains also are drowned in the Red Sea . . . Your right hand, O Lord, is glorious in power; Your right hand, O Lord, has dashed in pieces the enemy . . . The enemy said, I will pursue, I will overtake, I will divide the plunder . . . You blew with Your wind, the sea covered them; they sank as lead in the mighty waters . . . Who is like You, O Lord, among the gods? Who is like You, glorious in holiness, fearful in praises, doing wonders? You stretched out Your right hand, the earth swallowed them . . . You in Your mercy have led forth the people whom You have redeemed . . . You shall bring them in, and plant them in the mountain of your inheritance, in the place, O Lord, which You have made for You to dwell in, in the Sanctuary, O Lord, which Your hands have established . . . The Lord shall reign forever and ever.*

It's interesting to see the way in which a Torah scribe writes the verses of this song in the Torah scroll. The verses are set up to look like a brick wall (see Figure 5-1). Remember that there are strict and exact laws for writing a Torah (see Chapter 14 for details). In the case of the Song at the Sea, it must be written in 30 lines exactly the way it has been written since the beginning of the writing of Torah scrolls.

Figure 5-1:
The Song at the Sea, as it appears in a Torah scroll.

After the Song at the Sea appears in the Torah, Miriam, the sister of Moses and Aaron, is mentioned by name for the first time. The Torah says that "Miriam took a drum in her hand, and all the women followed her with drums and dancing" (Exodus 15:20). According to Torah commentators, Miriam's drum was more like a tambourine or a timbrel.

Gathering manna from heaven and water to drink

After the Children of Israel crossed the Red Sea and were in the desert, they faced new challenges, one of them being hunger. The Torah says that the whole community began to complain and protest to Moses and Aaron. They said, "If only we had died by the hand of God in Egypt. At least in Egypt we could eat. But you brought us into the desert and you will kill us all through starvation" (Exodus 16:3).

God told Moses that food would fall from the sky but also that this food would be the basis of a test of faith for the Children of Israel. The Israelites were instructed to go out each day and gather enough food for themselves for one day. The hungry people would be tempted to gather more than they needed for a day, but God promised that the food would be replenished for each day's gathering. The only exception would be Friday, when God would provide a double portion of food so that the Israelites wouldn't have to work on Saturday (Shabbat; see Chapter 11 for more about this day).

The food appeared each morning in the form of dew with little grains underneath called *manna* in English; in Hebrew, the word is **mun** (muhn). Each day, the people were instructed to gather a quantity called an **omer** (*oh*-mare; approximately two quarts). If someone gathered a little less or a little more, he or she would still have the perfect amount. Any manna that was left over to be eaten the next day would spoil and become putrid.

Although the food problem was solved, the Israelites complained that they were thirsty and had no water. Once again, they asked Moses why he had brought them out of Egypt, where they'd had water. When they insisted that he provide them with water, Moses cried to God and asked God what to do. Moses was frightened that the people would stone him. God told Moses to march in front of the people, take his trusty staff that had served him well until then, and strike a large boulder to produce flowing water from it. Moses named the place **Massa U'Merrivah** (*mah*-sah oo-muh-*ree*-vah; testing and argument).

Fighting the war against Amalek

After the Israelites' food and water issues were resolved, Amalek, a tribe who descended from Esau (see Chapter 4), suddenly attacked the Israelites from behind. Moses told his assistant Joshua to prepare for battle against Amalek. Moses told Joshua that during the battle he (Moses) would stand on the top of the hill overlooking the battle and have God's staff in his hand. As long as Moses held his hands up, the Israelites would be winning, but if he put his arms down, Amalek would gain strength. The battle began, and Moses kept his arms up, but after a while he grew tired. Aaron and another person helped Moses keep his hands up, and the Israelites were victorious.

Over the centuries, the memory of the evil Amalek has persisted among the Jewish people, and the Torah presents a paradox regarding Amalek that's often addressed: The Torah says to remember to obliterate the memory of Amalek. Moses said, "God shall be at war with Amalek for all generations" (Exodus 17:16). In fact, the enemies of the Jewish people are often referred to as "Amalek." For example, Hitler has been referred to as "Amalek" among the Jewish people.

Appointing judges

Moses's father-in-law, Yitro, heard about the Israelites' exodus from Egypt and traveled to be with Moses and the people. Yitro brought along Moses's wife Tzipporah and their two sons, Gershom and Eliezer. Moses updated his father-in-law on all that had occurred since they last saw each other.

There were inevitable conflicts among the Israelites as they continued to travel, and Moses spent his days listening to their cases and acting as a judge. After some observation, Yitro told Moses, "You are going to wear yourself out . . . you cannot do it all alone" (Exodus 18:18). He suggested that Moses share his wisdom with the people and then appoint God-fearing men, "men of truth who hate injustice" (Exodus 18: 21), to listen to disputes and make judgments. This arrangement became the basis of the court system of the Jewish people (see Chapter 10) and court systems throughout history. Yitro said, "You must appoint them over the people as leaders of thousands, leaders of hundreds, leaders of fifties, and leaders of tens" (Exodus 18:21). Moses only served as the judge of the toughest cases; the minor cases were left to the God-fearing judges.

Arriving at Mount Sinai

Three months into the Israelites' journey from Egypt, they arrived at Mount Sinai; I discuss the momentous events that happened there (including the receipt of the Ten Commandments and the Torah) in the following sections.

Connecting with God

The Torah says that when the Israelites arrived at Mount Sinai, Moses "went up to God" (Exodus 19:3), and Torah commentators say that this means that Moses connected directly with God by way of meditation. The message Moses received from God was a pivotal moment in the history of the Children of Israel. God said to Moses, "This is what you must say to the Children of Israel":

- ✔ "You saw what I did in Egypt."
- ✔ "If you obey Me and keep My covenant you shall be My special treasure."
- ✔ "You will be a kingdom of priests and a holy nation to Me."

The Children of Israel responded, "All that God has spoken we will do" (Exodus 19:8).

God told Moses that in three days He would descend on Mount Sinai. The Children of Israel then prepared for the momentous time by setting a boundary around the mountain.

Going up the mountain to get the Ten Commandments

Three days after Moses received God's message, thunder, lightning, and smoke were heard and seen. A loud trumpet blast from a ram's horn was sounded, and the Divine Presence was perceived by all who were at Mount Sinai. God instructed Moses to ascend to the peak of the mountain. Moses climbed up the mountain but then came down to warn the people not to cross over the boundary they had set around the mountain. Moses cautioned that people could die if they got too close to Mount Sinai.

God then spoke the Ten Commandments. Some Torah commentaries claim that all the gathered Israelites heard the Voice of God as He spoke all Ten Commandments, whereas others insist that everyone heard the first two commandments from the voice of God and Moses taught them the remaining eight. Following is a summary of the Ten Commandments (Exodus 20:1–14) (check out Chapter 17 for a more-complete discussion of the Ten Commandments):

1. I am the Lord your God.

2. Do not have any other gods or idols.

3. Do not take God's name in vain.

4. Remember the Sabbath and keep it holy.

5. Honor your father and your mother.

6. Do not murder.

7. Do not commit adultery.

8. Do not steal.

9. Do not bear false witness (don't lie!).

10. Do not be envious of your neighbor.

God gave Moses two tablets, which Jewish tradition says were written on by God's finger. Jewish commentaries differ as to what was written on the tablets. One opinion says that of the Ten Commandments, five were written on one tablet and five on the other. Another opinion suggests that all Ten Commandments were written on each of the two tablets. The Talmud also indicates that there were two miracles regarding these tablets:

- The writing went right through the stones but could be read from either side.

- The central parts of some of the letters, even though they weren't connected, didn't fall out but floated.

You can find out what happened to these tablets in the later section "Aaron and the Incident of the Golden Calf."

Returning with the Torah

When Moses returned from Mount Sinai after 40 days (Exodus 34:28–29), in addition to the Ten Commandments, he had received an enormous number of teachings from God. Some of these teachings are recorded in detail in the Torah, resulting in the Five Books of Moses. Many other teachings were to remain oral and became the basis of the Oral Law of the Jewish people. In a very real sense, Moses received two Torahs on Mount Sinai: a Written Torah and an Oral Torah (eventually to be known as the Talmud; see Chapter 3). Both are essential parts of the Torah of the Jewish people.

As a whole, the Five Books of Moses contains 613 laws scattered throughout the text (see Appendixes B and C for full details on these laws), but a great number appear in the book of Exodus in particular. Some of these laws relate to the following issues:

- Prohibition against idolatry
- How to treat indentured servants
- Capital crimes such as murder, injuring or cursing your parents, and kidnapping someone
- The laws of damages
- The laws of stealing
- Proper wages
- Prohibition against occult practices
- Treatment of widows and orphans
- The laws of money lending
- The laws of court procedure

Aaron and the Incident of the Golden Calf

While Moses was still on the mountain speaking with God (see the previous section), the Israelites were getting restless. They felt that Moses was taking quite a long time (wouldn't you be impatient after 40 days?), so they gathered around Moses's brother Aaron and asked him to make them an idol to worship.

Aaron instructed the people to give the women's gold earrings to a designated goldsmith, who melted the gold and formed it into the shape of a calf. The Torah says that some people actually said of the calf, "This is the god who brought us out of Egypt" (Exodus 32:4). When Aaron saw and heard the people's reactions, he built an altar before the golden calf and announced a festival to be held the next day. (The great Torah commentators indicate that Aaron really didn't believe in or condone the building of a golden calf idol; he was merely buying time, hoping that Moses would return soon.) The next morning, the people awoke and prepared for a festival. They brought sacrifices to be burned, and they ate, drank, and had a great time.

God saw what was going on among Aaron and the Israelites and told Moses that the people were becoming corrupt. God said, "They are quick to forget what I commanded of them and they have made an idol." God described the Children of Israel as a "stiff-necked people" (Exodus 32:9). A great Torah commentator points out that describing the Jewish people as stiff-necked is not a negative comment; the commentator explains that this stubborn trait is a positive trait when the Jewish people get it right and are stubborn about the right things.

Moses tried to plead to God on behalf of the people and managed to convince God to be patient with them. Moses went down the mountain, holding the two tablets with the Ten Commandments, and saw the golden calf and the dancing. In anger, Moses smashed the tablets and destroyed the golden calf by melting it and grinding it into powder. He scattered the powder into the water of a brook and forced the people to drink the water.

Moses and Aaron spoke about the incident with the golden calf, and Moses understood that Aaron had actually restrained the people. Moses also saw that it was only a small minority of people who had led the rest astray. In a bold act of housecleaning, Moses ordered the rebellious leadership to be killed, and on that day, 3,000 people were executed.

The Torah indicates that Moses and God had an intimate chat about the whole sinful golden calf affair, the way two friends would. During this conversation, Moses asked God if he could see God, but God replied that no man could see Him and survive. God then instructed Moses to create a duplicate set of the Ten Commandments. Moses did as God asked and then recited words that became one of the most sacred prayers of the Jewish people: "God, God, Omnipotent, merciful and kind, slow to anger, with tremendous love and truth. He remembers deeds of love for thousands of generations, forgiving sin, rebellion and error" (Exodus 34:6–7).

Building a Movable Worship Tent

In the book of Exodus, the Torah describes in rather precise detail the structure of the movable place of worship that accompanied the Children of Israel. In English, it's known as the *Tabernacle,* which comes from the Latin word for "hut," but the Hebrew term **mishkan** (*mish*-kahn; to dwell), describes it more accurately. The Hebrew word "mishkan" is from the same root as the Hebrew word **shechinah** (sheh-*khee*-nah; God's presence). The mishkan was the focal point of worship for the Children of Israel as they worked their way from Egypt to the land of Israel where the Holy Temple was eventually built in Jerusalem. The layout of the sanctuary in synagogues today is based on the description of the mishkan in the Torah.

Six chapters in the book of Exodus offer the details of the mishkan (the books of Leviticus and Numbers also discuss the Tabernacle; see Chapters 6 and 7 for details). The Exodus chapters speak of many of the details of the mishkan, including:

- ✔ **The materials required to build the Tabernacle** (Exodus 25:1–9 and Exodus 35:4–9)

    Moses tells the people which materials God has instructed be used to build the Tabernacle and asks that the people make offerings of these materials if they have them. The materials included gold, silver, copper, various-colored wool, animal skins and hides, acacia wood, lamp oil, fragrances to make incense, and precious stones.

- ✔ **The details of the Ark of the Covenant** (Exodus 25:10–22 and Exodus 37:1–9)

    The Torah says that the chief architect of the Tabernacle was an artist named **Bezalel** (betz-ah-*layl*). Bezalel made the Ark of acacia wood with a layer of pure gold on the inside. The Torah describes its precise dimensions (2½ cubits by ½ cubits and 1½ cubits in height; a *cubit* is the ancient yardstick that measures from the tip of the middle finger to the tip of the elbow). The Torah also describes the two gold cherubs that decorated the top of the Ark. The Ark of the Covenant was where the tablets of the Ten Commandments were kept.

- ✔ **The table** (Exodus 25:23–30 and Exodus 37:10–16)

    The table in the Tabernacle was also made of acacia wood and layered with pure gold. Once a week, freshly baked bread made of the finest flour was placed on the table as part of the divinely directed ritual. Echoing this today are the two loaves of bread called **challah** (*khah*-lah) that are on the Shabbat table in Jewish homes each week.

- ✔ **The menorah** (Exodus 25:31–40 and Exodus 37:17–24)

    Bezalel created the seven-branched lamp called the **menorah** (meh-*no*-rah; lamp) by hammering one single piece of pure gold. On each side of the central shaft were three branches. Each branch was decorated with three cups, a sphere, and a flower. The central shaft had even more of these decorations. All the details of the menorah design were dictated by God, and it's rich in its symbolism. The menorah that was used in the second Temple in Jerusalem was brought to Rome when Rome conquered the Holy Land. In Rome today, you can see a sculpted representation of this event on the Arch of Titus.

- ✔ **The copper altar** (Exodus 27: 1–8 and Exodus 38:1–7)

  This altar was made of acacia wood plated with copper. Located outside the Tabernacle itself, it was the location of the offerings of sacrifices, the major activity at the Tabernacle site. The Torah describes it as a square, 5 cubits by 5 cubits and 3 cubits in height.

- ✔ **The clothing of the priests** (Exodus 28: 1–43 and Exodus 39: 2–31)

  The priests' vestments were ornate and looked like garments created for royalty. In Exodus 28:2, the Torah says that the vestments were designed for "glory and splendor," regarding the priests as well as for the honor God.

- ✔ **The incense altar** (Exodus 30:1–10 and Exodus 37:25–29)

  This altar was made of acacia wood and plated with gold. It was a square, 2 cubits by 2 cubits and 3 cubits tall. Incense burned morning and night in the Tabernacle.

- ✔ **The washstand** (Exodus 30:17–21 and Exodus 38:8)

  In the courtyard of the Tabernacle was a big copper basin filled with water. The priests were required to wash their hands and feet at this basin before each sacrificial service. Many pious Jews today also wash their hands before a prayer service.

The Ark of the Covenant (yes, the one Indiana Jones looked for)

In Hebrew, the Ark of the Covenant is known as **Aron Habrit** (*ah*-rone ha-*brit*). It's the container that stored the tablets containing the Ten Commandments. The Ark included two **cherubim** (cheh-*roo*-beem; forms or images of angels) situated on the top of the Ark. The Torah states that Moses was able to receive teachings from God by standing beneath and between these two cherubim. See Exodus 25:10–22 for the Torah's description of this famous object.

The Holy of Holies

The **kodesh hakodashim** (*kow*-desh ha-koh-dah-*sheem*; the Holy of Holies) was the most sacred spot in the mishkan because it was the location of the Ark of the Covenant. As such, the voice of God spoke to Moses in this place. Many years later, when the Holy Temple stood on the Temple Mount in Jerusalem, it too had a Holy of Holies. Only on one day of the year (Yom Kippur) was the High Priest permitted to enter this most sacred space.

Why do Jews avoid the Dome of the Rock?

In photographs of present-day Jerusalem, one structure that dominates the skyline is the Dome of the Rock, part of an Islamic mosque in Jerusalem's old city. Jewish tradition teaches that this mosque was built on the very spot where the Holy of Holies is located. It isn't just for political reasons that Jews today don't visit that mosque or the area surrounding it. Because it isn't known precisely where the Holy of Holies is (the spot was located by means of prophecy), Jews avoid that area in order to not enter this sacred space.

The menorah

The seven-branched candelabra known as the menorah is one of the major pieces of furniture in the mishkan (and ultimately in the Holy Temple). The Torah goes into precise detail about the menorah's construction. Included in this detail are the following requirements:

- ✔ It must be pure gold.
- ✔ It is formed by hammering.
- ✔ It must be one single piece of gold.
- ✔ There must be seven lamps.
- ✔ On each side of the central branch are three branches.
- ✔ Each branch must have three cups with a sphere and flower on each.

The menorah's structure is filled with symbolic significance and has been the subject of a lot of commentaries over the centuries.

The priests, their special garments, and their rituals

Moses's brother Aaron was designated as the first High Priest of the mishkan, and along with his sons, he arranged for the menorah to burn and to oversee the other activities in the mishkan (and eventually in the Holy Temple). To this day, Jewish men who trace their ancestry to Aaron refer to themselves as priests called **kohanim** (ko-ha-*neem*) and have special roles in the synagogue service (see Chapter 13 for details of this service). The Torah goes into great detail about the responsibilities and rituals performed by the priests and their descendants as well as the special clothing worn by the priests. The Torah includes the following information about the priests' clothing:

- The basic garment, called the *ephod*
- The design of the ephod
- The breastplate, including the material to be used
- The precious stones on the breastplate
- The robe worn under the ephod
- The forehead plate and its details
- The head covering or turban

Remember that the main activity in the mishkan was the offering of sacrifices. These weren't bribes to God by primitive people. Rather, a sacrifice was a profound ritual. When you study the details and symbolism of each sacrifice, or when you experience the emotional, intellectual, and spiritual impact on those involved with the sacrifice, the results are deep spiritual connections with God and profoundly personal religious experiences.

Chapter 6

"And He Called": The Book of Leviticus

In Hebrew, the book of Leviticus is called **Vayikra** (vah-*yih*-krah). It's the first word of the book, and it means "and He called," referring to God. In every Torah scroll, the word "Vayikra" consists of five letters, the fifth of which is the "aleph," the first letter of the Hebrew alphabet. In every accurate Torah scroll, the aleph in the first word is written extra small, and all the surrounding letters are normal size.

Jewish tradition teaches that the small aleph serves as a reminder of the major character trait of Moses: humility. Jewish tradition teaches that Moses was the most humble man in the world. Because of his humility, Moses wouldn't enter the Tabernacle unless he was called by God. Moses also is known by Jews to be the greatest prophet and greatest teacher who ever lived. The message is clear: In order to receive God, you must humble yourself. The book of Leviticus begins with a call from God, and the way to receive God's call is to diminish your ego and make room for the Divine.

The third of the Five Books of Moses is known as Leviticus because it's largely about the Levites, the descendants of Jacob's son Levi. When the Children of Israel entered the Promised Land (the Land of Israel), each received a part of the land to call their own. But the descendants of Levi received no land; rather, they worked in the Holy Temple, assisting the **kohanim** (koh-hah-*neem*; priests) and supporting themselves with donations from those who came to the Temple. The Levites also were the singers in the Holy Temple. The book of Leviticus, as you find out in this chapter, details the holy duties that the Levites were responsible for carrying out. In this chapter, you also find out that the book of Leviticus deals with many of the most basic moral commandments in the Torah that pertain not only to the priests and Levites but to all the Children of Israel.

Drawing Near to God: The Laws of Sacrifices

A major part of the first section of the book of Leviticus deals with the sacrifices, or offerings, that the Israelites brought to the **mizbaiach** (miz-*bay*-akh; altar) in the **mishkan** (*mish*-khan; to dwell). (Turn to Chapter 5 for more about the mishkan, or Tabernacle.) Whether they were animal, vegetable, or baked items, the sacrifices were burned in the mishkan. A sacrifice wasn't intended as a bribe to God. After all, it's foolish to think that God would be forgiving or loving in response to an animal slaughtered on the altar, for example. And what would the Creator of the Universe want with the smoke of a burnt pigeon?

So what's the purpose of a sacrifice? The answer starts with the word itself. The Hebrew word for "sacrifice" is **korban** (*core*-bahn; to draw near). The purpose of the Tabernacle was to give the people an opportunity to focus all their attention on God and to feel closer to God. So the Tabernacle in general and the sacrifices in particular were designed to draw one near to God.

There were a number of aspects to every sacrifice:

✔ It created a pleasurable smell, offered with heartfelt and sincere love and devotion to God.

✔ It was offered in the place of the person who offered the sacrifice. By offering the sacrifice, the person was saying, "I offer myself to You, God, with utmost sincerity and completeness, just as this sacrifice is being completely offered."

Hearing God's call through sacrifice and education

In the Jewish world today, it's considered a deed of the highest order to help others get involved in Jewish life, study the Torah, and deepen their faith in God. Performing acts of outreach and trying to influence family, friends, and others to reconnect with Judaism is called **Kiruv** (*kee*-roov). Every Hebrew word is based on a root that's usually three letters. The word "kiruv" shares the same root as the word "korban" (sacrifice).

Just as the purpose of the sacrifice is to bring a person near to God, the efforts to educate other Jewish people in the ways of Judaism are really an effort to also bring them near. A person hears the call of God and is inspired to call out to others and to bring a person's soul closer to the Divine.

✔ It was usually an animal that represented a life; the sacrifice was symbolic of a total offering of life itself and an acknowledgment that life is a gift from God.

✔ It was burned completely because the sincerity of a sacrifice had to be total. (In some cases, part of the sacrifice was eaten by the priests who performed the ritual sacrifices on behalf of others.)

According to the teachings of the sages, every sacrifice requires a special inner attitude on the part of the individual involved in the ritual. This order reflects the order in which all people, not just priests, are supposed to serve God:

1. The person opens himself to God and hears God's call.

2. The person must come close to God and be ready to give his whole being to God.

3. In place of giving his own life, the person offers the sacrifice.

In the following sections, I describe the many kinds of sacrifices detailed in the book of Leviticus.

Burnt offerings

In the book of Leviticus, the most common sacrifice or offering is the **olah** (oh-*la*; burnt offering), which symbolically represented one's complete devotion to and submission to God (Leviticus 1:1–17). The root of the word "olah" means "ascension."

Burnt offerings consisted of different kinds of animals; the choice of animal was based on what a person could afford. The person's first choice, according to the Torah, would be a fine bull, cow, sheep, or goat. But if he couldn't afford such an animal, a bird (such as a pigeon or a turtledove) was used. If the person wasn't able to afford any animal, a meal offering was permissible.

Meal offerings

A meal offering is known as **korban mincha** (*core*-bahn *min*-khah) (Leviticus 2:1–3). The meal offering was supposed to be made of the finest flour available mixed with oil and frankincense, but it was an inexpensive offering used by those who were too poor to use more expensive items such as animals. Because grain is the basic ingredient for prepared food, it's the sustainer of life. Symbolically, the meal offering expressed the fact that the true source and sustainer of all life is God. The person making the sacrifice gave the korban mincha to a priest who took a part of it and burned it on the altar. The rest was available to be eaten by the priests. Various types of meal offerings are detailed in Leviticus, including

- Baked offering
- Pan (fried) offering
- Deep-fried offering
- Grain offering using the first reaping

Peace offerings

A peace offering (Leviticus 3:1–17) is an expression of gratitude to God. It's an offering of thankfulness for all that God has given and gratitude for God's generosity. In Hebrew, a peace offering was known as **zebach sh'lamim** (*zeh*-bakh sheh-la-*meem*) or simply **sh'lamim,** which is connected to the Hebrew word "shalom," which means meaning "peace" or "whole." According to the Torah, people offered peace offerings after surviving life-threatening situations or fulfilling vows. Peace offerings had nothing to do with sins or regret.

The objects of peace offerings included

- Cattle
- Sheep
- Goats

As with other sacrifices, the animal was cooked. A portion was eaten by the person making the offering, a portion was eaten by the priests, and a portion was burned.

Sin offerings

A sin offering serves as an expression of regret for a sin. This kind of sacrifice, called **chatat** (khah-*tat*), was only appropriate for a sin that was unintentional. One of the Hebrew words for "sin" is **chayt** (khayt) which actually means "to miss the mark."

There were several kinds of offerings made by different people or groups who committed sins as described in Leviticus 4:1–35. Here are some examples:

- The sin offering made by a High Priest who sinned was a young bull.
- The sin offering made by a community that sinned was a young bull.

> ✔ The sin offering made by a king who sinned was an unblemished male goat.
>
> ✔ The sin offering made by commoner who sinned was an unblemished female goat.

Guilt offerings

A guilt offering, known as an **asham** (ah-*shahm*), is an offering to atone for possible sins. When a person thought that perhaps he or she had sinned but wasn't completely sure, he or she made a guilt offering. A guilt offering was also made when knowledge of a past sin was later realized. The Torah requires a variety of items for the sacrifice depending upon what the person could afford (Leviticus 5:1–13). The wealthiest people offered a female sheep or goat. If that couldn't be afforded, the other choices were two turtledoves, two common doves, and, for the poorest people, a portion of wheat meal.

The purpose of sacrificing animals

The great Torah sage known as the Ramban (see Chapter 16) says in his Torah commentary that when a person's animal sacrifice is being slaughtered and burned on the altar, his or her thoughts should include the knowledge that it's God's mercy and generosity that allow us to substitute a sacrifice in our place (Leviticus 1:9).

Animal rights advocates have a problem with this subject, asking why it's necessary to kill a poor animal in order to feel closer to God? A few things need to be remembered regarding the Jewish view toward animals:

✔ In principle, animals are in the world to serve people.

✔ Slaughtering an animal must be done in the most painless way possible. Jewish laws go into great detail about how an animal is slaughtered. To this day, an animal is kosher (see Chapter 12) because of the type of animal it is, how it's prepared, and how it's slaughtered.

✔ Hunting for sport isn't permissible.

✔ Pets and animals raised for food must be treated humanely while they're alive, and you must feed your animals before you feed yourself.

Sacrifice on the altar in the Tabernacle or the Holy Temple is an ancient ritual intended to raise one's consciousness and to purify one's soul. Humans are considered the central actors on the world stage, and sacrificial animals serve humans in a process that's mysterious, deeply psychological, deeply spiritual, and ultimately for the purpose of elevating the human spirit.

Because God spared the firstborn Children of Israel during the last plague in Egypt (see Chapter 5 for details), the Torah teaches that all firstborn animals have a special connection to God. While all Creation obviously belongs to God, firstborn animals are said by the Torah to "belong" to God in a more profound way.

Surveying the Priestly Duties

The Torah designates Aaron, the brother of Moses, as the source of all future priests. Aaron was the High Priest and his sons were the first actual priests who worked in the Tabernacle (in the desert) and in the Holy Temple in Jerusalem. They supervised the daily and holy day sacrifices. Many of the verses in the book of Leviticus offer details about the vestments and activities of the priests and the High Priest. Here are some examples:

✔ Priests must have no contact with corpses other than close relatives (Leviticus 21:2).

✔ Priests must never use God's names in vain (Leviticus 21:6).

✔ Priests must not marry divorced women (Leviticus 21:7).

✔ The High Priest must have no rips in his clothing (Leviticus 21:10).

✔ The High Priest must wear special clothing or vestments (Leviticus 16:4 and Leviticus 21:10). The details of these vestments are in Exodus 28.

In addition to details about priestly vestments and duties, the book of Leviticus tells of a powerful and troubling incident concerning the two oldest sons of Aaron, **Nadav** (nah-*dahv*) and **Avihu** (ah-*vee*-who). The Torah says that these two priests offered a "strange fire" to God during their sacrificial activities. The Torah is blunt and dramatic about it, saying, "Fire came forth from God and consumed them and they died before God" (Leviticus 10:2).

Tracing your lineage back to Aaron, the first High Priest

In Hebrew, the word for priest is **kohen** (*ko*-hayn). The popular Jewish surname Cohen comes from this word, as do surnames like Kahn and Kahane. Although not completely guaranteed, it's usually the case that a Jewish person with one of these names is a descendant of the original priests — and therefore of Aaron himself. The status of the kohen is passed down in a patrilineal way (from father to son), and an unbroken chain exists for 3,300 years and more than 100 generations! In fact, in the synagogue Torah service (see Chapter 13), the first person to be called to the Torah during its public reading is a direct descendant of Aaron. As amazing as it seems, Jewish families today usually know if they descend from Aaron or from the Levites. A Jew who isn't a descendant of either is consider an Israelite.

Genetically, if two people have the same ancestor, a genetic marker is present in both of their DNA. An article published in 1997 in the highly regarded science journal *Nature* reported that DNA analysis revealed that, of 188 Jewish men who had been told that they were descendants of Aaron, 98.5 percent of these men shared the same ancient genetic marker. Since that report, many other studies have been done and indicate a clear tradition of shared descent among most of those today who claim descent from Aaron.

The Torah also clearly says that their "strange fire" was part of a ritual that was unauthorized and not part of the specific instruction in the Torah.

This incident is the subject of much commentary among the Torah sages throughout the centuries. The major accusations against the two brothers and sons of Aaron are as follows:

✔ They didn't first consult with Moses.

✔ Their offering was supposed to be the activity of only the High Priest.

✔ They may have been drunk at the time of their offering, according to one Talmudic opinion (see Chapter 3 for more about the Talmud). Drinking wine before participating in the service was forbidden.

✔ They used items that were privately owned. According to the Torah, the utensils used in offerings must be communally owned.

✔ They entered the Holy of Holies, which was forbidden to all except the High Priest one day a year (Yom Kippur.) See Chapter 5 for more about this sacred space in the Tabernacle.

Apart from the specific accusations against Nadav and Avihu, the general problem is clear: Jewish tradition leaves much room for creativity and fluidity, but when the Torah provides very specific instructions, it's unacceptable for someone in authority to say, "I'm going to do it a different way."

The Laws of Purity and Impurity

The book of Leviticus contains many of the details that make up the ritual life of the Jewish people. It also covers many of the laws that comprise the backbone of Jewish family life. In the Torah, they're referred to as *laws of purity and impurity.* Many of the 613 commandments also appear in the book of Leviticus; for more about these commandments, see Appendixes B and C.

Clean and unclean animals

Many aspects of Jewish life have made the Jewish people distinctive among the other families of the world, and the laws of **kashrut** (kahsh-*root*; kosher) are prominent among them. The book of Leviticus outlines a great number of details of the laws of eating kosher food; some of these major commandments are

✔ Among mammals, only those with split hooves and those who chew their cud are permitted. (Cows are in, but pigs are out.)

✔ Only sea animals with fins and scales are permitted. (Salmon is okay, but lobsters are out.)

- ✔ All insects are forbidden.

- ✔ Certain birds are acceptable as food, but others listed in the Torah are not acceptable. (Chickens and ducks are permitted, but eagles, hawks, owls, and falcons are not. See Leviticus 11:13–18 for details.)

- ✔ Only animals that have been slaughtered properly can be eaten. For example, you can't shoot an animal and eat it, nor can you eat an animal that has died of natural causes.

You can find a more detailed discussion of the Torah's kosher laws in Chapter 12.

Ritual cleanliness

One of the most misunderstood and maligned parts of Jewish law has to do with the concept of ritual impurity. The Torah addresses this subject at length, including the rules about pouring water on one's hands after leaving a cemetery and after waking up in the morning, as well as the necessity for married women to enter and submerge in a mikvah after their menstrual cycles each month (see Chapter 14 for more about mikvahs). The book of Leviticus contains instructions regarding a time period after a woman gives birth when she's considered to be "ritually impure" (Leviticus 15:19–28).

These laws and commandments about ritual cleanliness have nothing whatsoever to do with physical uncleanness, and they don't imply that a woman is inferior, dirty, or in need of a washing after giving birth. These Torah commandments are all of a symbolic and spiritual nature. They have to do with rebirth, transformation, and renewal. They're also the original sources for the Christian practice of baptism.

The laws of tzarat (some call it leprosy)

The book of Leviticus provides an interesting example of how the Torah has been mistranslated and how mistranslations often get passed from one edition to the next and from one century to the next. A rather large number of passages in this section of the Torah deal with a physical condition called **tzarat** (tzah-*raht*). Scholars have determined that this condition is absolutely not leprosy, yet that's what it's called in most English translations of the Torah. Although there are some similarities between tzarat and leprosy, there are also enough significant differences to prove conclusively that the Torah isn't speaking of leprosy. The condition presented in the book of Leviticus is marked by white spots on the skin as well as on sheets, houses, and other surfaces.

The important thing about tzarat isn't the name of the disease but rather the causes of it. The Torah considers it a punishment for certain disobedience of Torah commandments, and the Talmud teaches that the infractions include murder, pride, and theft. But the major wrongdoing that Jewish tradition says causes tzarat is the sin of **lashon hara** (la-*shone* hah-*rah*; evil speech). Abusive language is a serious crime according to Jewish law, and I go into detail about this in Chapter 9.

The laws concerning tzarat are complex, and while the Written Torah addresses tzarat a great detail, the Oral Torah is even more expansive on the topic. Essentially, it's the role of the priesthood to identify tzarat, to declare the person or object as clean or unclean, and to quarantine the person or object outside the camp for various lengths of time. As with all suffering, the Torah views the appearance of tzarat mainly as a signal to an individual with tzarat to examine his or her deeds and to repent.

Yom Kippur, the Day of Atonement

One of the most well-known Jewish holy days is **Yom Kippur** (yome kee-*poor*), also known as the Day of Atonement. In the Torah, this holy day is discussed in the book of Leviticus (as well as in other places). For example, permission is given to the High Priest alone to enter the Holy of Holies, the most sacred place in physical space, and to pray to God on behalf of the people. Leviticus 16:1–34 provides some of the details of the Yom Kippur Service as performed in the Tabernacle, including the sacred vestments required of the High Priest as well as special Yom Kippur sacrifices and rituals made on behalf of the community. The hope on Yom Kippur is that the rituals and offerings symbolize the personal repentance and purification on the part of all the people. For more on Yom Kippur, see Chapter 11.

Sexual laws

Leviticus outlines many of the commandments for men that deal with forbidden sexual relations. It's forbidden for men to have sexual relations with the following people:

- ✔ Parents
- ✔ Stepmother
- ✔ Sister
- ✔ Grandchildren
- ✔ Half sister
- ✔ Aunt
- ✔ Daughter-in-law
- ✔ Sister-in-law

This section of the Torah also contains a controversial commandment directed at men: "Do not lie with a male as you would with a woman" (Leviticus 18:22). There are many interpretations of this passage, but Torah commentaries make it relatively clear that this commandment refers specifically to anal intercourse between men. (Chapter 9 has more information about sexual laws.)

Holiness laws

The book of Leviticus contains some of the most well-known and highly admired commandments that form the basis of civilization. The Torah indicates that observance of these commandments is the basis of a righteous, pure, and holy lifestyle. These commandments include:

- Respect your parents.
- Observe the Sabbath.
- Don't make idols.
- Don't steal.
- Don't lie.
- Pay employees on time.
- Don't gossip.
- Don't hate people in your heart.
- Admonish your neighbor.
- Don't bear a grudge.
- Love your neighbor as you love yourself.
- Be honest with your weights and measures.
- Honor the elderly.

These commandments are followed by a number of commandments that aren't obvious moral ideas but are just as important in Jewish tradition. They include:

- Don't plant fields with different species in them.
- Don't wear garments that contain a mixture of linen and wool.
- Don't eat blood.
- Don't follow astrology.
- Don't shave the corners of your beard or the corners of your head (which is why many Jewish men wear beards!).
- Don't wear tattoos.

Appendixes B and C cover these and other commandments found throughout Leviticus and the rest of the Torah.

Priestly laws

Toward the end of the book of Leviticus, the Torah reviews some of the laws that specifically pertain to the priesthood. For example, the laws deal with whom priests are and aren't allowed to marry, forbidden contact (a priest can't have contact with a corpse, for example), and conditions that disqualify a priest, such as certain physical blemishes that prohibit a priest from participating in an offering (Leviticus 21:16–23).

After presenting these details, Leviticus outlines the major Jewish holy days including:

- **Shabbat:** This is a weekly day of rest.

    "For six days labor may be done, and the seventh day is a day of complete rest." (Leviticus 23:3)

- **Passover:** This holy day period commemorates the exodus from Egypt.

    "You shall eat matzos for a seven day period." (Leviticus 23:6)

- **Shavuot:** This holy day commemorates the receiving of the Torah.

    "This day shall be celebrated as a sacred holy day." (Leviticus 23:21)

- **Rosh Hashanah:** This holy day is a the start of a new year and begins an intense ten-day period of prayer and introspection.

    "The first day of the seventh month shall be a day of rest." (Leviticus 23:24)

- **Yom Kippur:** This holy day is known as the Day of Atonement and is the climax of the intense ten-day period of self-reflection and prayer.

    "It is a day of atonement, when you gain atonement before God." (Leviticus 23:28)

- **Sukkot:** This holy day period commemorates the Children of Israel's experience of wandering in the desert and living in temporary shelter.

    "The fifteenth of the seventh month shall be the festival of Succot." (Leviticus 23:33)

- **The Sabbatical Year:** The Torah requires that the farmland in Israel rest every seventh year.

    "For six years you may plant your fields, prune your vineyards, and harvest your crops. But the seventh year is a Sabbath of Sabbaths for the land." (Leviticus 25:3)

- **The Jubilee Year:** This year, according to the Torah, is when debts are canceled out and people return to the lands that their ancestors originally owned.

    "You shall count seven sabbatical years, that is seven times seven years." (Leviticus 25:8)

Each Jewish holy day or holy day period has its own customs, laws, history, and significance. But all have one thing in common: the constant goal of inner refinement and purification. The details of each holy day ultimately focus on these goals. I discuss these days in more detail in Chapter 11.

Reward and punishment

The book of Leviticus ends with an exploration of reward and punishment. Essentially, the Torah says that if you live a pure life and follow the divine commandments in the Torah, you'll reap rewards. And if you don't live such a life, you'll suffer consequences.

It's important to keep in mind the great Jewish sages' teaching that a fundamental principle in Jewish tradition is reincarnation. The idea is that your soul existed before your current body, and when you die, the soul drops that body. If you haven't fulfilled your tasks in this lifetime, you come back and get additional chances. (For a full exploration of this concept in Jewish thought, see my book *Kabbalah For Dummies,* published by Wiley).

Reward and punishment don't occur immediately. Ultimately, God is the True Judge as well as the ultimate bestower of understanding and compassion. God knows what's in your heart, what you're capable of, and what you ultimately deserve.

Chapter 7

"In the Wilderness": The Book of Numbers

*L*ike each of the other books in the Torah, the book of Numbers has a different name in Hebrew: **Bamidbar** (*bih*-mid-*bar*; in the wilderness). It's somewhat understandable that the Greek translation is "the book of Numbers" because the book begins with a lengthy census of the Children of Israel in the desert. But the book of Numbers is really an account of the 40 years the Israelites spent wandering from Egypt to the Promised Land, the Land of Israel.

The trip didn't have to take as long as it did. If the Children of Israel had followed a straight route, the journey would have taken far less time. But the 40 years in the desert, which I describe in this chapter, transformed the Children of Israel into a nation capable of defending itself and establishing itself as an organized group. The trials in the desert (of which there were many) forged them into a nation with a deep commitment and faith and obedience to God. Also, enough time passed in the desert for a new generation to be born — a generation without the slave mentality that those who left Egypt unfortunately couldn't fully shake.

Counting the Children of Israel

The book of Numbers begins with a command by God to Moses and his brother Aaron to take a census of the Israelites. In the following sections, I explain the results of the census of the Twelve Tribes of Israel and tell you about an exception to the census: the tribe of Levi.

Organizing the Twelve Tribes of Israel

The purpose of the census was to count those members of each major family (sometimes called a *tribe*) who were qualified for military duty, defined by the Torah as all males over age 20. Each of the Twelve Tribes of Israel descends from one of the 12 sons of the patriarch Jacob, whose name was changed by God to "Israel." The sons of Jacob/Israel were literally the "fathers" of the tribes, as each tribe bore the name of one of the sons. When the Children of Israel left Egypt, they did so as tribes — that is, as huge family groups each of whom descended from one of the sons of Israel. When the Children of Israel arrived at Mount Sinai to receive the Torah, they camped around the mountain as tribes. When they finally arrived in the Holy Land, they settled in separate areas as tribes. Each tribe had its own flag, traits, special abilities, and other distinctive characteristics.

Each tribe also was organized *patrilineally,* or by the father, during the census. My last name, for example, is Kurzweil because it's customary to take the last name of your father, who took the last name of his father, and so on. This is exactly how the census and the tribes of Israel in the book of Numbers were organized — by the father: "Take a census of the entire community of the Children of Israel and do it following the paternal line" (Numbers 1:2).

Here's the result of the census:

- Asher: 41,500
- Benjamin: 35,400
- Dan: 62,700
- Ephraim: 40,500
- Gad: 45,650
- Issachar: 54,400
- Manasseh: 32,200
- Naphtali: 53,400
- Reuven: 46,500
- Shimon: 59,300
- Yehuda: 74,600
- Zebulun: 57,400

The total came to 603,550 male Israelites over 20 years of age divided among 12 tribes. In Jewish literature throughout the ages, this number is often rounded to 600,000.

It has been taught that the word "Israel," which actually means "a person of God," can also be an acronym for the phrase **Yesh Shishim Ribo Otiot LaTorah,** which means "There are 600,000 letters in the Torah." In Chapter 14, which covers writing a Torah scroll, you see that this claim isn't literally true. There are actually a little over 300,000 letters in the Torah. But Jewish spiritual tradition suggests that the figure of 600,000 comes from a special way of counting not only the letters but also other marks that appear on a Torah scroll. The Jewish people are taught to see themselves as "letters in the Torah" and as part of a whole. It's a goal in life for each Jewish person to find his or her own letter — that is, his or her own special task that belongs to nobody else.

Appointing the Levites to serve in the Tabernacle

The only people not counted in the census were those from the tribe of Levi, who were put in charge of the Tabernacle and its holy items. (The Tabernacle was the portable holy space set up each time the Israelites stopped their wandering in the desert; see Chapter 5 for more details about the Tabernacle.) The beginning of the book of Numbers says, "Take a census of the entire assembly of the Children of Israel according to their families, according to their fathers' household" (Numbers 1:2). After the Torah gives the numerical results of the census of each tribe, it says, "The Levites according to their fathers' tribe were not counted among them" (Numbers 1:47). The text of the Torah goes on to say, "God spoke to Moses saying 'But you shall not count the tribe of Levi, and you shall not take a census of them . . . you shall appoint the Levites to be in charge of the Tabernacle'" (Numbers 1:48–50). The tribe of Levi was divided into two groups:

- ✓ **Kohanim** (ko-ha-*neem*; priests) were the priests who served in the Tabernacle and performed the ritual sacrifices (see Chapter 6 for more about these sacrifices).

- ✓ **Leviyim** (leh-vee-*eem*; the priests' assistants) took the Tabernacle apart before the Israelites traveled, carried the parts of the Tabernacle as they traveled, and constructed the Tabernacle when the Israelites stopped. The Leviyim also sang every day in the Tabernacle.

When the Tabernacle was built, each tribe had a specific spot around the structure of the Tabernacle in which to set up camp (see Figure 7-1). The Torah provides detailed instructions as to how the Tabernacle was to be set up at each rest stop:

- ✓ The Tabernacle was built in the middle.

- ✓ The Levites set up their tents around the Tabernacle.

- ✓ The other families set up their tents around the tents of the Levites in a precise formation detailed in the Torah.

- ✓ A special flag assigned to each tribe by God was displayed.

Figure 7-1:
The
arrangement
of the
Tabernacle.

The Torah doesn't give reasons for the arrangement of the tribes in their precise configuration, but Torah commentators throughout the ages have weighed in on the issue and have come up with many ideas, from the mystical to thoughts about the creation of order itself. Some commentators point out that the beginning of the Torah speaks of the original chaos of existence and that the precise details of the layout of the camp of tribes suggest that it's a task of humankind to bring order to the world, to harness its energy and elevate it.

Looking at a Few Important Laws

The Torah has a habit of sticking important commandments and laws in seemingly strange places. Right in the middle of one subject you can find a divine edict that appears to have little to do with the surrounding text. But every detail of the Torah has divine intention; nothing in the Torah is left up to chance. Many commentators throughout the ages have offered insights to explain why it is that, on the surface, some passages don't seem to fit, but when you look at them on deeper levels, the connections are meaningful.

A good example of this characteristic of the Torah is the number of important teachings that appear in the book of Numbers right after the census. I review some of the most prominent and important ones in the following sections.

Confessing sins

The Torah teaches the importance of confession. If you do something wrong to another person, you have to make it up to the person by abiding by the instruction of Jewish law. For example, when something is stolen, in some cases the thief has to pay double the value of the object. But he also has to confess, out loud, to God.

The book of Numbers says, "He must confess the sin he has committed" (Numbers 5:7). The great Jewish sage Maimonides defines the process of confession in his writings. According to Jewish law, that process has three essential parts:

- ✔ Acknowledgment of the sin
- ✔ Remorse for the sin
- ✔ Resolution that the sin will never be committed again

Every infraction of the Torah deserves confession. If you gossip, steal, desecrate Shabbat, eat non-kosher food, lie, slander, worship idols, embarrass someone publicly, fail to give charity, judge someone too harshly, commit adultery, and so on, confession is essential.

Addressing adultery

Like it or not, polygamy was practiced in ancient times. Specifically, it was the practice of a husband with more than one wife, not the reverse. Suspicion of adultery, therefore, meant suspicion that a wife was intimately involved with a man other than her husband. In Numbers 5:11–29, the Torah outlines what's done in the case of a suspected adulteress.

The central part of the process is this: A priest created a special mixture that the suspected woman had to drink. If she was guilty, the drink caused her belly to burst and her sexual organs to rupture. The suspected woman was allowed to refuse the drink and proceed to dissolve the marriage. It's likely that a woman of faith *who was guilty* wouldn't want to drink the formula and would probably confess.

Throughout the ages, commentators have offered a variety of ways to look at this process, most of them focusing on the importance of the sanctity of marriage. The procedure has traditionally been seen as one involving divine intervention; it worked by way of a miracle. But the fear that the ritual procedure would actually work surely served as a deterrent.

The laws of the Nazirite

Numbers 6:1–21 presents an interesting option for someone who wanted to enter into an intense state of discipline, constraint, and spiritual devotion. The category is known as **nazir** (*nah*-zeer; separated or consecrated), and the person who made a vow to be a nazirite had to commit himself to do the following for at least 30 days:

- ✔ Abstain from wine
- ✔ Refrain from cutting one's hair and beard
- ✔ Avoid dead bodies and graves

Jewish tradition teaches that the primary purpose of entering into this state is to combat sexual temptation. But becoming a nazirite was also part of a process of fighting pride as well as acquiring spiritual gifts and even the power of prophecy (according to some).

The Priestly Blessing

One of the most well-known passages in the entire Torah is the Priestly Blessing. In the book of Numbers, God directs Moses to tell Aaron and his sons (all of whom are priests) to bless the Israelites with the following words:

> *May God bless you and keep you.*
>
> *May God shine His face upon you and be gracious to you.*
>
> *May God direct His providence toward you and give you peace.*
>
> Numbers 6:24–27

Jewish tradition teaches that the priests held their arms up over the people as they blessed them. They also held their fingers in a special way and brought their hands together, as shown in Figure 7-2. When the fingers of each hand are positioned properly, they form the Hebrew letter "shin," which is the first letter of **Shaddai** (shah-*die*), a name for God that implies God's infinite power and strength. Do you remember how *Star Trek*'s Mr. Spock held his hand when he gave the Vulcan sign and said, "Live long and prosper"? Leonard Nimoy, the actor who played the part, based this hand configuration on the blessing of the priests as taught in Jewish tradition.

A number of laws are connected to the Priestly Blessing, including the following:

- ✔ While customs vary, the blessing is part of the daily liturgy and is also part of the liturgy of most major Jewish festivals.
- ✔ A priest must not be under the influence of alcohol when he recites the blessing.
- ✔ Many parents recite the blessing each Friday evening at the Shabbat table to bless their children.

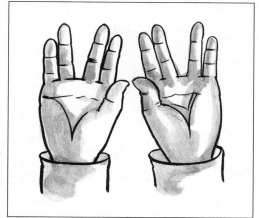

Figure 7-2:
The Priestly
Blessing.

Witnessing Some Wild Events in the Desert

The book of Numbers records many incidents that took place as the Children of Israel traveled through the desert during the 40 years of wandering. It's understandable that an experience like wandering in the desert for so many years could provoke rebellion and impatience. Much of the book of Numbers describes these kind of incidents, all of which were ultimately designed by God to strengthen the Israelites' faith, resolve, and trust in God. God was grooming Israel not simply to be a nation but to be a holy nation, steadfast in its faith and dedication to God and God's commandments.

Complaining about manna

One incident occurred when some of the Israelites complained that they were fed up (no pun intended) with eating manna every day (see Chapter 5 for more about manna). Even though the manna was delicious and one tradition says that it would taste like anything one wanted it to taste like, some of the Children of Israel wanted meat. They said, "We also remember the fish we ate in Egypt, along with cucumbers, melons, leeks, onions and garlic."

Moses spoke to God and told Him that some of the people were complaining bitterly. God told Moses to tell the people to prepare to receive all the meat they wanted. In fact, the Torah says, "God is going to give you meat and you will have to eat it. You will not eat it for a day or two, nor five nor ten nor twenty days. You will eat it for an entire month until you are stuffed and sick of it" (Numbers 11:18–20). And that's just what happened. The Torah records that lots of people became ill and died.

The journey in the wilderness for 40 years was designed by God to forge the Children of Israel into a spiritual nation steadfast in its faith and trust in God. God's reaction to their petty complaints served, as most good punishments should, to strengthen the people and to show them that the best approach is to trust God.

Miriam's sin and punishment

A brief but important incident involving the siblings of Moses, Miriam and Aaron, is recorded in Numbers 12:1–15. Miriam spoke privately to Aaron about Moses, questioning the state of Moses's marriage and also questioning whether Moses was the only one to whom God spoke. This gossip was punishable by God, so God punished Miriam by giving her the condition known as tzarat (see Chapter 6 for more about tzarat as a punishment for evil speech and gossip in particular).

Aaron pleaded with Moses, asking him to pray on behalf of Miriam. Moses said, **El nah refa nah-la** (ehl *nah* reh-*fah nah*-lah; O Lord, make her well). Moses prayed, and in a week Miriam was cured.

This story isn't an illustration of a cruel and harsh God but rather of the process of purification, discipline, and the highest standards necessary to prepare the Jewish people for their task and role as a priesthood for the world.

The report of spies to the Holy Land

The Torah indicates that God's intention was to get the Children of Israel from Egypt to the Holy Land as soon as possible, but entry into the Promised Land took preparation, from the hardships in Egypt to the trials in the desert. After all, the Promised Land is unlike anywhere on earth; for the Jewish people, it's the focal point of physical life.

When the Israelites were getting close to their destination, God instructed Moses to send out a group of men to take a peek at the Promised Land. Moses gathered one representative from each of the 12 tribes (I cover these tribes earlier in this chapter) and gave them the assignment to find out the following:

- ✔ What kind of land is it?
- ✔ Are the people living there strong or weak?
- ✔ Are they few or many?

- ✔ Are their communities open or fortified?

- ✔ Is the land good or bad?

- ✔ Is the soil rich or weak?

- ✔ Are there trees?

- ✔ Bring back some samples of the fruit growing there

The men set off to investigate the Promised Land. The Torah describes their 40-day journey in Numbers 13:1–14:10. When they returned, they issued their report to Moses, Aaron, and the entire community; here's what they found:

- ✔ The land is flowing with milk and honey.

- ✔ The fruit is terrific.

- ✔ The people are aggressive types.

- ✔ Their cities are fortified.

- ✔ The people are giants. We felt like tiny grasshoppers.

When the people heard the report, they shouted, complained, and wept. As was their practice (see Chapter 5), they complained to Moses and told him that they wished they had never left Egypt. They wanted to know why God would bring them to a place where they would be killed, and they even considered deposing Moses, appointing a new leader, and going back to Egypt! At this point, the Torah says that Moses and Aaron "fell on their faces" (Numbers 14:5).

Two of the 12 spies spoke up and gave this minority report:

- ✔ The land we explored is fantastic.

- ✔ If God brought us this far, we can enter the land.

- ✔ It is indeed flowing with milk and honey.

- ✔ Don't rebel against God.

- ✔ Don't be afraid of the people who are there.

- ✔ God is with us — don't be afraid.

The community didn't much care for this report and threatened to stone the two spies to death.

By this time, the Torah indicates, God was growing impatient. "How long shall this nation continue to provoke me? How long will they not believe in Me, despite all the miracles that I have done?" (Numbers 14:11). Moses pleaded with God to forgive the people, and his words included one of the most important descriptions of God: "God is slow to anger, great in love, and forgiving of sin and rebellion" (Numbers 14:18).

Moses was successful in convincing God to forgive the Israelites' rebellion. But God said, "I will grant forgiveness as you have requested . . . but I will punish all those who tried to test me . . . They will not see the land I promised to their ancestors" (Numbers 14:20–23). The only exceptions were Caleb and Joshua, the two spies who issued the minority report. They saw the Promised Land. The rest of the Children of Israel wandered in the desert for 40 years and eventually died. Only the children and grandchildren, who weren't in Egypt and weren't part of all the rebellions against God in the desert, entered the Land of Israel.

Who does Moses think he is? Korach's rebellion

As the book of Numbers makes clear in verses 16:1–35, things didn't go smoothly for Moses, and Korach's rebellion was just one more headache. Korach was a great grandson of Levi and therefore a great grandson of the patriarch Jacob. He was also a wealthy man who decided to gather some followers and stage a rebellion against Moses. Why? Korach challenged Moses's leadership and expressed the desire to be the High Priest. He said to Moses, "All the people in the community are holy . . . why are you setting yourself above everyone else?" (Numbers 16:3). The Torah says that Korach had 250 followers, and among them were some of the most well-known leaders of the Israelites.

The great Torah commentators are actually somewhat sympathetic to Korach. After all, Korach wanted to serve God and wanted to participate more fully in the spiritual activities in the Tabernacle. But someone else got there first when Moses selected Aaron to be the High Priest at the direction of God.

In the face of Korach's rebellion, Moses prayed for divine guidance and then told Korach that he and Aaron should both bring pans of fire and burn incense on the altar. They did as Moses had instructed, and ultimately the ground opened up and swallowed Korach and his cohorts. Then a fire descended from heaven and destroyed all the people who supported the rebellion.

The Torah reports that the entire community protested so much that God was about to destroy them too. Aaron offered a sacrifice, and although 14,700 people died, the plague against them stopped.

The great Torah commentators have a lot to say about Korach and his rebellion. They make a major point: Korach acted based on jealousy and ego, not on a pure desire to do God's will. The moral of this story from the book of Numbers is made clear in the famous book of the Oral Torah called *The Sayings of the Fathers*: "Any controversy which is for the sake of Heaven will endure; and that which is not for the sake of Heaven will not endure. What is a controversy that is for the sake of Heaven? The controversy between Hillel and Shammai.

And which is not for the sake of Heaven? The controversy of Korach and all his faction" (Avot 5:17). In other words, there's nothing wrong with questions or challenges of authority — as long as the motives are pure.

Getting water from a rock

The book of Numbers relates that at a certain point the Children of Israel didn't have any water (Numbers 20:2–12). The people once again "gathered against Moses and Aaron" (Numbers 20:2). As they had in the past, the people demanded to know why Moses brought them into the wilderness from Egypt, where they had enough to eat and to drink, to the desert, which they described as a "terrible place" (Numbers 20:5). Moses and Aaron prayed to God for guidance.

God told Moses to take the staff and gather the people. God then instructed Moses to speak to the rock and promised that water would come out of the rock; God said that the rock would provide enough water for the people and for their animals. Moses angrily said to the people, "Listen to me, you rebels. Shall we bring water from this rock?" (Numbers 20:10). At that moment, Moses lifted his hands and struck the rock twice with the staff. A great quantity of water began flowing from the rock, providing the community with plenty of water.

But God didn't tell Moses to strike the rock in anger; God asked Moses for faith. As a result of the anger that Moses expressed by striking the rock, he and Aaron were punished. God said them, "Because you did not believe in Me . . . you will not bring this congregation to the Land that I have given them" (Numbers 20:12). This episode in the Torah has great significance, not only as a story about the importance of having faith in God but also as an illustration that Moses was just a human being. Unlike other religious traditions in which followers end up revering and even worshipping their leaders, in Judaism, Moses may have been the greatest prophet and teacher but he also was mortal, imperfect, and punished for his errors.

The death of Aaron

The death of Aaron, brother of Moses, High Priest, and ancestor of all priests forever, seems like an aside in the Torah text. Numbers 20:27–29 says, "Moses did as God commanded in full view of the whole community. They went up Mount Hor. Moses stripped Aaron of his robes and gave them to Aaron's son, Eleazar. Aaron died there on the mountaintop. When Moses and Eleazar came down from the mountain, the Israelite community saw that Aaron had died and the people mourned for thirty days."

And that's about it. The rest is up to the Oral Torah (known as the Talmud; see Chapter 3), which fills in the blanks and helps you to picture the scene. One well-known story from the oral tradition teaches that Moses woke up early and approached his brother Aaron. Moses told Aaron that during the night he (Moses) was studying the story of Adam and Eve and was thinking about the fact that Adam brought death into the world through his sin. Moses told Aaron that death was inevitable for both of them and asked Aaron how much more time he thought they had. Aaron said that he didn't think they had too much longer to live, and then Moses told Aaron that God said it was Aaron's time to die.

Judaism is a tradition that considers life to be sacred and holy, and yet it faces death realistically. When God decides that it's a person's time to die, it may be sad for those left behind, but it's different for the deceased, whose soul continues on beyond the body. (Check out Chapter 12 for more about Jewish views on death.)

Balak and Bilaam

Belief in angels is an important part of Jewish life. The Torah story of **Balak** (bah-*lahk*) and **Bilaam** (bih-*lahm*) is partly about an angel (Numbers 22:1–24:25). After almost 40 years in the desert, the Children of Israel were finally close to the Promised Land. The rich and successful King of Moab, Balak, felt threatened by Moses and the Israelites because they'd successfully battled a few kings during their wandering (see Chapter 5 for an example). Balak contacted Bilaam, a prophet, and told him to curse the Children of Israel. Bilaam refused after God told him not to do it. After repeated orders from Balak to curse the Children of Israel, Bilaam continued to receive prophetic messages from God to refrain from cursing the Israelites.

Bilaam traveled to see Balak, but on the road his donkey suddenly stopped, refused to continue, and veered off the road. Bilaam beat the donkey until it began to speak, telling Bilaam that it had never failed him, so the beating wasn't justified. The donkey said that it stopped moving because it saw an angel standing before them wielding a sword. Bilaam then saw the angel as well and knew that it was sent by God. Had the donkey not stopped, Bilaam would have been killed by the angel's sword.

Like every story in the Torah, the episode of Balak and Bilaam is rich with meaning. One of my teachers says that a major moral of the story of Balak and Bilaam is that everyone ultimately answers to God. Balak used his position as King to attempt to pressure and use a prophet of God for his own evil reasons. Jewish tradition addresses the question of why good things happen to bad people in different ways. The Torah utilizes the story of Balak and Bilaam to remind the reader that the sinner will ultimately fail, even if he's a king with everything going for him today. A benevolent God will give him enough rope and then exact a penalty. Napoleon met his Waterloo, and Bilaam was disgraced by his she-ass.

One of the most well-known verses in the Torah comes from Bilaam (Numbers 24:5). When Balak sent Bilaam to the top of a mountain to curse the Israelites, God caused the opposite to happen: Bilaam saw the Israelites and said, **Ma-tovu oha-leicha Ya'akov** (mah toe-*voo* oh-*ha leh*-khah *ya-ah-cove*; How good are your tents, O Jacob). These are the very words that Jews recite whenever they enter a synagogue to pray.

The boundaries of the Holy Land

Near the end of the book of Numbers, the Torah defines the precise boundaries of the Holy Land. Needless to say, the impact of these verses continues to reverberate today. After centuries, the Jewish people have reclaimed the Holy Land, and in 1948, with the support of the United Nations, the Jewish people established the modern state of Israel. Some Jews have lived in the region throughout history, but since the destruction of the Holy Temple in Jerusalem in 70 CE, the Jewish people have mostly lived in exile. But they've held onto the dream of returning to the Holy Land promised by and given by God as recorded in the Torah.

Chapter 34 of the book of Numbers provides the exact details of the boundaries of the Holy Land. The Torah begins by defining the extreme southeast border, then the western boundary, followed by the north, east, and south boundaries. One of the reasons the precise boundaries are important is that there are some commandments in the Torah that are only applicable for people who are actually in the Holy Land. One example is the Sabbatical Year. In Leviticus 25:1–6, the Torah states that God says, "When you come to the land that I am giving you, the land must be given a rest period. For six years you may plant your fields . . . but the seventh year is a Sabbath of Sabbaths for the land. It is God's Sabbath during which you may not plant your fields nor prune your vineyards. . . ."

This is just one of many Torah commandments that's dependent on precise knowledge of the boundaries of the Holy Land. Of course, the precise boundaries also have profound political implications. The Holy Land is the ancient homeland of the Children of Israel. Since the time when the Jewish people were conquered and banished, Jews have been well-known victims in the lands of other people. The worst chapter of Jewish history occurred a mere 65 years ago during the Holocaust, when one out of every three Jews in the world was murdered. Today, the Jewish people have reclaimed their Promised Land and have a security that they haven't known for many centuries.

Chapter 8

"Words": The Book of Deuteronomy

. . . .

In This Chapter

▶ Listening to Moses review the major teachings of the Torah

▶ Reviewing the Ten Commandments and the major Jewish statement of faith

▶ Revisiting some of the most important laws in Jewish life

▶ Witnessing the death of Moses

. . . .

*L*ike those of the first four books of Moses, the name "Deuteronomy" comes from the Greek translation known as the Septuagint. In Greek, "Deuteronomy" means "the repetition of the law" or the "second law." In large part, this book of the Torah records three speeches by Moses as he bids farewell to the Children of Israel before his death; in the three speeches, Moses repeats many of the things he has previously taught.

The Jewish people refer to Deuteronomy as **Devarim** (deh-vah-*reem*; words). The book begins, "These are the words which Moses spoke to all of Israel." Very little "happens" in the fifth book of the Torah, and yet I can easily argue that the book of Deuteronomy is the richest of the Five Books of Moses. The first four books are filled with drama and intrigue: The universe is created, the patriarchs and matriarchs of the Jewish people establish the Jewish family, the Children of Israel are slaves in Egypt (and finally find their freedom), the people rebel many times, they fight their enemies, and they encounter God at Mount Sinai, among many other things.

But the book of Deuteronomy, as its Hebrew title suggests, is mostly words. These words are basically a long sermon in which Moses, knowing that he would soon die, tried one last time to teach the Torah to the Children of Israel. The Children of Israel gathered on the east bank of the Jordan River, and, as the Torah says, "Moses spoke to the Israelites regarding all that God had commanded" (Deuteronomy 1:2).

The First Discourse of Moses

Moses began the first of three discourses to the Children of Israel by reminiscing. It isn't surprising that he started his farewell speech by remembering what he and the people had been through together. It's also natural that Moses, who knew that he would die soon, then focused on the fact that he wasn't going with the people to the Promised Land. It's as though he said to them, "This is where I get off." But before he "went," Moses started telling his people of the foundations of Judaism, and he stressed that God is at the center of all being.

Recalling 40 years of wandering in the desert

With the Children of Israel camped at the banks of the Jordan River overlooking the Land of Israel (the Promised Land), Moses began the first part of his talk by looking back at some of the major events that took place following the exodus from Egypt. Included in Moses's summary are these key points:

- **God gave the Promised Land to the Jewish people.**

  "I have placed the land before you," said Moses. "Come and occupy the land that God swore He would give your fathers, Abraham, Isaac and Jacob, and to their descendants." (Deuteronomy 1:8)

- **Moses, not being able to settle all the conflicts among the people by himself, established a system of courts to settle disputes.**

  "Designate people who are wise, understanding and known to your tribes and I will appoint them as your leaders." (Deuteronomy 1:13)

- **Moses assured the people many times not to be afraid but rather to trust in God.**

  "Do not be afraid and do not be concerned." (Deuteronomy 1:21)

- **Moses sent spies to check out the land to which they were headed and instructed them to report back on what they had found.**

  "I appointed twelve men, one from each tribe." (Deuteronomy 1:23)

- **Moses reminded the Children of Israel of their frequent rebellions.**

  "You rebelled against God, your Lord." (Deuteronomy 1:26)

- **God saw that most of those who were slaves in Egypt weren't spiritually ready to live in the Promised Land, so He decided that the generations born after the exodus would enter the Promised Land.**

  "Nobody of this evil generation will see the good land that I swore to give to your fathers." (Deuteronomy 1:35)

✔ **Moses was forbidden to enter the Promised Land.**

"You also will not enter the Land." (Deuteronomy 1:37)

✔ **While wandering toward the Promised Land, the Children of Israel encountered hostile foes. They avoided some of them, fought victoriously against others, and finally arrived at the Promised Land.**

"The Lord, your God, has given you this land as a heritage." (Deuteronomy 3:18)

Asking permission to enter the Promised Land (permission denied)

My teacher is fond of teaching that in Judaism there are no "plastic saints." What my teacher means by that is that there are no perfect heroes in Judaism. Every person, including Moses — the greatest teacher and prophet who ever lived — is imperfect. Moses had moments of weakness and made lots of mistakes. It was because of one of these flaws that Moses wasn't permitted to enter the Promised Land. While wandering in the desert, God told Moses to speak to a rock in order to get water from it. Instead, Moses struck the rock with his rod, displaying not only anger but also a lack of faith. As punishment, God refused to let Moses enter the Land of Israel. (You can read more about this story in Chapter 7.)

Moses asked God to change this decree on a number of occasions. In the book of Deuteronomy, Moses reminded the Children of Israel that he prayed to God, asking to be permitted to enter the Land, but that God refused. God, like a parent who says "I'm not going to say it again," tells Moses, "Do not continue to speak with Me about this matter" (Deuteronomy 3:26).

Instead of entering the Land of Israel, God instructed Moses to climb on top of a mountain so that he could see the land that the Children of Israel would inherit for all eternity.

Teaching the foundation of faith

The bulk of the book of Deuteronomy consists of teachings and laws. Moses makes a number of declarations that are fundamental to Judaism. I paraphrase some of the more important ones here:

✔ When you listen to the teachings of the Torah and do them, you will remain alive (Deuteronomy 4:1).

In Jewish thought "alive" and "dead" have much more profound meaning than the literal senses of the words. Someone alive can be considered dead and vice versa. Jewish thought sees a person as an eternal soul with a temporary body, so if that person follows God's teachings, he will surely die physically, but his soul will remain alive. Likewise, a person who lives a life of sin is alive but in Jewish thought can be considered dead.

✔ **Don't add or subtract from the word of God (Deuteronomy 4:2).**

The Torah is considered perfect. According to Jewish tradition, it's unthinkable for someone to come along claiming that the Torah includes verses that it's never had or that there are verses that don't belong in the Torah.

✔ **Keep all the commandments (Deuteronomy 4:2).**

The Torah urges Jews to observe all the commandments that are possible for them to perform. In fact, it's impossible for everyone to keep all the commandments. For example, some commandments are just for women or just for men, and some can only be performed in the Holy Land. Others can only be performed by the King of Israel (when there is one).

✔ **Safeguard the laws (Deuteronomy 4:6).**

Jewish law has developed many ancillary laws that serve to protect the laws. For example, although some say it's technically permissible to play a musical instrument on Shabbat, it's not permissible to tune the guitar on Shabbat because that would involve altering the world. To insure that a person doesn't transgress and unconsciously tune the instrument, a safeguard is added to the law forbidding that the instrument be played.

✔ **When the Children of Israel follow God's teachings, the nations of the world will see them as a great nation, wise and understanding. (Deuteronomy 4:6)**

Jewish thought conceives of the nations of the world as different parts of one single body, so when any part of the body is injured or ill, it impacts the entire body. The Jewish people are a vital organ of the body.

✔ **Do not forget the history of the Jewish people (Deuteronomy 4:9).**

It is a principle of Jewish life that its family history be recalled. The Jewish holy day of Passover, when families gather to retell the story of the Children of Israel and their exodus from Egypt, is just one of many times when Jewish law commands that history be remembered.

✔ **Teach your children and your children's children the ways of God (Deuteronomy 4:9).**

Universal education has always been a fact of Jewish life. All Jewish children are required to be literate in order to spend a lifetime learning the teachings of the Torah. The Jewish people have had an almost 100 percent literacy rate for centuries.

✔ **Do not depict God with any physical image or symbol. God is not like an animal, nor is God male or female (Deuteronomy 4:16).**

My teacher taught me that it's difficult to be Jewish. As he said, "One must establish a personal relationship with a God that you cannot conceive of." My teacher also taught me that if you ever think you know God, one thing is certain: You're wrong. God is beyond anything a person can imagine.

✔ Do not bow down to the sun nor the moon nor the stars (Deuteronomy 4:19).

The prohibition of idolatry is at the core of Jewish life. This prohibition not only pertains to the creation of statues; many people seem to worship money, for example, and this is a modern form of idolatry.

✔ Do not forget the covenant the God made with the Children of Israel (Deuteronomy 4:23).

The Torah is, in a sense, a contract between God and the Jewish people. The idea of a covenant is frequently discussed in Jewish texts, beginning with the Torah. God basically says to Abraham and to all the Jewish people: If you keep My teachings, I'll do my part for you.

Stressing allegiance to God

The Jewish people are a theocentric family, which means that God is at the center of all being and is the center of life. In the book of Deuteronomy, Moses stresses the fundamental importance of the Children of Israel remaining loyal to God and God's teachings. For example, Moses teaches that

✔ If the Children of Israel become idolaters, they will be banished from the Holy Land (Deuteronomy 4:25–26).

✔ If the Children of Israel become idolaters, they will be scattered among the nations and will serve man-made gods, but when "you will begin to seek God, and pursue God with all your heart and soul, you will find God" (Deuteronomy 4:29).

✔ When the Children of Israel stray from God but then try to return to God, they will be able to do so (Deuteronomy 4:30).

✔ God will never abandon or destroy the Children of Israel; God will not forget the promises He made to them (Deuteronomy 4:31).

Moses concludes his first discourse by saying, "Realize today and ponder it in your heart that God is the Supreme Being in heaven above and on earth below. There is no other. Keep God's decrees and commandments that I am presenting to you today, and God will be good to you and to your children. Then you will exist for a long time in the land that the Lord, your God, is giving to you for all time" (Deuteronomy 4:40).

The Second Discourse of Moses

The second of the three discourses delivered by Moses to the Children of Israel is really the heart of the book of Deuteronomy. In this second speech, Moses repeats the Ten Commandments (they're enumerated earlier in the Torah), teaches the most important prayer and declaration of faith in all Jewish life (known as the Shema), and reviews many of the core teachings to be found in the Torah and Judaism.

Reviewing the Ten Commandments

Moses begins his second discourse to the Children of Israel by demanding that they listen to him. Moses insists that the people learn what the Torah is teaching and uses a form of a key Hebrew word, **shomor** (shoh-*more*; to guard or protect). It's not enough to learn a law and follow it; Jewish tradition urges Jews to protect the Torah's laws. How does a person guard a law? By reviewing it, repeating it, focusing on its meaning, and sometimes by adding additional customs to make sure that the law is followed.

Moses reminds the Children of Israel that God made a deal with them at Mount Sinai, where He gave them the Ten Commandments (see Chapter 5). It's interesting and important to note that at this point in his discourse Moses was speaking to many people who didn't actually stand at Mount Sinai but were born afterward. Nevertheless, Moses says, "Not with our forefathers did God seal this covenant, but with us — we who are here. All of us who are alive today" (Deuteronomy 5:3). This verse in the Torah implies and teaches at least two things:

- ✔ There are 600,000 primary souls of the Children of Israel, all of whom stood at Mount Sinai and heard God. Today, with over 12 million Jews in the world, the traditional Jewish notion is that the original 600,000 souls spread out and are within the Jewish people as a whole. The traditional Jewish belief in reincarnation includes the assumptions that all Jews throughout history stood at Mount Sinai and that these 600,000 original souls still "live" within Jews throughout time.

- ✔ The Torah was given at Mount Sinai thousands of years ago, yet the Torah is constantly being given by God to the Jewish people. Every Jew has the responsibility to symbolically stand at Mount Sinai and reach to hear God's teachings.

Here's a loose translation of the words of Moses as he recounted the Ten Commandments in his second discourse (Deuteronomy 5:1–18):

- ✔ I am the Lord, your God, Who has taken you out of the land of Egypt, from the house of bondage.

- You shall not have any other gods before Me. Do not make images of other gods, do not bow down to them. I, God, demand that you worship Me exclusively.

- Do not take the name of the Lord, your God, in vain.

- Safeguard the Sabbath to keep it holy. You can work during the six days and do all that you must, but the seventh day is the Sabbath to God, so do not do any work. This prohibition against work also includes your children, your male and female servants, your animals, and the foreigners in your gates.

  In the version of the Ten Commandments in the book of Exodus, the fourth commandment says, "Remember the Sabbath" (Exodus 20:8). Jewish tradition teaches that the Children of Israel heard the words "safeguard" and "remember" at the same time.

- Honor your father and your mother.

- Do not commit murder.

- Do not commit adultery.

- Do not steal.

- Do not be a false witness against your neighbor.

- Do not desire your neighbor's wife, house, fields, servants, animals, or anything that belongs to your neighbor.

Presenting the most important Jewish statement of faith: The Shema

In the middle of the second discourse, Moses repeats the statement of faith known as the **Shema** (sheh-*mah*; listen or hear). The Shema is a crucial part of the morning and evening prayer services every day of the year. It can be recited in any language the reciter can understand. It's traditional for a person on his or her deathbed to recite the Shema, and it's also customary to recite the first paragraph of the Shema before going to sleep at night.

Here's the text of the Shema:

> *Listen, Israel, God is our Lord. God is One.*
>
> *You shall love the Lord, your God, with all of your heart, with all of your soul, and with all of your resources.*
>
> *And these words that I command you today shall be upon your heart. You shall teach them thoroughly to your children and you shall speak of them while you sit in your home, while you walk on the way, when you lie down*

and when you rise up. Bind them as a sign upon your arm and let them be ornaments between your eyes. And write them on the doorposts of your house and upon your gates.

Deuteronomy 6:4–9

Often a Jewish person who knows absolutely no Hebrew can still recite the very first line of the Shema in Hebrew because it's such a common part of Jewish life and is heard so often. It's usually the first prayer taught to children. This first line, as pronounced in Hebrew, is "sheh-*mah* yis-row-*ale* ah-doe-*noy* eh-low-*hay*-new ah-doe-*noy* eh-*khahd.*"

Trusting, loving, and remembering God

The Talmud (see Chapter 3) contains a discussion about what the Children of Israel actually heard when standing at Mount Sinai. Some say they heard the whole Torah, whereas others say they heard the Ten Commandments. Of the various opinions recorded, all agree that the Children of Israel heard the first two of the Ten Commandments. The first is the commandment to know God. The second is the commandment to know that idolatry is a great temptation.

Throughout the Torah, Moses warns against idolatry in all its forms, and in his second discourse, Moses repeats this prohibition. In the eighth chapter of Deuteronomy, Moses presents the teaching against idolatry in the harshest of terms: "If you ever forget God and follow other gods, worshipping and bowing to them, I bear witness to you today that you will be totally annihilated" (Deuteronomy 8:19).

Along with this fierce warning, Moses reviews some basic Jewish beliefs and commandments related specifically to God:

- Remain in awe of God (Deuteronomy 6:13).
- Don't follow the gods of other nations (Deuteronomy 6:14).
- Don't test God (Deuteronomy 6:15).
- Do what is good and upright in God's eyes (Deuteronomy 6:18).
- Don't intermarry with other nations (Deuteronomy 7:3).
- God loves you (Deuteronomy 7:8).
- God is the one and only Supreme Being (Deuteronomy 7:9).
- Have confidence in God (Deuteronomy 7:18).
- Don't be afraid of other nations, even if they're bigger than Israel, because God is always with you (Deuteronomy 7:17–21).
- Thank God after each meal for the food He has given to you (Deuteronomy 8:10).

✔ Don't forget God, God's laws, and teachings (Deuteronomy 8:11).

✔ Don't be haughty when God gives you what you need (Deuteronomy 8:14).

✔ All life's trials and tests are from God (Deuteronomy 8:16).

✔ Don't think that what you've accomplished is your own doing. God is involved in everything (Deuteronomy 8:17).

✔ If you're prosperous, don't forget that God made it that way (Deuteronomy 8:18).

✔ Don't be self-righteous and think that you can accomplish anything with God's help (Deuteronomy 9:4).

✔ Be in awe of God, cling to God, and serve God (Deuteronomy 10:20).

✔ Love God always (Deuteronomy 11:1).

Making the right choices

One of the great paradoxes within the Torah is this question: Do humans have free will or is everything determined by God? The great Talmudic sage Rabbi Akiva (see Chapter 15) states the Jewish solution succinctly: "All is foreseen and free will is given" (Mishnah, Ethics of the Fathers 3:19). On the one hand, nothing happens without God allowing it to happen. On the other hand, God gave humans one of the divine aspects: free will.

The Torah urges students to constantly be aware that God is the moving force behind everything (yes, everything!). At the same time, paradoxically, each person is to be aware that he's always facing choices and that the basic trial of life is to make the right choices. The importance of this challenge — that you're always free to choose — appears in a number of places in the Torah; in his second discourse in the book of Deuteronomy, Moses repeats it: "I present before you today a blessing and a curse. The blessing: that you listen to the commandments of God that I command you today. And the curse: if you do not obey the commandments of God and you stray from the path that I command you, to follow the gods of others" (Deuteronomy 11:26–28).

Recounting the laws of Judaism

Although the entire book of Deuteronomy is really a last-ditch effort on the part of Moses to teach the Children of Israel the ways of God, the second discourse summarizes and reviews several broad areas of Jewish law. (Flip to Part III for more about these laws.)

Dietary laws

The kosher laws are those teachings in the Torah that explain what's permissible and forbidden to be eaten by Jews. The details of these laws are found in the Oral Torah, mainly in the Talmud. These teachings include the following:

- Only fish with fins and scales may be eaten (Deuteronomy 11:10).

- Certain birds may be eaten and others may not (Deuteronomy 11:11–18).

- Animals must be properly slaughtered in order to be fit to eat (Deuteronomy 11:21).

- Meat and dairy products may not be eaten together (Deuteronomy 11:21).

- The only mammals that can be eaten are those that have split hooves and chew their cud (Deuteronomy 14:6).

- Consuming pork isn't permissible under any circumstances (Deuteronomy 14:8).

Laws of charity

Giving charity, or **tzedakah** (tseh-dah-*kah*; justice), is one of the most important practices in Jewish life. The Torah requires that one-tenth of one's income go to charity, and specific laws in the Torah explain how this is calculated (Deuteronomy 14:22–23). The important idea is that you have a responsibility to see to it that people in need have what's needed to survive.

A variety of other laws

As Moses continues to review the major teachings of the Torah in his second discourse, he touches upon the following topics, most of which are also dealt with elsewhere in the Five Books of Moses:

- Lending money (Deuteronomy 15:7–11): Be generous, and don't charge interest when lending to family members.

- A justice system (Deuteronomy 16:18–20): Don't bend justice, don't take bribes, always pursue perfect honesty, and don't give special consideration to anyone, rich or poor.

- The laws of waging war (Deuteronomy 20:10–18): If you have just built a new house or have planted a vineyard and not had a first crop yet, or if you've just gotten married, or if you're terrified of fighting, in all these cases you're exempt from military service. The Torah also has detailed laws about taking captives and the proper ways to treat them.

- Returning lost objects (Deuteronomy 22:1–3): If you find a lost object, you must make every effort to find the owner and take care of the object until you locate its owner.

- How to deal with a rebellious child (Deuteronomy 21:18–21): Be strict.

✔ Cross-dressing (Deuteronomy 22:5): Don't do it.

✔ Keeping vows (Deuteronomy 23:22–24): If you make a promise using God's name, you had better keep your word.

✔ Divorce (Deuteronomy 24:1–3): Divorce is permissible, and the parties may remarry others.

✔ Weights and measures (Deuteronomy 25:13–16): Be accurate.

The full range of topics and teachings in the book of Deuteronomy can be found in Appendixes B and C, where I list all the positive and negative commandments in the Five Books of Moses.

A warning against breaking laws

At the end of the second discourse, Moses warns that disobeying the Torah will result in curses (while obedience results in blessings). Moses stresses the following sins (Deuteronomy 27:11–28:68):

✔ Idolatry

✔ Disrespect to parents

✔ Moving fixed boundaries

✔ Misdirecting the blind

✔ Mistreating orphans, widows, and foreigners

✔ Sexual misconduct (in particular, sex with one's father's wife, with animals, or with one's mother-in-law)

✔ Hurting a neighbor secretly

✔ Taking a bribe to convict an innocent person

The Final Discourse of Moses

The third and final discourse by Moses (before he says farewell and dies) in the book of Deuteronomy is most familiar to me because it's the part of the Torah that I chanted in public in my synagogue when I was 13 years old and marking the time of my Bar Mitzvah. Because my birthday is in August, I received a Torah portion close to that date in the annual cycle of the public reading of the Torah. (You can find more on the Bar and Bat Mitzvah in Chapter 12 and more about the annual public reading of the Torah in Chapter 13.) In this section of the Torah, Moses makes many important statements, including:

✔ Everyone stands before God at all times (Deuteronomy 29:9).

✔ The covenant with Abraham, Isaac, and Jacob will always exist for all their descendants — past, present, and future (Deuteronomy 29:11–14).

> ✔ All Jews stood at Mount Sinai and all Jews must avoid worshiping anyone but the true God, the God of Israel (Deuteronomy 29:15–17).
>
> ✔ When you make a mistake and repent, God accepts your repentance (Deuteronomy 30:1–4).
>
> ✔ The Torah isn't some remote document that's too difficult to understand. Rather, it's available to all who want to learn from it (Deuteronomy 30:11–13).
>
> ✔ All the Children of Israel have free choice (Deuteronomy 30:15–20).

The third discourse wraps up with the final days of Moses, as you see in the following sections.

God asks Moses for a song

Toward the end of the book of Deuteronomy, God tells Moses that the time is coming for him to die. God tells Moses to send for Joshua, who will take over as leader of the people. God then informs Moses that the future will be a challenge for the Jewish people: "When you go and lie with your ancestors, this nation shall rise up and stray after alien gods . . . they will abandon Me and violate the covenant . . . I will hide My face from them" (Deuteronomy 31:16–17). God knows that there will be many times in history when the Jewish people will stray from the covenant and will feel as though God has abandoned them. (I talk more about the covenant in the earlier section "Teaching the foundation of faith.")

God instructs Moses to write a song for Him — a song that Moses will sing before the people and teach to them. The song, known as **HaAzinu** (ha-ah-zee-new; listen), is both a warning and a promise.

> ✔ The warning tells of how easy it will be for the Children of Israel to stray from the holy covenant with God.
>
> ✔ The promise speaks of the final redemption, when the Children of Israel will be faithful to God and the enemies of Israel will crumble.

Moses blesses each tribe for the last time

At the end of the Five Books of Moses, God speaks one final time to Moses, instructing Moses to climb a mountain and telling him that he will die on that mountain. God permits Moses to see the Holy Land, but only from afar.

From the mountaintop, Moses looks out on the Children of Israel and blesses each of the tribes one last time. God says, "This is the land regarding which I made an oath to Abraham, Isaac and Jacob, saying 'I will give it to your descendants.' I have let you see it with your own eyes but you will not cross the river to enter it" (Deuteronomy 34:4).

The death of Moses

The Torah records that Moses was 120 years old when he died and states that "No man knows the place that he is buried even to today" (Deuteronomy 34:6). The people mourned him for 30 days. When the mourning period was over, Joshua took over. The Torah says that "Joshua was filled with a spirit of wisdom because Moses had laid his hands on him" (Deuteronomy 34:9). The word for "laid his hands" is of the same root as **semichah** (she-mee-*khah*; ordination). Thus, when a rabbi is ordained, it's said that he receives semichah.

It's interesting to note that as important as Moses is to the Jewish people, his burial place is unknown. Some commentators suggest that the location of his grave is unknown because his greatness may have inspired people to worship him. As I say throughout this book, Judaism has no concept of the perfect person. As great as Moses and the patriarchs were, they were human, with failings and mortality. Here's how the burial of Moses is described in the Torah: "So Moses the servant of God died there in the land of Moab, by the mouth of God. And He buried him in the valley in the land of Moab, opposite Beth-peor; but no man knows his burial place to this day" (Deuteronomy 34:5–6).

The Torah ends with the following words: "Never again has a prophet like Moses arisen in Israel who knew God face to face. Nobody else could reproduce the signs and miracles that God let Moses display in the land of Egypt, to Pharaoh and all his land, nor any of the mighty acts or great sights that Moses performed before the eyes of all Israel" (Deuteronomy 34:10–12).

Part III

The Torah: An Operating Manual for Planet Earth

The 5th Wave

By Rich Tennant

"We don't need to consult the Torah. I'm the mother, and when I say 8:30 is bedtime, that's the law."

In this part . . .

More than a book of theological and spiritual ideas, the Torah is a plan for action in the world. Although the Torah does concern itself with sublime and profound concepts about the meaning of existence, it's far more concerned with human behavior, both between people as well as between humans and God. In this part, I show you how this ancient book is an instruction manual for healthy, ethical, righteous living, and you come to understand how simple statements in the Torah are actually the foundation for huge areas of human life and law.

Chapter 9

Keeping Your Personal Behavior in Line with the Torah

*I*n Judaism, there are lots of holidays, lots of rituals, and lots of profound theological concepts. But the heart of Judaism, as taught by the Torah, is a combination of faith and deeds. The Torah is emphatic about it: Faith without deeds is bankrupt. It's never enough to simply believe.

Here's a story that illustrates this concept: A man who was once a thief went to my teacher to tell him that he had changed his ways. The former thief admitted his past failings and announced proudly that he had become a new person. He had repented in his heart and had found God. My teacher wasn't terribly impressed, and the former thief could tell. It wasn't the response that the former thief had anticipated, so he asked, "Aren't you pleased with my new turn?" My teacher responded, "When you were a thief, didn't you take lots of things that belonged to other people?" "Yes," said the repentant man. "Well," said my teacher, "when you find those people and repay them, then you can come back to me and be so proud of yourself."

In this chapter, I discuss some of the many ways the Torah speaks to your personal deeds in this world. By the way, every time you do a good deed, the sages say that you create a good angel who will be your advocate when your case arrives at the heavenly court.

Defining the Essence of the Torah

The term "Torah" implies far more than the Five Books of Moses (which I describe in Part II). It's also far more than the Holy Scriptures (commonly referred to as the Bible). And it's far more than the Oral Torah (generally known as the Talmud; see Chapter 3). "Torah" includes the vast body of Jewish teachings throughout the ages and even includes what a Jewish teacher will teach tomorrow!

Nevertheless, many attempts have been made to define the essence of the Torah, and the definition best known in Jewish tradition sounds very much like the Golden Rule — but with a difference. But like the Golden Rule, this definition in Jewish tradition focuses on a person's own behavior.

The most frequently quoted attempt to define the Torah comes from a famous story found in the Talmud. A certain non-believer came before a great teacher named Shammai and said to him, "I will convert to Judaism on the condition that you teach me the whole Torah while I stand on one foot." Shammai impatiently chased him away with the builder's measuring stick in his hand. When the same man came before another great teacher named Hillel and asked the same question, Hillel replied, "What is hateful to you, do not do to your neighbor: that is the whole Torah while the rest is commentary; go and learn it."

It's interesting to note that the famous Golden Rule spoken by Jesus of Nazareth expresses almost the same notion but in the positive: "Do unto others what you would have others do unto you" (New Testament, Luke 6:31). Historians point out that Jesus almost surely knew this teaching of the great sage, Hillel.

And what, exactly, should be hateful to you so that you don't do it to others? You can start to figure out this concept with the help of two popular expressions: One is "God is in the details," and the other is "the devil is in the details." For Judaism and the Torah, it's surely true that "God is in the details." As I explain many times in this book, it's never enough to look into the Five Books of Moses to see what Judaism says. A simple verse like "Love thy neighbor as thyself" prompts many questions: What is "love"? Who is one's "neighbor"? In what way does one love oneself? These kinds of questions inspire significant discussion and detail in Jewish thought. The Torah in its broadest sense is the result of that ongoing, eternal pursuit for an understanding of what it is that God wants from His creation.

In light of this pursuit, a basic guiding principle for Jewish life and personal behavior based on the Torah is to imitate God. Just as God is charitable, so must people be charitable. Just as God is merciful, so must people be merciful. This idea is based on a verse in the Torah: "God will establish you to Him as a holy people as He swore to you, if you guard the commandments of the Lord your God, and you walk in His ways" (Deuteronomy 28:9).

Be a Mentsch: Some Basic Torah Principles about Personal Behavior

In Judaism, trying to be a good person — a mentsch — isn't enough. Jewish life requires a lifetime of Torah study to continue to learn and to constantly refine your actions and personal qualities. But there are some basic principles that guide personal behavior in Judaism; as you may have already figured out, they're based on important verses found in the Torah.

Good works

Ma'asim tovim (mah-ah-*seem* toe-*veem*; good works) is the general term for good actions and attitudes. The divine command to be a good person appears in many forms in the Torah, including:

- "You shall not take revenge, and you shall not bear a grudge for the people of your nation, and you shall love your fellow man as yourself." (Leviticus 19:18)
- "You shall not hate your brother in your heart, and you shall reprove your friend and not carry a sin because of him." (Leviticus 19:17)

Acts of kindness

Gemilut chasadim (geh-meh-*loot* khah-sah-*deem*; acts of kindness) is the general Hebrew term for being nice to others. There are many hundreds of verses in the Torah that obviously reflect this attitude, but the great Torah sages point out that the proverbial kindness shown to people tends to be expressed as kindness to "orphans and widows," as found in the Torah: "Every widow and orphan you shall not oppress" (Exodus 22:21).

Some guidelines taught by the Torah and the sages regarding acts of kindness include:

- Speak kindly to people.
- Offer people words of comfort.
- Judge people positively.
- "Love your neighbor as yourself." (Leviticus 19:18)
- Pursue peace actively.
- Greet people cheerfully.

Hospitality

Hachnasat orchim (hakh-nah-*saht* ore-*kheem*; inviting guests) is an important commandment that every Jewish person and family must make every effort to fulfill. Jewish lore tells of the great patriarch Abraham and his wife Sarah, and their exceptional reputation for welcoming guests into their home. While the stories about Abraham and Sarah and their habit of inviting guests has inspired generations of Jews, the basis of this custom is found in the Torah: "You shall love the stranger, for you were strangers in the land of Egypt" (Deuteronomy 10:19). (I go into more detail about treating strangers and other people fairly later in this chapter; I share the general story of Abraham and Sarah in Chapter 4.)

The Torah teaches the following details regarding hospitality:

- Seek out guests; don't just wait for people to show up.

- Make your guests feel wanted.

- Make sure your guests feel comfortable about their need for food, drink, and washing facilities.

- When guests arrive, give them time to get relaxed and rested after their journey to see you.

- Make sure your guests don't feel like they're an imposition.

- Treat guests royally.

- Tend to your guests' needs as quickly as possible.

- Teach your children to do this mitzvah.

Charity

The Hebrew word for "charity" is **tzedakah** (tzeh-dah-*kah*), which really means "justice." The Torah view of charity is that justice is being served when a person gives charity to someone in need. Many verses in the Torah command that you give charity, including: "If there will be in your midst a poor person, from among your brothers, in one of your cities, in your land which the Lord your God has given you, you shall not harden your heart, or close your hand from your poor brother" (Deuteronomy 15:7). The Torah also teaches: "For the poor shall not cease to exist from amidst your land, therefore I have commanded you, saying, 'You shall surely open up your hand to your brother, to the poor and to the destitute in your land'" (Deuteronomy 15:11).

The Torah's laws regarding charity to the poor also deal with the realities of an agricultural society and the obligation of farmers to leave some of the crops for the poor and needy. Here are a couple relevant verses:

✔ "When you reap the harvest of your land, you shall not reap entirely the corner of your field, and the gleanings of your harvest you shall not gather." (Leviticus 19:9)

✔ "When you gather your harvest in your field and you forget a bundle in the field, you shall not return to take it, for the stranger and the orphan and the widow it shall be in order that the Lord your God shall bless all the work of your hand. When you beat your olive tree, you shall not remove its splendor from behind you; for the stranger and the orphan and the widow it shall be." (Deuteronomy 24:19–20)

Visiting the sick

The act of visiting the sick is known in Hebrew as **bikkur cholim** (*beer*-khoor *khoh*-leem). Interestingly, there's no verse in the Torah that explicitly tells you to visit the sick. However, the great Torah sages have noticed that God visits Abraham just after Abraham circumcises himself in the book of Genesis (see Chapter 4). Based on the principle of "walking in God's ways" that I describe in the earlier section "Defining the Essence of the Torah," just as God visits Abraham when he's healing, so should you visit people when they're sick or trying to heal.

Evil speech

The Torah disagrees with the last phrase in the adage that "sticks and stones will break my bones but words will never harm me." The Torah represents the view that words can surely harm a person. Jewish thought, as based on the Torah, recognizes many sins concerning speech. One is **lashon hara** (lah-*shone* ha-*rah*; evil tongue), which the rabbis define as telling someone something true about a third party, with the result that the person who hears what was said diminishes his or her opinion of the person being described (Leviticus 25:17). This is different from lying, which is its own sin (Exodus 23:7).

Other sins of speech include making a vow and ignoring it, embarrassing someone in public, telling tall tales — "You shall not be a talebearer amongst your people" (Leviticus 19:16) — and one of the Ten Commandments, "You shall not bear false witness" (Exodus 20:16).

Look Sharp! Dressing Appropriately

The Oral Torah explains that one of the ways to understand the word "humble" in the description of Moses in the Torah as being "exceedingly humble, more than any man in the world" (Numbers 12:3) is in terms of modesty. The teachings of the Torah include principles and concerns about the virtues of behaving modestly. The Hebrew term for "modesty" is **tzniut** (tsnee-*oot*), and it includes guidelines for appropriate and inappropriate dress.

The Oral Torah teaches that both men and women should dress modestly, with particular concern about avoiding the exposure of the body publicly in provocative ways. Jewish practices concerning modesty have always been flexible and are often influenced by local custom.

Everything Is Relative: The Torah's Family Rules

It isn't surprising that the Torah places great value on the family unit; after all, the Jewish people as a whole are considered to be a family, as implied by the phrase "the Children of Israel." Even though a few million people stood at Mount Sinai to receive the Torah (as I describe in Chapter 5), the entire group knew itself to be one large family, with all descended from Jacob, the patriarch. In a sense, the entire Torah is really the rules and history of one large family, but within the Torah you find many specific commandments designed to regulate the individual family unit.

Be fruitful and multiply

The Torah contains 613 commandments (take a look at them in Appendixes B and C), and the first one found in the first chapter of the first book is the commandment to have children: "And God blessed them, and God said to them, 'Be fruitful and multiply and fill the land and conquer it, and you shall rule over the fish of the sea and the birds of the sky, and all the animals that move upon the earth'" (Genesis 1:28).

Honor your father and mother

Honoring your father and your mother is known in Hebrew as **kibbud av v'em** (kih-*bood* ahv vah-*eem*). It's one of the Ten Commandments, but there are other verses in the Torah that also concern themselves with how to treat your parents. They are as follows:

- ✔ "Honor your father and your mother in order that your days shall be lengthened upon this land that the Lord your God has given you." (Exodus 20:12)

- ✔ "He who smites his father or his mother shall surely be put to death." (Exodus 21:15)

- ✔ "He who curses his father or his mother shall surely be put to death." (Exodus 21:17)

- ✔ "A man, his mother and his father shall he fear, and my Sabbaths shall he guard, I am the Lord your God." (Leviticus 19:3)

Just married? Take a year off

An unusual set of commandments in the Torah pertains to a newly married couple. The Torah teaches that a newly married husband shall be free for one year to rejoice with his wife: "When a man takes a new wife, he shall not enter military service, nor shall he be charged with any business; he shall be free for his house one year, and shall cheer his wife whom he has taken" (Deuteronomy 24:5).

The wife's rights are just as important as the husband's

The Torah protects the rights of wives in many ways. To mention just one example, Jewish law states that if a husband wants to change careers, his wife can forbid him to do so if it means that he will be away from home more often and therefore will not be able to make love as often as the wife would like. The Torah states, "If he takes a wife, her food, her clothing, and her conjugal rights, he shall not diminish" (Exodus 21:10).

Steer clear of forbidden relationships

According to the Torah, sexual relations are confined to being between a husband and wife. It's forbidden to have sex with another person outside of the marriage as well as to have sex with an animal. Here are the relevant verses:

- ✔ "And you shall not lie carnally with your neighbor's wife, to defile yourself with her" (Leviticus 18:20). Note that although the technical definition of adultery according to the Torah only pertains to the wife, tradition also forbids extramarital relations by the husband because, at one time, polygamy was a common practice.

- ✔ "And you shall not lie with any beast to defile yourself with it; neither shall any woman stand before a beast, to lie down with it; it is perversion." (Leviticus 18:23)

In addition, incest is defined as forbidden sexual relations within a family. According to the Torah, there are many such forbidden combinations, including sex with your mother, father, daughter, sister, father's wife, father's daughter, son's daughter, daughter's daughter, father's sister, mother's sister, father's brother's wife, wife's daughter, and daughter-in-law. (Did you get all that?) These prohibited sexual relations and others are detailed in Leviticus 18.

All You Need Is (A Lot More than) Love: Treating Everyone Fairly

According to Jewish tradition, treating people fairly doesn't mean to simply love everyone. The great Torah sages understand life to be far more complex than that. One of the fundamental principles in Jewish thought and life, and one of the biggest differences between Christianity and Judaism, is that no emotion is defined intrinsically as good or bad. Love isn't always good, and hate isn't always bad. Sometimes hate is good (the Torah teaches to hate evil and to hate evil people, for example) and sometime love is bad (for example, the Torah says that there's no sense in loving an enemy who hates you). Every pharmacist knows that the fine line between a medicine and a poison has to do with timing and dosage; these rules also apply to love and hate. But the Torah does teach some important principles that guide you in the general way to behave toward others, as you find out in the following sections.

One basic principle underlying all Jewish law is the assumption that being honest is the way to be. One exception in Jewish law, though, is the permissibility of telling a white lie to spare someone pain. For example, when you walk in to a hospital room to visit a patient, you aren't supposed to say, "You look like you're about to die." Similarly, when a bride asks you how she looks in her gown, you don't say, "It makes you look terrible." In cases in which the truth is likely to hurt, a white lie is the way to go.

Be kind and welcoming to strangers

One of the most important Jewish values has to do with being fair, kind, and welcoming to strangers. The Jewish people know from hard experience that being a stranger in a strange land can be a difficult and precarious situation. Jews have been in such a situation countless times, beginning with slavery in ancient Egypt and continuing through the centuries in exile from the Promised Land. Several verses in the Torah stress the value of sensitivity to strangers:

- "The stranger you shall not taunt or oppress for you were strangers in the land of Egypt." (Exodus 22:20)

- "You shall love the stranger, for you were strangers in the land of Egypt." (Deuteronomy 10:19)

The commandment to invite guests and welcome strangers is a topic that countless sages have discussed throughout history. Jewish tradition identifies the patriarch Abraham as a master of hospitality. The Torah says, "God appeared to Abraham while he was sitting at the entrance of the tent in the heat of the day. Abraham lifted his eyes and he saw three strangers standing near him. When he saw them from the entrance of his tent, he ran to greet them, bowing down to the ground" (Genesis 18:1–2). The following verses indicate that Abraham and his wife Sarah did several things. They

✔ Ran to help them (Genesis 18:2)

✔ Brought them water (Genesis 18:4)

✔ Washed their feet (Genesis 18:4)

✔ Offered them a place to rest (Genesis 18:4)

✔ Fed them (Genesis 18:5)

✔ Fed them the finest food (Genesis 18:6–7)

✔ Attended to them while they ate (Genesis 18:8)

These details found in the verses of the Torah form the basis of the attributes of a good host. The sages teach that hosts must provide physical comfort to guests, must feed them as best as they can, and must be alert to their needs.

Don't just stand there — do something for someone in need

Several times in the Torah, God commands people not to stand idly by while someone is in need. The Torah's answer to the question, "Am I my brother's keeper?" is "yes." In fact, there's a special commandment concerning your responsibility to try to correct the ways of others around you: "You shall not hate your brother in your heart, and you shall reprove your friend and not carry a sin because of him" (Leviticus 19:17). Other verses in the same spirit include:

✔ "If you see the donkey of your enemy crouching under its burden, shall you refrain from helping him? You shall surely help him!" (Exodus 23:5)

✔ "You shall not be a talebearer amongst your people. You shall not stand by while your friend's blood is shed. I am God." (Leviticus 19:16)

✔ You shall not see the donkey or the ox of your friend falling along the road and hide yourself from them. You shall surely stand them up with him [your friend]." (Deuteronomy 22:4)

Keep the vows you make

The Torah recognizes the power of words and holds people responsible for what they say. Within Torah law is the concept of the vow, which is a solemn promise. One Torah commandment says, "That which has gone out of your lips you shall observe and do" (Deuteronomy 23:24).

The Hebrew word for "vow" is **neder** (*neh*-dehr), and an entire section of the Oral Torah (see Chapter 3) is called **Nedarim** (neh-*dah*-reem; vows). Detailed laws are explained and explored in Nedarim.

When a person states something and uses God's name in the statement, the words spoken are considered a vow. According to the Torah, if you make a vow and don't fulfill it, you're breaking a divine command: "When a man vows a vow to the Lord . . . he shall not break his word; he shall do according to all that came out of his mouth" (Numbers 30:3). Keeping a vow made in God's name is so important to the Torah that it's actually mentioned four times. Here are the other three verses:

- ✔ "You shall not take the name of the Lord your God in vain; for the Lord will not hold guiltless one who takes His name in vain." (Exodus 20:7)

- ✔ "And you shall not swear by My name falsely, so that you profane the name of your God: I am the Lord." (Leviticus 19:12)

- ✔ "You shall fear the Lord your God; Him shall you serve; and to Him shall you cleave, and by His name shall you swear." (Deuteronomy 10:20)

B'li neder (bih-*lee neh*-dehr) is a common expression that I've heard countless times; it's used by religious Jews when they've expressed something but don't want it to be considered a solemn vow. For example, if I tell you that I will call you tonight, I may say, "I will call you tonight b'li neder." Although I have every intention of calling you, I also want to cover my back so that I'm not breaking a vow if I can't make the call.

Honor and respect your elders

The Torah teaches that you must honor people who are elderly and people who are wise. The Hebrew word for "honor" is **kovod** (kah-*vode*). But the word "honor," which is also used to refer to the commandment to honor your parents (which I discuss earlier in this chapter), doesn't mean "obey." As an adult, you aren't obligated to obey your parents. For example, if your parents tell you to do something that's wrong, you certainly don't have to do it. Whether it's your parents or an elderly person or a wise person, honoring them means displaying respect and kindness to them according to the Torah.

One of the ways to show honor and respect is to stand up. When an elderly or wise person enters a room and surely when he or she approaches you, the Torah urges you to rise out of honor. As the Torah says: "Before an old person shall you arise, and you shall honor the face of an elder, and you shall fear your God, for I am the Lord" (Leviticus 19:32).

Showing Kindness to Furry Friends

Several verses in the Torah form the basis of a Torah attitude of being kind to and preventing the suffering of animals. One well-known aspect of this attitude among Jews is the absolute necessity to minimize the suffering of an animal being slaughtered for food. The sharpest knife must be used, and the skill of the person who does the slaughter must include the ability to be swift and painless.

It's also a Jewish law that you feed your animals (including pets, of course) before you feed yourself. Other Torah verses dealing with kindness to animals include:

- "And whether it be cow or ewe, you shall not kill it and its young both in one day." (Leviticus 22:28)

- "If a bird's nest happens to be before you in the way, in any tree or on the ground, with young ones or eggs, and the mother sitting upon the young, or upon the eggs, you shall not take the mother with the young." (Deuteronomy 22:6)

- "You shall not muzzle the ox when he treads the corn." (Deuteronomy 25:4) In other words, let the animal eat and enjoy!

Chapter 10

Living by the Word of the Torah in the Community

In This Chapter

▶ Understanding universal laws in the Torah

▶ Exploring the laws of the Torah that guide business

▶ Appreciating the Torah's respect for property rights

▶ Grasping the Torah's commandments on courts

In Chapter 9, I explain the Torah laws that apply to personal behavior, but Judaism isn't just the spiritual path for individuals. The Torah also is concerned with the community at large — both Jews and those who aren't Jewish. As you find out in this chapter, the Torah has lots to say about the general community, how it functions (especially in business and law), and how it should behave.

It's Universal: The Seven Laws of the Sons of Noah

Some religions give the impression that it's their way or no way. Either you believe in their religion or you're going about your life all wrong. Judaism has a different point of view. According to Jewish tradition, the Torah certainly pertains to everyone, but Jews have a responsibility to the Torah that others do not. The whole meaning of the concept of the chosen people is 3that God has chosen the Jewish people to carry extra burdens in this world. If you aren't Jewish, Judaism doesn't require you to change your ways and accept the Jewish way.

But the Torah is a message to all humankind and does have requirements for people who aren't Jewish. These requirements amount to seven universal laws called the *seven laws of the sons of Noah,* also called the **Noahide** (no-uh-*khayd*) laws.

Applying common sense from the Torah

There's no denying that much of the Torah is simply common sense. The general principle is "Be nice and be fair to others." And an ancillary principle is this: Take what you have learned and apply it to life situations.

My oldest daughter, who was raised as a traditional Jew and follows a traditional Jewish lifestyle, was once told by a non-traditional Jew, "It must be easy being Orthodox. The books tell you what to do and you just do it." My daughter explained that the traditional Jewish way is usually misunderstood. The books can't possibly anticipate every situation and set of circumstances that one experiences in life. It's actually quite difficult to be a traditional Jewish person because you spend a lifetime studying the Torah, but when you go out and live your life, you're basically on your own. You have to take what you've learned, apply common sense, and try to do what you think is best in light of your Torah studies.

According to the Torah, Noah and his wife are the ancestors of all humankind. The Jewish people originally descend from one branch of Noah's family — from Shem, one of his three sons. (The name Shem is the source of the word "Semite.") The Noahide laws are required of all the descendants of Noah — in other words, everyone.

Jewish tradition teaches that both Jews and non-Jews must follow seven rules in order to be considered righteous. The seven laws expand on two verses in the Torah: "And God said to Noah and his sons with him saying, 'And as for Me, I establish My covenant with you and your offspring after you'" (Genesis 9:8–9); and "remember the covenant between God and every living being" (Genesis 9:16). The Oral Torah details the seven universal laws, consisting of six prohibitions and one positive commandment:

- Do not commit the sin of idolatry.
- Do not commit blasphemy.
- Do not murder.
- Do not steal.
- Do not engage in sexual immorality.
- Do not eat from the limb of a living animal.
- Establish courts of justice.

Doing Better Business

A fundamental principle of Jewish law as found in the Torah regards honesty in business. The Torah says, "And if you sell anything to your neighbor, or buy from your neighbor's hand, you shall not wrong one another" (Leviticus 25:14). The notion of honesty in business, known in Jewish law as **ona'ah** (oh-nah-*ah*; fraud), is examined in great detail in the Talmud. Overcharging or underpaying, for example, are considered serious infractions. The Torah teaches several principles about doing better business, and the following sections help you understand some of those important principles.

Lend money compassionately

In the Torah, God encourages people to lend money to those who need it (Exodus 22:24). Lending money to someone in need is considered a great and meritorious act. But the Torah adds something to the subject and strictly forbids a person to charge interest on a loan to a relative. So if a family member needs money and you can afford it, you must lend the money and not charge interest, even if the family member offers to pay it. As the Torah says plain and simple, "Do not charge interest on a loan to a family member" (Leviticus 25:37).

The Torah also insists that if you loan someone money, you must be compassionate and liberal about the situation. You must not demand that a poor person who owes you money pay if you know that he or she can't. The Torah also warns that you must not pressure the person to pay (Exodus 22:24).

Exploding a myth about Jews lending money

Jews have often been viewed in a negative light as moneylenders, and the fact is that there were periods in history when Jews were frequently in the business of lending money. Ironically, this profession *was imposed on Jews* during a time when they were forbidden to be landowners or participate in most professions. In addition, Jews who were moneylenders were severely restricted regarding how much interest they could charge (it was a very small percentage). So, while others were landowners and thrived in many kinds of businesses, Jews were restricted to lending money at a small profit. They had money but little opportunity to use it to build a good life. A Jewish moneylender was actually a very poor person.

Many discussions recorded in the Talmud and many laws in the Code of Jewish Law concern aspects of paying back a loan. Here are a couple examples:

✔ Written agreements with witnesses are recommended for loans in which the two parties agree explicitly to the rate of payback.

✔ As great as loaning money is, you shouldn't feel obligated to give a loan to someone if you have good cause to believe that he or she will squander the money.

Make sure your scales and weights are correct

Years ago, I worked in a store that sold gourmet foods and cheeses. I'll never forget the day when another employee showed me how to read the scale. In fact, the person was teaching me how to cheat people by tipping the scale. I was taught that it was easy to make difficult customers literally pay for their obnoxious behavior.

As you can imagine, the Torah objects to this horrible practice (and so do I, for the record!). The Torah emphatically says, "Just balances, just weights, both dry measures and liquid measures, shall you have: I am the Lord your God, who brought you out of the land of Egypt" (Leviticus 19:36). The principle of accurate scales and weights is so important that it's considered both a positive and a negative commandment: On the positive side, the Torah calls for "Just balance and weights," and on the negative side, it teaches not to possess inaccurate measures and weights by saying, "You shall not have in your bag weights of different inaccurate sizes, a great and a small" (Deuteronomy 25:13).

This is an area of Torah law in which the Talmud demonstrates that the Five Books of Moses can easily be applied to every era of history and to every new development. The word in the Written Torah for "just weights" — meaning accurate ones — actually represents the Torah's requirement for honesty in every conceivable way that you can measure things.

Treat your employees well

The Torah is concerned with all life, and it's said that everything is contained in the Torah. This includes something as (seemingly) mundane as how employers treat their employees. In fact, the Torah urges employers to be fair and supportive of the people who work for them and identifies some specific ways to do so.

Pay wages on time

One of the important aspects of the employer-employee relationship has to do with when to pay the employee. The Torah is clear: Unless you (the employer) and your employee have agreed upon some other schedule, you must pay your employee at the end of each day. This doesn't mean that you can't arrange for weekly payments, as many do. But if that's the agreement, you must fulfill it promptly. It's not permissible to delay payment; as the Torah says, "Thou shall not oppress your neighbor, or rob him; the wages of a hired servant shall not stay with you all night until the morning" (Leviticus 19:13).

When Moses repeats the laws of the Torah in the book of Deuteronomy, he again stresses this point of prompt payment and says, "In the same day you must give him his pay, the sun shall not go down upon it; for he is poor, and is counting on it: lest he cry against you to the Lord and it will be a sin for you" (Deuteronomy 24:15).

Allow a worker to eat what he or she is reaping

A very positive aspect of my work experience in a gourmet food and cheese store long ago has to do with a fascinating law found in the Torah. The management of the store permitted employees to eat as much as they wanted from the store free of charge during the workday. The Torah describes much the same approach:

- A hired laborer may eat from the produce of the field he or she is working on (Deuteronomy 23:25–26).
- The hired laborer must not take more than he or she can eat (Deuteronomy 23:25).
- The hired laborer shall not eat produce that is not being harvested (Deuteronomy 23:26).

Slavery in the Torah

The Torah explores the subject of slavery in detail. The Hebrew word for "slave" is **eved** (ehved), but the Torah's notion of a slave is quite different than what you may imagine. You may think of a slave as someone who's oppressed and treated cruelly. Such is not the case in the Torah. A slave was a servant who was obligated to the person he or she worked for, but the eved had rights and was carefully protected by the laws of the Torah. For example, a slave owner is severely punished if he strikes a slave (Exodus 21:20–21), and the slave must be housed, clothed, and fed in a most satisfactory way.

Finally, the Torah stipulates that a slave isn't a slave forever; after a specified period of time (no more than seven years), a slave must be freed of his status. When a slave is released, he must be given gifts and additional support to help him become independent. The Torah says, "When you send him away free you shall not send him away empty-handed. Adorn him generously from your flocks, from your threshing floor, and from your wine cellar. As God has blessed you, so shall you give him" (Deuteronomy 15:13–14).

Property Rights: What's Mine is Mine, What's Yours Is Yours

An ancient saying found in one of the most popular books of the Oral Torah, *The Ethics of the Sages,* describes four categories of attitudes:

- An average person thinks, "What's mine is mine and what's yours is yours."
- A fool thinks, "What's mine is yours and what's yours is mine."
- A righteous person thinks, "What's yours is yours and what's mine is yours."
- An evil person thinks, "What's yours is mine and what's mine is mine."

Although the way of the righteous person is the spiritual ideal, Jewish law is satisfied by the position of the average person, with the mindset "What's mine is mine and what's yours is yours." Certainly you should reach as high as possible spiritually, but if you can simply be respectful of others and their property, the Torah law is satisfied. I share a couple of guidelines regarding property rights in the following sections.

Don't be sneaky and change boundaries

One important principle in the Torah concerns itself with boundaries. For example, if you own a piece of land and the community knows that your land extends to a large boulder in a field, it would be a transgression of the Torah for someone to move the boulder in an attempt to cheat you. As the Torah states, "You shall not remove your neighbor's landmark" (Deuteronomy 19:14).

Other laws in the Torah dealing with property include:

- Be honest when dealing with the property of others (Leviticus 19:11). For instance, the Oral Torah includes detailed discussion about buying and selling, with particular focus on the question of the precise moment that a transaction and transfer of property takes place.
- Don't steal the property of others (Leviticus 5:23).

A sacred obligation: Return lost objects

A large section in the Talmud expands on the teaching in the Written Torah about lost objects. According to Torah law, it's your responsibility to make conscientious efforts to locate the owner of a lost object that you've found.

The Torah verse on which the whole body of law regarding lost objects is based is, "You shall not see your brother's ox or his sheep driven away, and hide your eyes from them; you shall surely bring them back to your brother" (Deuteronomy 22:1). The Torah is so serious about this that there's another verse teaching that you can't pretend to overlook a lost object because you don't want the responsibility of finding the owner: "And so shall you do with his donkey; and so shall you do with his garment; and so shall you do with every lost thing of your brother's, which he has lost, and you have found; you may not hide yourself" (Deuteronomy 22:3).

When I lived in Brooklyn and spent most evenings for ten years studying Torah in a local **Beit Midrash** (bait mid-*rahsh*; house of Torah study), I often saw notices on the bulletin board in the lobby from people who had found lost objects like pens or books or overcoats. The finders placed announcements attempting to find the items' owners. The laws of the Torah were taken very seriously; to try to find the owner of a lost object was as much a sacred duty as studying, praying, or observing any other religious laws.

Order in the Court — the Torah Way

As I explain in Chapter 5, the Torah tells of Moses not being able to keep up with all the disputes between and among the Children of Israel. With many hundreds of thousands of people wandering in the desert, no one person could possibly keep up with all the disagreements that arose. That's why Moses's father-in-law **Yitro** (*yit*-row; Jethro) suggested that Moses set up a court system to handle the cases. When Moses gave his farewell speeches to the Children of Israel (see Chapter 8), he reminded them of the necessity of a court system and said, "Accept the rulings of every court in Israel and do not rebel against the orders of the court" (Deuteronomy 17:11). I survey some important court guidelines in the following sections.

The appointment of judges

In order for a court system to work, it needs the full cooperation of the citizenry. Judges need to be appointed, and respect for the judges must be maintained. The Torah instructs the Children of Israel "to appoint judges and officers in every community of Israel" (Deuteronomy 16:18) and also to make sure that the judges are qualified. The Torah states that the people must not appoint as a judge a person who isn't well-versed in the laws of the Torah even if he's expert in other branches of knowledge (Deuteronomy 1:17). In addition, the Torah instructs the people not to curse a judge (Exodus 22:27). One reason for this is that a judge and his court are surrogates for God's judgments, so cursing the judge is blasphemy.

The rules of testimony

Setting up a court system isn't a simple task. Rules, regulations, and guiding principles must be in place for the system to work. The Torah deals with many aspects of a functioning court system, a primary one being the rules of testimony. These Torah rules, which sometimes appear in the Written Torah and sometimes are clearly stated in the Oral Torah, include the following:

- If you have some evidence, you must testify (Leviticus 5:1).
- Be honest in your testimony (Exodus 20:13).
- The court can't accept the testimony of a close relative, and a parent can't be punished for a child's crime (Deuteronomy 24:16).
- When testimony is heard, all parties involved must be present (Exodus 23:1).
- Witnesses must be examined thoroughly (Deuteronomy 13:15).
- One witness isn't enough (Deuteronomy 19:15).
- No one gets special treatment (including great people or poor people) (Leviticus 19:15 and Exodus 23:3).
- Beware of bribes (Exodus 23:8).
- Don't be impressed or intimidated by people in court (Deuteronomy 1:17).

Punishments for wrongdoings

Another aspect of a court and legal system is punishment. When a person is found guilty of a crime, an appropriate punishment must be ordered. The Written Torah and the Oral Torah establish a complex and thorough system for punishment, compensations to victims, and all the many details that go into constructing an effective and just penal system.

Corporal punishment

The Torah teaches that corporal punishment is sometimes appropriate. For example, the Torah says, "If a wicked man has incurred the penalty of flogging, the judge shall make him lean over and have him flogged (whipping or beating) with a fixed number of lashes for his crime" (Deuteronomy 25:2). The crimes whose punishment is flogging include idol worship, breaking one's vow, perjury, and crimes of sexual immorality.

Theft and price fraud

Someone found guilty of stealing must pay the person back, and in some cases must pay double or more. For example, the Torah says, "If someone steals an ox or sheep and then slaughters or sells it, he must repay five oxen for each ox and four sheep for each sheep" (Exodus 21:37). If the thief can't afford to pay, he's forced by the court to work for the person from whom he stole. As the Torah states, "A thief must make full restitution. If he is unable to pay, he is sold as a slave for his crime" (Exodus 22:2).

Another extensive area of Torah law is called **ona'ah** (oh-nah-*ah*; fraud, overcharging, underpaying). As with each area of law, the laws of fraud grow out of a verse in the Torah: "When you buy or sell to your neighbor, do not wrong one another" (Leviticus 25:14). In cases of fraud and all other monetary crimes, the Oral Torah teaches how to evaluate the extent of the crime and what the restitution should be.

Bodily injury and monetary compensation

As I explain in Chapter 18, the verse in the Torah that states "an eye for an eye, a tooth for a tooth" is one of the most misquoted and misunderstood passages in the Torah. It's absolutely forbidden to understand this verse-literally, meaning that you may never take physical revenge on a person who has injured you physically.

In the book of Exodus, the true Torah attitude is revealed that a person who inflicts a bodily injury shall pay monetary compensation to the victim: "And if men argue, and one strikes the other with a stone, or with his fist, and he does not die, but is confined to his bed; if he rise again, and walk abroad with his staff, then he that struck him shall be quit, only he must pay for the loss of time, and shall cause him to be thoroughly healed" (Exodus 21:18–19).

Capital punishment

The Torah describes four types of capital punishment (the Oral Torah connects these methods with the Torah verses that I indicate):

- Decapitation with the sword (Exodus 21:20 and Leviticus 26:25)
- Strangulation (Leviticus 20:10)
- Burning with fire (Leviticus 20:14)
- Stoning (Deuteronomy 22:24)

It's extremely important to recognize that in the annals of Jewish history, when the Jewish system of courts was functioning, there was almost never a case for which capital punishment was actually used. Although capital punishment is certainly a part of Torah law, it's extremely difficult to fulfill all the essential requirements needed to enact such punishment. For example, it's almost impossible for two witnesses to see the capital crime and the murderer to have been clearly warned of the implications of his deed before he did it. The system is constructed so that the punishment is on the books as a deterrent and as a way to express the severity of the illegal acts. But in actuality, capital punishment is rarely used.

Rabbi Elazar ben Azarya states in the Talmud: "More than one person executed in 70 years would be called a murderous court." Rabbi Tarfon and Rabbi Akiva state: "If we had been members of the Supreme Court, no defendant would ever have been executed."

Part IV
The Importance of the Torah in Judaism

The 5th Wave   By Rich Tennant

"It's the brand-new iTorah. I'm organizing my mitzvahs into shuffle mode."

In this part . . .

The Jewish People are called "the people of the book," and that book is the Torah. There are many important books in Jewish life, but the Torah is the most important book in all of Judaism. It contains basic instructions for Jewish holy days and Jewish religious practice and serves as the central focus of the synagogue Sabbath service. In this part, I explain how the Torah impacts all of Jewish life, ultimately focusing on the study of the Torah, a daily practice among all traditional Jews. You find out why the study of the Torah is so crucial for Jews and how to take the necessary steps to engage in Torah study yourself (whether or not you're Jewish).

Chapter 11

Observing the Holy Days in Torah Time

In This Chapter

▶ Grasping the Torah's view of sacred time

▶ Understanding the Torah's rules of observing Shabbat

▶ Brushing up on the Jewish holy days established in the Torah

*I*n case you hadn't noticed, Jews have lots of holy days. They aren't *holidays* — they're *holy* days. Whereas a holiday is a day off, a Jewish holy day is a day devoted to prayer, study, meditation, celebration, rituals, and family gatherings. All the activities of Jewish holy days are ultimately about God and the teachings of the Torah. As you find out in this chapter, Jews see special holy days that are placed on the calendar by God and taught in the Torah as ways to elevate oneself spiritually.

Time in general is an important category of thought in Jewish tradition. Time has its own unique ability to provide people with opportunities to connect with God and receive divine awareness and delight. In this chapter, I explain the ways the Torah and Judaism look at different units of time.

Breaking Down Time According to the Torah

The Jewish sages teach that holiness — connection to and awareness of God — is possible to attain through vehicles of time. The day, the week, the month, the year, and multiyear cycles of time each have a special ability to connect people with God and raise their consciousness.

The day: "It was evening and it was morning, one day"

The very first verses in the Torah, found in the book of Genesis (see Chapter 4), contain a precise description of the events leading up to the creation of the first Day and the first Night.

These five verses have been the object of Jewish meditation for millennia. Each verse is full of meaning and secrets, some that have been uncovered and others that remain to be discovered by some scholar of the future.

God creates the heaven and the earth

The first verse of the Torah, "In the beginning when God created the heaven and the earth" (Genesis 1:1), is understood by one of my teachers to mean that in Jewish tradition a person's spiritual work includes the struggle to grasp the paradox that God created existence and therefore existed before existence. God is beyond all time, space, or any concepts you can possibly think of (refer to Chapter 2 where I explore the Torah's view of God in more detail).

God hovers over the earth when the world is still formless and void

The second verse of the Torah is, "The earth was without form and empty, with darkness on the face of the deep and God's spirit moved on the surface of the waters" (Genesis 1:2). This verse contains a profound mystery of the Torah that only the greatest of scholars have pierced over the centuries: The phrase **tohu v'vohu** (*toe*-who v'*voh*-who), which is often translated as "darkness on the face of the deep," is the subject of contemplation particularly among Kabbalists (see my book *Kabbalah For Dummies*, published by Wiley, in which I describe the Kabbalistic teachings on the Torah). Much of the scholarly discussion focuses on what the terms literally mean. Some say that the terms can be translated as "formless and void." The very words "tohu v'vohu" rhyme, similar to a phrase like "topsy-turvy."

The image of a world that's formless and void is impossible to picture. As one great Torah teacher writes, existence is based on "divine non-being," which is also quite a challenge to grasp. Modern cosmologists also play with ideas like non-being as the basis for all creation.

God creates light

The third verse of the Torah states that "God said 'Let there be Light,' and there was Light" (Genesis 1:3). The Light that was created, called **Ohr** (oar), isn't the same as the light that we know, which comes from the rays of the sun, our local star. But neither the stars nor the sun (nor the moon) were created until the fourth day, according to the Torah. So what's going on? Jewish tradition considers what's sometimes called "the primordial light" to be the divine emanation that forms the basis of creation. In short, God didn't create the world out of nothing; rather, creation is a contracted and sculpted emanation of Light from God (see Chapter 2 for more details).

God divides light and darkness

The fourth verse of the Torah introduces the concept of the "day" as being a cycle of light and darkness: "God saw that the light was good, and God divided between the light and the darkness" (Genesis 1:4). The rhythm of the two, which corresponds to the rhythm of each day of your life, is the framework for much of Jewish life. A person has certain responsibilities every day in Jewish life, and the Torah fixes that rhythm as an eternal pattern of time.

God puts evening before morning

The fifth verse contains the statement, "And there was evening and there was morning, one day" (Genesis 1:5). This biblical phrase, putting "evening" first, is the basis of the fact that Jewish holy days begin at sundown. A Jewish "day" begins in the evening, which is why Shabbat begins at sundown on Friday night and ends the following sundown, Saturday night. (I discuss Shabbat in more detail later in this chapter.)

Each day contains three prayer sessions (see Chapter 2 for details):

- **Ma'ariv** (*mah*-ah-reeve; evening)
- **Shacharit** (*shah*-khah-reet; morning)
- **Mincha** (min-*khah*; afternoon)

The Torah also teaches that the famous prayer, the Shema (you can read it in Chapter 2), is to be said every evening and every morning. The prayer commands people to speak of God "when you lie down and when you rise up." The order reflects the fact that the Jewish day begins at night.

The week: Torah time is a spiral, not a straight line

The round nature of the week in Jewish life is based on the story of creation found in the entire first chapter of the book of Genesis. According to the Torah, God creates the world in six days. After the sixth day comes Shabbat, which isn't even considered a day in Jewish life; it's more of a unique category, an oasis in time, with special activities, restrictions, customs, and goals.

The Sabbath, called **Shabbat** (shah-*baht*), is essentially a day of rest. God creates the world in six days and rests on the seventh, and the Torah instructs the Jewish people to do the same. The cyclical nature of the Jewish week creates a spiral so that the week always returns to Shabbat. One of my Torah teachers suggests that the passing weeks should be seen as a spiral or helix rising. The weeks go around and around, returning to the same place but hopefully with participants who are spiritually elevated and who feel closer to God with each new cycle.

The Torah laws of Shabbat are complex and lengthy, as I explain in the later section "Shabbat: Observing the Holiest of Holy Days." But all these laws are ultimately part of a design for a day of peace, rest, prayer, tranquility, and delight every week.

The month: When the moon hits your eye

The concept of the month in the Torah is based on the cycle of the moon. The moon looks like it changes and grows each month, going from a narrow crescent to a full moon and then back to a reversed narrow crescent. In the book of Genesis, God creates the moon on the fourth day, but the significance of the moon in the marking of months appears much later. In Exodus 12:1–2, the Torah refers to the establishment of the Jewish calendar and the counting of months by the cycle of the moon.

On Shabbat before the new moon each month, the new Hebrew month is announced during the weekly synagogue Shabbat service. There are also some additional prayers added to the synagogue service as well as special readings from the Torah on the occasion of the beginning of the new month. The day beginning the new month is called **Rosh Chodesh** (rowsh *khowe-desh*; the head of the month).

Here's the order of the Hebrew months and their equivalents in the solar calendar:

- Tishre (September/October)
- Heshvan (October/November)
- Kislev (November/December)
- Tevet (December/January)
- Shevat (January/February)
- Adar (February/March)
- Adar II (the leap month)
- Nisan (March/April)
- Iyar (April/May)
- Sivan (May/June)
- Tammuz (June/July)
- Av (July/August)
- Elul (August/September)

Each month has to have full days, not fractions of days, so each Hebrew month has either 29 or 30 days in it, adding up to 354 days in the year. This is 11 days less than a solar calendar with 365 days in a year. To balance things out so that

Jewish holy days stay in the same season instead of move around the calendar, the Jewish calendar has a leap *month* called Adar II. It's added to the calendar seven times every 19 years.

Why is all this important? Because holy days described in the Torah can be scheduled properly only by establishing each new month. For instance:

✔ Rosh Hashanah is observed on the first day of Tishre. It's the day when the creation of the world was completed (Leviticus 23:24).

✔ Yom Kippur is observed on the tenth day of Tishre (Leviticus 23:26).

✔ Sukkot is in Tishre, from the 15th to the 21st (Leviticus 23:34).

✔ Passover is observed from the 15th to the 21st of Nisan (Leviticus 23:6).

The year: When holy days abound

According to the Torah, the Jewish year begins on the first day of the month Tishre, the anniversary of God's completion of the creation of the world. In Jewish time, the years go around and around with the celebration of the New Year being not only the start of the year but also the anniversary of existence itself. The Jewish New Year, Rosh Hashanah (which I cover later in this chapter), is a sacred occasion.

During the year, the Jewish calendar is filled with holy days that are all about God and the Torah's teachings. In addition to Shabbat (celebrated weekly), Rosh Chodesh (celebrated monthly), and the holy days that I discuss later in this chapter, holy days include those in Table 11-1.

Table 11-1	Sampling of Jewish Holy Days	
Holy Day	*Description*	*Date(s)*
Ten Days of Awe	A period of intense introspection and prayer from Rosh Hashanah to Yom Kippur	1st to 10th of Tishre
Hanukkah	Festival of Lights	24th of Kislev to 1st of Tevet
Tenth of Tevet	A day of fasting connected to the destruction of the Temple	10th of Tevet
Tu B'shvat	New year of the trees	15th of Shevat
Purim	Festival of Lots	14th of Adar
Sefirah	Counting of the Omer	21st of Nisan to 6th of Sivan

(continued)

Table 11-1 (continued)

Holy Day	Description	Date(s)
Lag B'Omer	A festive day connected to the sages of the Talmud	33rd day of the counting of the Omer; the 18th of Iyar
17th of Tammuz	A day of fasting connected to the destruction of the Temple	17th of Tammuz
The Three Weeks and the Nine Days	Days of mourning leading up to Tisha B'Av	17th of Tammuz to 9th of Av
Tisha B'av	A day of fasting, commemorating the destruction of the Temple	9th of Av

The seven-year cycle: Giving the land and debtors a break

The Torah describes cycles of seven years as having great significance. The seven-year cycle, mentioned several times in the Torah, is called **sh'mita** (sheh-*mee*-tah). There are two main parts of sh'mita:

- ✔ After six years, farmed land is given a year of rest.
- ✔ After seven years, debts among the Children of Israel are canceled out.

Here are a few of the verses that teach about the sh'mita year:

> *It is permitted for six years to plant your land and gather crops. But during the seventh year, you must leave it alone and withdraw from it.*
>
> Exodus 23:10–11

> *God spoke to Moses at Mount Sinai and told him to speak to the Children of Israel and say to them: When you come to the land that I am giving you, the land must be given a Sabbath rest for God. For six years you may plant your fields and prune your vineyards and harvest your crops, but the seventh year is a Sabbath of Sabbaths for the land.*
>
> Leviticus 25:1–4

> *At the end of every seven years you shall institute the remission year. Here is the point: every creditor shall remit any debt owed by his neighbor and brother when God's remission year comes around.*
>
> Deuteronomy 15:1–2

The basic idea of sh'mita is still alive and well among the Jewish people:

- ✓ Many religious Jews in Israel allow their farming land to rest for a year.
- ✓ It's considered an act of great merit to offer a free loan to someone in need.

The 50-year cycle: When all land belongs to God

In ancient times, the Children of Israel observed the **Yovel** (*yoh*-vail; jubilee) in accordance with this Torah verse: "You shall count for yourself seven cycles of Sabbatical years, seven years seven times . . . it shall be the Jubilee year for you . . . You shall not harvest, you shall not sow" (Leviticus 25:8–12).

The details of the Jubilee are complex and haven't been observed for centuries, but the basic, profound idea behind the concept of the Jubilee year is the assumption that land ultimately belongs to God.

Shabbat: Observing the Holiest of Holy Days

There's an old saying among Jews that more than Jews keep Shabbat, Shabbat has kept the Jews. Shabbat is the most important Jewish holy day (contrary to popular belief, it's not Yom Kippur) and is so holy that it isn't even considered a real day among the Torah sages but rather is a special creation by God as a gift to His children. Shabbat is a day of liberation, when Jews are free from the routine of the workweek. Keeping Shabbat is even one of the Ten Commandments (see Chapter 17); passages about it appear in both the book of Exodus and the book of Deuteronomy.

In the following sections, I explain the basic rules of observing Shabbat according to the Torah, including forbidden activities.

The Torah's basic Shabbat instructions

Shabbat is like a dance in that it has certain steps to follow. Looking at any one moment of a dance doesn't reveal much about the dance as a whole. You have to watch an entire dance performance to appreciate its wholeness. The same is true of Shabbat. When you participate in it from the inside, and participate fully, you're able to grasp the holiness of Shabbat.

The laws of Shabbat are complex and numerous, but they all grow out of verses in the Written Torah that the great Torah sages and Talmudic scholars have supplemented with the Oral Torah. The basics consist of the following commandments and their corresponding verses in the Torah:

- ✔ **Stay close to home on Shabbat.**

 "Let no man go out of his place on the seventh day." (Exodus 16:29)

- ✔ **Make Shabbat a special day.**

 "Remember the Shabbat day, to keep it holy." (Exodus 20:8)

- ✔ **Don't "work" on Shabbat.** (See the later section "The 39 things you can't do on Shabbat" for specifics.)

 "But the seventh day is Shabbat for the Lord your God, in it you shall not do any manner of work: You, nor your son, nor your daughter, nor your male servant, nor your maidservant, nor your cattle, nor the stranger that is within your gates." (Exodus 20:9)

- ✔ **Rest on Shabbat.**

 "Six days shall you do your work, but on the seventh day you shall rest; that your ox and your donkey may have rest, and the son of your handmaid, and the stranger, may be refreshed." (Exodus 23:12)

 "Six days shall you work, but on the seventh day you shall rest; in plowing time and in harvest you shall rest." (Exodus 34:21)

The activities within the Tabernacle were altered on Shabbat, and parallel or similar alterations in the liturgy on Shabbat can be seen in synagogue services today. For example:

- ✔ **Offer up an additional sacrifice every Shabbat (two lambs).** Today, this is represented in the Shabbat synagogue service by the addition of a relatively brief service called **mussaf** (*moo*-sahf; addition) at the end of the morning service.

 "And on the Shabbat day, two male lambs in their first year without blemish, and two tenth parts of an ephah of fine flour for a meal-offering, mingled with oil, and the drink-offering with it." (Numbers 28:9)

- ✔ **Set the showbread (12 loaves representing the tribes of Israel) and the frankincense before God every Shabbat.** Every Shabbat table includes at least two loaves of challah (bread). Some Shabbat tables include 12 loaves to reflect the ancient practice.

 "And you shall set upon the table showbread before Me always." (Exodus 25:30)

The start of Shabbat

Shabbat begins at sundown on Friday evening. Just before the sun sets, Shabbat candles are lit in Jewish homes. Traditionally, Jewish families gather for a festive meal on Friday night to usher in Shabbat. The meal includes the singing of sacred songs, blessing the children of the household, reciting a special prayer over a cup of wine in honor of Shabbat, and then partaking in the festive meal, which always begins with ritual hand washing and a special blessing before Shabbat challah loaves are eaten. The Written and Oral Torahs provide the basis of Shabbat customs and rituals. They include the following:

1. **Candle lighting.**

   Traditionally, the woman of the household lights at least two candles, one for each of the two important references to Shabbat in the Torah: "Remember Shabbat" (Exodus 20:8) and "Observe Shabbat" (Deuteronomy 5:12).

2. **Blessing the children of the household (see Figure 11-1).**

   This custom is based on a verse in the Torah describing how Jacob blessed his grandsons Ephraim and Menashe (Genesis 48:20).

Figure 11-1:
A father puts his hands on his children while blessing them.

3. Reciting the blessing over a cup of wine.

The Oral Torah explains that the way to fulfill the Torah's command to "remember" Shabbat is by reciting the special prayer called the **Kiddush** (kih-*doosh*; sanctification) over wine. Figure 11-2 shows a Kiddush cup.

Figure 11-2: A Kiddush cup.

4. Washing hands before reciting the blessing to eat bread.

Although it's not explicitly in the Written Torah, the oral tradition bases this custom on two verses: one from the Written Torah (Leviticus 15:11) and the other from Psalms 26:6. Each verse refers to rinsing hands for purification purposes (Figure 11-3 shows a cup used for rinsing hands).

Figure 11-3: A cup for washing hands.

Two loaves of challah are used on Shabbat to commemorate the two portions of manna that God provided the Children of Israel before Shabbat each week when they were in the wilderness. You can see a loaf of challah in Figure 11-4.

Figure 11-4:
A loaf of challah.

The 39 things you can't do on Shabbat

With regard to Shabbat, one verse in the Torah states, "For six days you may perform melachah, but the seventh day is a day of complete rest, holy to the Lord" (Exodus 31:15).

The great rabbis and sages of Jewish tradition explain that the word **melachah** (meh-lah-*khah*; work) actually means far more than work. The oral tradition teaches that melachah consists of 39 categories of work that correspond to 39 activities, most relating to the building of Tabernacle, that appear in the Torah (see Chapter 5 for more on the Tabernacle). They can be better understood as four general categories (which I cover in the following sections), all related to the physical activities performed by the Children of Israel as they wandered in the desert.

The following 39 activities are actually terms that represent more than their literal meaning. Jewish tradition teaches that each of these 39 categories of work have what's known as **toledot** (toll-*dote*; offspring). For example, the fifth melachah, threshing, means any extraction of something from something else. In other words, squeezing a lemon for its juice isn't permitted on Shabbat because it falls into the category of threshing.

Baking bread

The first category consists of activities that were part of the process of baking bread. The book of Exodus describes how the Children of Israel didn't gather manna (food sent from heaven) on Shabbat but instead gathered two portions of manna on the day before Shabbat (see Chapter 5). The preparation of food is forbidden on Shabbat, so the food for Shabbat is prepared in advance. The following activities are necessary for making the basic food — bread — and so they're forbidden on Shabbat:

- Zoreah (sowing)
- Choresh (plowing)
- Kotzair (reaping)
- M'amair (gathering)
- Dush (threshing)
- Zoreh (winnowing)
- Borer (sorting)
- Tochain (grinding)
- Miraked (sifting)
- Lush (kneading)
- Ofeh; Bishul (baking; cooking)

Creating clothing

The second category is based on the fact that in the Tabernacle the Priests wore special clothing described in detail in the book of Exodus. The materials in these beautiful garments were created by the following activities, which are forbidden on Shabbat:

- Gozez (shearing)
- Melabain (whitening)
- Menafetz (disentangling; combing)
- Tzovayah (dyeing)
- Toveh (spinning)
- Maisach (mounting the warp)
- Oseh Beit Batai Neirin (preparing to weave)
- Oraig (weaving)
- Potzai'ah (separating threads)
- Koshair (tying a knot)

✔ Matir (untying a knot)

✔ Tofair (sewing)

✔ Ko'reah (tearing)

Making leather and parchment

The third category relates to the creation of leather, an essential part of the physical Tabernacle in that it was used for the roof of the structure, as well as to the creation of parchment for writing. As a verse in Exodus says, "Make a roof for the tent out of reddened rams' skin. Above it, make a roof out of the blue processed hides" (Exodus 26:14). These materials require the following activities that are forbidden on Shabbat:

✔ Tzud (trapping)

✔ Shochet (slaughtering)

✔ Mafshit (skinning)

✔ M'abaid (salting; tanning process)

✔ Mesharteit (tracing or scratching lines)

✔ Memacheik (smoothing; scraping)

✔ Mechateich (cutting to shape)

General types of work

The last category includes writing as well as various general kinds of labor. There are no explicit references to these activities in the Written Torah, but the Oral Torah, specifically the section of the Mishnah called *Shabbat,* lists these prohibited activities as well as all 39 categories considered "work" on Shabbat:

✔ Kotaiv (writing two or more letters)

✔ Mochaik (erasing two or more letters)

✔ Boneh (building)

✔ Soiser (demolishing)

✔ Mechabeh (extinguishing a flame)

✔ Ma'avir (kindling)

✔ Makeh B'Patish (completing; putting on finishing touches)

✔ Hotza'ah (transferring from domain to domain)

The end of Shabbat

There are no specific instructions in the Torah for the conclusion of Shabbat, but over the centuries a brief ritual developed called **havdalah** (hahv-dah-*lah*; separation). The ritual, usually performed at home, includes the recitation of verses from the Torah and other sacred Jewish writings as well as lighting a decorative candle, saying a blessing over a cup of wine, and smelling sweet spices.

Celebrating Holy Days Appearing in the Torah

Earlier in this chapter, I describe the way the Torah looks at various units of time: those that are seemingly natural, like the day, the month, and the year; and those more-human inventions, like the week, the cycle of seven years, and the cycle of 50 years. The Torah considers all these cycles of time to be "natural" and woven into the fabric of God's universe.

The Jewish holy days that appear in the Torah also are considered to be embedded within the rhythm of time itself; I discuss these holy days, in order of their appearance on the Jewish calendar, in the following sections. In the view of the Torah, each holy day, even those that seem to simply commemorate historical events, is a part of the creation itself.

The Jewish concept of time isn't linear and, as such, isn't so easy to grasp. As my teacher explains, time is more like a spiral or a helix rising up from Creation. There's always a certain return to the past; the past is never a condition that has gone by and is no more. Each year, Creation returns in a sense to the same place. Each holy day is considered to be a part of the pattern of time and is built into Creation itself.

It may surprise you to know that the holy days of Chanukah and Purim don't appear in the Torah. Both days commemorate historical events that occurred after the Torah was given to Moses at Mount Sinai.

Rosh Hashanah: Happy birthday, dear universe

The Jewish New Year celebration, **Rosh Hashanah** (rowsh hah-*shah*-nah; head of the year), is the anniversary of the creation of the universe and begins a period of ten days of profound introspection and prayer. Jews celebrate it on the first day of the month of Tishre (I discuss the months of the Jewish year earlier in this chapter). The Torah instructs several things about the observance of Rosh Hashanah that form the basis of Rosh Hashanah practice today.

There are a few different "new years" in Judaism, so although Rosh Hashanah is in the month of Tishre, which is sometimes seen as the first month of the year, you should note that the Torah says that Rosh Hashanah is in the seventh month. This may seem strange to you, but in modern life in the United States there are also a few different "beginnings" of the year. There's January 1st, which is the beginning of the calendar year. There's September, which is the beginning of the school year for most students. There's also a fiscal year, which varies from company to company. The Jewish calendar year actually begins with the Hebrew month of Nisan.

It's a day of rest

Like Shabbat (also known as the Sabbath, which I cover earlier in this chapter), there are many laws and customs on Rosh Hashanah that help to create an atmosphere contrary to the hustle and bustle of ordinary days. One of the primary laws stresses that the holy day is a day of rest. (Keep reading to find out some of these laws and customs.)

> *Speak to the children of Israel, saying, "In the seventh month, in the first day of the month, shall be a solemn rest for you, a memorial proclaimed with the blast of horns, a holy convocation."*
>
> Leviticus 23:24

You can't work, but you can make food

Jewish law requires that almost all the restrictions appropriate for Shabbat also pertain to Rosh Hashanah. One of the exceptions allows for food preparation on this holy day.

> *You shall do no manner of work, and you shall bring a fire offering to the Lord.*
>
> Leviticus 23:25

Hear the sound of the shofar

The **shofar** (show-*far*; ram's horn) is blown in the synagogue on Rosh Hashanah, and a highlight of the day is hearing its blasts.

> *And in the seventh month, on the first day of the month, you shall have a holy convocation: you shall do no manner of work; it is a day of blowing the horn for you.*
>
> Numbers 29:1

Offer an additional sacrifice

Although the Temple is no longer standing, the synagogue service reflects the Torah's injunction for an additional sacrifice. The Rosh Hashanah liturgy includes an additional part of the prayer service that substitutes for the additional sacrifice. Today, there are no sacrifices at all because the Holy Temple is not standing. Instead, prayers are offered.

> *And in the seventh month, the first day of the month shall be called holy for you . . . And you shall prepare a burnt-offering for a pleasant offering for the Lord.*
>
> Numbers 29:2–4

Yom Kippur: The day of at-one-ment

The climax of ten days of introspection, soul-searching, and prayer that begins on Rosh Hashanah (during the month of Tishre) is **Yom Kippur** (yohm kee-*poor*). It's a day of prayer and fasting and ultimately merging with God. The Torah teaches the following directives about Yom Kippur.

Observe the services appointed for the day

There are a number of special rituals performed on Yom Kippur, such as the eating of a festive meal before the holy day begins and the recital of the **Kol Nidre** (kohl nihd-*ray*; all vows) prayer, which is the first part of the synagogue service as the holy day begins. In this service, the individual asks God for forgiveness in the event that a vow made to oneself is not fulfilled.

> *"Aaron shall come into the holy place, with a young bull for a sin-offering, and a ram for a burnt-offering . . . And this shall be an everlasting statute for you, to make atonement for the children of Israel because of all their sins, once in the year." And he did as the Lord commanded Moses.*
>
> Leviticus 16:3–34

Observe a fast

For over 24 hours, Jews don't eat or drink on Yom Kippur as a symbol of the injunction in the Torah to "afflict your soul" on this holy day.

> *However, on the tenth day of this seventh month is the day of atonement; there shall be a holy convocation for you, and you shall afflict your souls; and you shall bring a fire offering to the Lord.*
>
> Leviticus 23:27

For whatever soul it be that shall not be afflicted on that same day, he shall be cut off from his people.

Leviticus 23:29

Rest and do no work

Yom Kippur is sometimes referred to as the Sabbath of Sabbaths. Like Shabbat (which I discuss earlier in this chapter), no work is done on this day.

You shall do no manner of work; it is a statute forever throughout your generations in all your dwellings.

Leviticus 23:31

It shall be to you a Sabbath of solemn rest, and you shall afflict your souls; on the ninth day of the month at evening, from evening to evening, you shall keep your Sabbath.

Leviticus 23:32

Offer an additional sacrifice

Because the Temple isn't standing in Jerusalem, the Yom Kippur liturgy includes an additional part of the prayer service that substitutes for the additional sacrifice. There are no sacrifices at all today because the Holy Temple is not standing. Instead, prayers are offered.

And the tenth day of the seventh month shall be called holy for you, and you shall present a burnt-offering to the Lord for a pleasant offering: one young bull, one ram, seven male lambs in their first year; they shall be for you without blemish.

Numbers 29:7–8

Sukkot: Recreating the exodus from Egypt

Sukkot (sue-*kote*; booths or huts) is a festival lasting several days in the fall (in the month of Tishre). Jewish families around the world build temporary dwellings reminiscent of the living conditions of the Children of Israel as they wandered in the desert before reaching the Promised Land. You can see a sukkah in Figure 11-5. The following sections point out the commandments in the Torah about Sukkot.

Figure 11-5:
A sukkah for the festival of Sukkot.

Celebrate three special festivals

The Torah singles out the three holy days of Passover, Shavuot, and Sukkot as special festivals to celebrate.

> *Three times during the year you shall celebrate a feast for Me.*
>
> Exodus 23:14

Rest and do no work on the first day of Sukkot

The Torah defines Sukkot as a seven-day holiday. The first of the seven days has a special status and is treated like Shabbat (except regarding food; on Shabbat, there are special restrictions about preparing food that don't apply on other holy days). The remaining days are still part of the holiday of Sukkot, and the customs and rituals apply to all the days.

> *On the first day shall be a holy convocation; you shall do no manner of work.*
>
> Leviticus 23:35

Rest and do no work on the day after Sukkot

The day after Sukkot is called **Shemini Atzeret** (sheh-*mee*-nee ah-*tzehr*-et; the eighth day of assembly). Although it's often thought to be the last day of Sukkot, the Torah defines it as a holy day in itself. In Israel, it's also called **Simchat Torah** (sim-*kaht* toe-*rah*). Outside of Israel, Simchat Torah is the day after Shemini Atzeret.

> *Seven days you shall bring a fire offering to the Lord; the eighth day shall be called holy to you; and you shall bring a fire offering to the Lord; it is a day of solemn assembly; you shall do no manner of work.*
>
> Leviticus 23:36

Shake four different plants

Each day between the first and eighth days of Sukkot, four species of plants — a date palm, the bough of a myrtle tree, a willow branch, and a lemon-like citrus fruit called an **etrog** (*eht*-rohg) — are taken together. They're shaken in six directions — north, east, south, west, up, and down — as an expression of the belief and faith that God is everywhere.

> *And you shall take for you on the first day the fruit of goodly trees, branches of palm-trees, and boughs of thick trees, and willows of the brook, and you shall rejoice before the Lord your God seven days.*
>
> Leviticus 23:40

Dwell in booths for seven days

Traditional Jews build temporary huts for Sukkot and at minimum eat meals in the hut during the festival. Some people sleep in them, too.

> *You shall dwell in booths for seven days; every native in Israel shall dwell in booths.*
>
> Leviticus 23:42

Offer an additional sacrifice

As I explain in regard to other holy days, the additional sacrifices that the Torah requires aren't offered today because there's no Holy Temple. Instead, an additional prayer service is placed at the end of the usual morning service.

> *And you shall present a burnt-offering, an offering made by fire, as a pleasant offering for the Lord: thirteen young bulls, two rams, fourteen male lambs in their first year; they shall be without a blemish.*
>
> Numbers 29:12–34

Rejoice during Sukkot

A key part of the observance of Sukkot is experiencing the feeling of joy. In fact, the holy days of Sukkot are also referred to as **ziman simchataynu** (zih-*mahn* sim-khah-*tay*-new; the season of joy).

> *And you shall rejoice in your feast, you, and your son, and your daughter, and your male servant, and your maidservant, and the Levite, and the stranger, and the fatherless, and the widow, that are within your gates.*
>
> Deuteronomy 16:14

Appear in the sanctuary during all the festivals

The holy days of Sukkot, Passover, and Shavuot are called the *Pilgrimage festivals* because Jews went to Jerusalem, and specifically to the Holy Temple, on these three occasions each year (if practical).

> *Three times a year all your males shall appear before the Lord your God in the place which He shall choose; on the Feast of Unleavened Bread, and on the Feast of Weeks, and on the Feast of Tabernacles; and they shall not appear before the Lord empty.*
>
> Deuteronomy 16:16

Simchat Torah: Let's hear it for the Torah!

Simchat Torah (sim-*kaht* toe-*rah*; rejoice in the Torah) isn't mentioned by name in the Torah. It's the day (on the 23rd of Tishre) when the Torah is finished and is begun again during the weekly public readings of the Torah (see Chapter 13). In the Torah, the holy day is called Shemini Atzeret, as I mention in the earlier section "Rest and do no work on the day after Sukkot." On Simchat Torah, Jews gather in synagogues and take turns dancing with the Torah.

Passover: The oldest Jewish holy day

The central event of the Torah is the story of the bondage of slavery, ultimate liberation, and the receiving of the Torah at Mount Sinai by the Children of Israel. The holy day of Passover (in the month of Nisan) is designed for observers to retell the story in great detail each year and be nourished by its lessons. Retelling this story each year on Passover is the oldest communal ritual in the tradition called Judaism. In many places throughout the text, the Torah explains how to observe the holy day of Passover.

Remove chametz from your home and property on the eve of Passover

Chametz (khah-*maytz*) is hard to define. Generally, it's any food that rises, such as breads and cakes that rise with yeast. The bread of Passover is matzah, which is unleavened bread. The basic framework of the observance of Passover comes directly from the Torah.

> *Seven days shall you eat unleavened bread; however the first day you shall put the leaven away, out of your houses; for whoever eats leavened bread from the first day until the seventh day, that soul shall be cut off from Israel.*
>
> Exodus 12:15

Don't possess chametz during Passover

On the days immediately before Passover, Jews prepare their homes by searching for, finding, and discarding all products that contain leavening agents as well as food products that the sages have added because of their similarity to food products that rise like leaven.

> *For seven days there shall be no leaven found in your houses; for whoever eats that which is leavened, that soul shall be cut off from the congregation of Israel, whether he be a sojourner, or one that is born in the land.*
>
> Exodus 12:19

> *Unleavened bread shall be eaten throughout the seven days; and no leavened bread shall be seen with you, nor shall there be leaven seen with you, in all your borders.*
>
> Exodus 13:7

Don't eat any food containing chametz on Passover

It's forbidden to have chametz in a Jewish home and also forbidden to eat these products during the days of Passover.

> *You shall eat nothing leavened; in all your homes shall you eat unleavened bread.*
>
> Exodus 12:20

> *And Moses said unto the people, "Remember this day, in which you came out from Egypt, out of the house of bondage; for by the strength of His hand the Lord brought you out from this place; there no leavened bread shall be eaten.*
>
> Exodus 13:3

Discuss the departure from Egypt on the first night of Passover

This law is the basis of the family Passover meal, known as the **seder** (*say*-der; order), when the story of the Exodus is told.

> *And you shall tell your son on that day, saying, "It is because of that which the Lord did for me when I came out of Egypt."*

> Exodus 13:8

Eat the flesh of the Paschal lamb with unleavened bread and bitter herbs

Unleavened bread (matzah) and bitter herbs are two of the important symbols that are essential to have on the table during the Passover feast (seder). Matzah is a symbol of the oppression of the Children of Israel in Egypt. The Israelites left Egypt quickly and didn't have time to wait until their bread had risen. The bitter herb is also a symbol of oppression; it reminds participants of the bitterness of slavery. In addition, a small shank bone is placed on the Passover table as a symbol of the Paschal lamb once offered as a sacrifice when the Holy Temple stood in Jerusalem.

> *In the second month on the fourteenth day at dusk they shall keep it; they shall eat it with unleavened bread and bitter herbs.*

> Numbers 9:11

Shavuot: When God gave the Torah to the world

The book of Exodus says "Three times during the year you shall celebrate a feast for Me" (23:14). One feast is Sukkot, one is Passover, and the third is Shavuot. Shavuot is the commemoration of the giving and receiving of the Torah at Mount Sinai; it's celebrated during the month of Sivan. It's customary for Jews to stay up all night and study the Torah on Shavuot. During the morning service on Shavuot, the Ten Commandments are publicly read. Following are the Torah commandments that address Shavuot.

Rest and do no work

As I discuss in the context of the other major Jewish holy days, most Jewish festivals forbid Jews from working. The holy days require special treatment; mundane activities are inappropriate.

> *And you shall make proclamation on the same day; it shall be called holy to you; you shall do no manner of work; it is a statute forever in all your dwellings throughout your generations.*

> Leviticus 23:21

Rejoice during the festivals

As with Passover and Sukkot, Shavuot is a day of rejoicing and festivity. It's not a regular workday, and the mood is always one of joy and celebration.

> *And you shall rejoice in your feast, you, and your son, and your daughter, and your male servant, and your maidservant, and the Levite, and the stranger, and the fatherless, and the widow, that are within your gates.*

> Deuteronomy 16:14

Chapter 12

Following Jewish Customs According to the Torah

In This Chapter

▶ Looking at life cycle traditions described in the Torah

▶ Checking out major Jewish symbols in the Torah

▶ Eating the Torah way

*I*t has been said that Judaism isn't a religion but a way of life. In this chapter, you see lots of evidence of this fact. Judaism, which is the so-called "religion" of the Torah, is far more than a set of spiritual beliefs and is also far more than a set of rules.

The Jewish people, originally known as the Children of Israel, are a family that grew into a nation. As a nation, the Jewish people have customs, folkways, legends, rituals, signs, symbols, history, and more. In particular, Judaism has a distinctive set of life cycle practices, a distinctive set of symbols, and an extremely distinctive set of laws and customs surrounding the most basic of human activities: eating.

Torah Traditions Related to the Cycle of Life

The five major life cycle events described in the Torah are

- ✔ Birth
- ✔ Becoming an adult
- ✔ Marriage
- ✔ Divorce
- ✔ Death

Each of these events is of concern to God, and each is explored at length starting in the Written Torah and then with more depth in the Oral Torah (see Chapter 3). As you find out in the following sections, the Torah is an instruction manual for life and all its many details.

Circumcision: A big issue over a little piece of tissue

When you think of circumcision, you probably think of the surgical procedure that removes the foreskin from a penis. But the Hebrew word for "foreskin," **orlah** (oar-*lah*), is used in more than one way in the Torah — and ultimately provides an explanation, or at least some insight, into the ancient Jewish practice of male circumcision. In the following sections, I go over the Torah's discussion of this ceremony and explain when and why it takes place.

The Torah's mention of circumcision

In the book of Deuteronomy, the Torah says, "You shall circumcise your heart" (Deuteronomy 10:16). According to the great Torah commentators, this verse means that a person must remove the barriers that dull the heart, which is the seat of compassion. Circumcision is a process of removing barriers, whether it's an emotional barrier that causes people to be insensitive to others or a physical barrier, like the foreskin of a penis.

The Hebrew term for circumcision is **brit milah** (b'rit mee-*lah*; covenant of circumcision). The word "brit" (or the more common pronunciation, "bris") means "covenant or agreement" and appears in the Torah in relation to Abraham, one of the patriarchs of Judaism, whom I discuss in Chapter 4.

The Torah relates that when Abraham was 99 years old, God appeared before him and told him to perfect himself. Even though perfection is a concept that really only applies to God, Judaism urges the Jewish people to participate in a lifelong pursuit of refinement and perfection. The Hebrew term **middot** (mee-*dote*; measures) refers to a person's character traits, such as compassion, empathy, or honesty; the goal of Torah study is to learn how to refine those traits, to deepen your understanding of those traits, and to ultimately elevate yourself spiritually. God commands Abraham to "walk before Me and be perfect" (Genesis 17:1).

In the Torah, right after God commands that Abraham perfect himself, God changes Abraham's name. (In Hebrew, Abraham is **Avraham**, pronounced ahv-rah-*hahm*.) In the Torah, his name was originally Avram, and God says, "Your name shall no longer be Avram, but your name shall be Avraham" (Genesis 17:5). Torah commentators point out that the name Avraham is actually a contraction of the words "av hamon," which means "father of a multitude." In other words, God sets in motion a transformation from Avram (which means "father of Aram," Aram being his former country) to Avraham, with Abraham ultimately becoming the head of a huge number of people and his family becoming a nation.

After God changes Abraham's name, God makes an eternal agreement with him — and with his descendants. God promises to give Abraham's offspring the Land of Canaan (Israel). Finally, God seals the deal with the ritual of circumcision and declares:

> *This is My covenant which you shall keep, between Me and you and the descendants after you. Every male among you shall be circumcised. And you shall be circumcised in the flesh of your foreskin; and it shall be a token of a covenant between Me and you. At eight days old every male among you shall be circumcised, every male throughout your generations . . . and My covenant shall be in your flesh for an everlasting covenant. And the uncircumcised male who is not circumcised in the flesh of his foreskin, that soul shall be cut off from his people; he has broken My covenant.*

> Genesis 17:10–14

Circumcision is a Jewish symbol and perhaps the most powerful Jewish symbol of all. It's a sign between each Jewish man and God, like the signing of an agreement or contract. What is the contract about? It's a promise to the Jewish people that God will never abandon them. And it's a promise to God that the Jewish people will never abandon Him. (I discuss other symbols of Judaism later in this chapter.)

The basics of the ceremony

The ancient practice of circumcision is a crucial ritual in Jewish life. On the eighth day of their lives, all Jewish boys are circumcised (unless the ritual needs to be postponed for some medical or developmental reason) and officially named. The Jewish sages point out that there's great significance in the fact that the Torah commands that the ritual be done on the eighth day. As I explain in Chapter 11, the cycle of seven days is the cycle of creation. God created the world in six days and rested on the seventh day, Shabbat. The eighth day is the first day of a new cycle, when humankind is charged with the task of taking over and perfecting the world. In the same spirit, the circumcision of a boy on the eighth day of his life is a symbolic act reflecting his lifelong assignment to perfect himself.

According to the Jewish view, the world is imperfect. This is a basic and important assumption on the part of the Torah sages. The Hebrew term for it is **tikkun olam** (tee-*koon* oh-*lahm*; repairing the world). God created the world unfinished, and it's humankind who must participate in the perfection of both the individual and also the world at large. The Jewish ritual of circumcision reflects this assumption that each person is a work in progress. And every part of a person, from inner personality traits to private physical form and sexuality, is in need of refinement.

Do Jewish girls undergo a special ceremony at birth?

There's no female equivalent to circumcision in Jewish practice. Female circumcision, as practiced in some cultures, involves the removal of the clitoris and is really a form of mutilation with profound and horrible results. A victim of such a procedure loses the pleasurable physical sensation that is the result of sexual stimulation. The Jewish ritual of brit milah, despite some claims to the contrary, has no such negative results among men. In fact, some people throughout history have suggested that circumcision actually has a health benefit. Recent studies prove conclusively that circumcision is effective in helping to stop the spread of AIDS.

A Jewish girl, however, is officially named shortly after her birth, just like a Jewish boy is named at his brit milah. A baby girl is customarily named on the first Shabbat after her birth during the Torah service when the baby's father is honored by being called to bless the Torah (see Chapter 13 for more on the public reading of the Torah).

Another form of celebration that has developed on the occasion of the birth of a girl is a party called a **brit bat** (b'rit baht; a daughter's covenant). It's usually a home celebration, but there's no set ritual. Either with the assistance of a local rabbi or by themselves, the baby's parents put together a ceremony with appropriate prayers and spiritual intention.

The Bar (or Bat) Mitzvah: Starting to accept responsibility when puberty sets in

A Bar Mitzvah or Bat Mitzvah ceremony commonly refers to the public Jewish "coming of age" ritual. The term **Bar Mitzvah** (bar mitz-*vah*) uses the Aramaic word **bar** (son), and literally means "son of the commandment." The female equivalent is **Bat Mitzvah** (baht mitz-*vah*); "bat" means "daughter" in both Aramaic and Hebrew.

The Written Torah doesn't mention Bar Mitzvahs (the actual plural, in Hebrew, isn't "Bar Mitzvahs" but rather "B'nai Mitzvah," pronounced bih-*nay* mitz-*vah*), but the process of becoming a responsible adult, beginning at the age of Bar and Bat Mitzvah, is built into the legal structure of the Oral Torah. According to Jewish law, when a boy reaches age 13 or a girl reaches age 12, the occasion marks the beginning of a process during which the young person takes on responsibility.

According to traditional Jewish belief, a baby isn't born "pure." On the contrary, children seem quite willing and able to participate in all kinds of forbidden and even destructive activities. It's parents' responsibility to educate their children, to refine their character traits, and to instruct them in the proper ways to behave and live. These proper ways are spelled out in the Torah and its commentaries.

Until the ages of Bar and Bat Mitzvah, Jewish children aren't considered (by Jewish law) to be responsible for their misdeeds. But when they hit the right age, responsibility begins to shift. From these teen years until the age of 20, Jewish law teaches that the heavenly court doesn't consider the individual to be fully responsible for his or her misdeeds. Full personal responsibility is a gradual process that reaches its climax after age 20. The Torah considers a 20-year-old man to be a full adult, and according to Jewish law, after age 20 the heavenly court begins to look at a person as fully independent.

A public or private ritual isn't essential to mark a Bar or Bat Mitzvah. It happens automatically, according to the Oral Torah, either when the young person reaches 13 (boys) or 12 (girls) or when physical signs of puberty appear. The Talmud specifically refers to the appearance of two pubic hairs.

One significant relationship between the Bar Mitzvah and the Torah is that when a boy turns 13, he's permitted to be called up to the Torah during the public reading of the Torah and is permitted to recite the Torah blessing. In liberal synagogues, this privilege is extended to girls of Bat Mitzvah age. See Chapter 13 for more about the Torah synagogue service.

Marriage: Two halves make a whole

To understand the Jewish concept of marriage, it's important to remember that God created humans by creating one person first. The original Adam was then split into two halves. In the first chapter of the Torah, Genesis 1:27 says, "God created man in His own image, in the image of God He created him; male and female He created them." The original person was androgynous. (See Chapter 4 for more details.)

Then, in the second chapter of the Torah, God said:

> It is not good for man to be alone; I will make him a helper suitable for him. Out of the ground God formed every beast of the field and every bird of the sky, and brought them to the man to see what he would call them; and whatever the man called a living creature, that was its name. The man gave names to all the cattle, and to the birds of the sky, and to every beast of the field, but for Adam there was not found a helper suitable for him. So God caused a deep sleep to fall upon the man, and he slept; then He took one of his sides and closed up the flesh at that place. God fashioned into a woman the side which He had taken from the man, and brought her to the man. The man said, "This is now bone of my bones, and flesh of my flesh; she shall be called Woman, because she was taken out of Man." For this reason a man shall leave his father and his mother, and be joined to his wife; and they shall become one flesh.

Genesis 2:18–24

The great Torah sages understand this passage to mean that each person's soul is really only half. The deeper meaning of marriage in Jewish tradition is a joining of two halves to form one whole soul. In Jewish tradition, marriage isn't for procreation. Procreation is certainly a Torah commandment; in fact, it's the very first actual commandment in the Torah ("Be fruitful and multiply" [Genesis 1:22]). But the purpose of marriage according to the Torah is companionship ("It is not good for man to be alone" [Genesis 2:18]).

In the following sections, I explain the procedure and duties of marriage according to the Torah.

The process of getting hitched

According to the Oral Torah, there are actually three possible marriage procedures:

- ✔ A man hands a woman an object of value (like a ring or a coin), which she accepts for the expressed purpose of creating a marriage.
- ✔ A man and woman sign a properly written marriage contract.
- ✔ A man and woman engage in sexual intercourse with the intention, by both parties, of creating a marriage.

Today, Jewish marriages are usually a combination of these three methods: a marriage contract (called a **ketubah,** pronounced keh-too-*bah*, which means "contract") is signed, a ring is given, and the marriage is consummated.

The duties of marriage

The Written Torah contains little detail concerning marriage. A verse in Exodus (21:10) indicates that a husband and wife have responsibilities to each other in three areas:

- ✔ Food
- ✔ Clothing
- ✔ Conjugal rights

However, the rights and responsibilities between a husband and wife are discussed in great detail in the Oral Torah, most specifically in the Talmud. One interesting aspect covered is sexuality. Jewish law is firm: A husband's one obligation during sex is to make sure that his wife is experiencing a pleasant encounter. In fact, if a husband wants to change careers, he must have his wife's permission if the change may result in his being home less and therefore less apt to make love with his wife.

Here are some additional teachings from the Torah regarding marriage:

- A newly married husband shall be free for one year to rejoice with his wife. A bridegroom shall also be exempt for a whole year from taking part in any public labor, such as military service.

  "When a man takes a new wife, he shall not enter military service, nor shall he be charged with any business; he shall be free for his house one year, and shall cheer his wife whom he has taken." (Deuteronomy 24:5)

- A husband who defames his wife's honor (by falsely accusing her of unchastity before marriage) must live with her throughout all his lifetime.

  "And they shall fine him a hundred shekels of silver, and give them to the father of the woman, because he has brought an evil name upon a virgin of Israel; and she shall be his wife; he may not divorce her all his days." (Deuteronomy 22:19)

Divorce: Fix it or get out

While some religious traditions forbid divorce, Judaism does not. In the Torah, divorce is viewed as a common and acceptable occurrence (Deuteronomy 24:1–4), and although the Talmud teaches that the "altar in heaven weeps" on the occasion of a divorce, there's no requirement that a husband and wife continue their marriage if they're miserable together. As one of my teachers advised me when I was considering divorce, "If you can fix it, fix it. If you can't fix it, get out."

A Jewish marriage has two levels: One is spiritual (as I explain earlier in this chapter), and the other is down-to-earth and quite practical. The practical aspect of marriage is reflected in the fact that Jewish marriages are finalized by a contract. The contract is mostly about the rights of the parties and the terms if a divorce occurs. Yes, when a Jewish couple gets married, they sign a document that has a lot to do with what happens in the case of a divorce. When a divorce occurs, the marriage contract is fulfilled and then destroyed, severing both the spiritual and the physical connections between the two people.

Here are some rules of divorce according to the Torah:

- A man may not divorce his wife concerning whom he has published an evil report (about her unchastity) before marriage (see the preceding section).

  "And they shall fine him a hundred shekels of silver, and give them to the father of the woman, because he has brought an evil name upon a virgin of Israel; and she shall be his wife; he may not divorce her all his days." (Deuteronomy 22:19)

- A divorce must be enacted by a formal written document.

"When a man takes a wife, and marries her, then it comes to pass that she does not find favor in his eyes, because he has found something unseemly in her, then he writes her a bill of divorce, and gives it in her hand, and sends her out of his house." (Deuteronomy 24:1)

The topic of divorce provides a good example of how the Torah can't simply be read literally (see Chapter 15 for details). Deuteronomy 24:1 makes it seem as though only a husband can initiate a divorce. The fact is that the Oral Torah explains how both husband and wife have rights and responsibilities in a marriage, including the right to go to a Jewish court to request that the marriage be dissolved.

✔ A man who divorced his wife shall not remarry her if she married another man after the divorce.

"Her former husband, who sent her away, may not take her again to be his wife. After that she is defiled, for that is an abomination before the Lord, and you shall not cause sin in the land which the Lord thy God gives you as an inheritance." (Deuteronomy 24:4)

Death: The end and the beginning

A common misconception about Judaism is that Jewish teachings don't say much about death and the afterlife. This is a gross distortion of Judaism based in part on the fact that the Written Torah has little to say about death. The Oral Torah, including the Talmud and the teachings of Kabbalah, is where you find extensive treatment of death and the afterlife. In the following sections, I discuss teachings about death and customs related to death as they're described in the Torah.

Torah teachings about death

A person is a combination of body and soul; the soul is immortal, but the body isn't. In the book of Genesis (see Chapter 4), the loss of immortality is one of the consequences of Adam and Eve eating from the Tree of Knowledge of Good and Evil. Had Adam and Eve obeyed God, eternal life would have been theirs. The verse in the Torah that describes the result of the primal sin is, "For you are dust and to dust you shall return" (Genesis 3:19). It establishes that humans are mortal; they are born, live, and die.

The Torah also teaches that death isn't the end. A verse in Genesis is the basis for the teaching that the soul, which God breathed into Adam's nostrils, continues on after death: "Abraham breathed his last and died in a ripe old age, an old man and satisfied with life; and he was gathered to his people" (Genesis 25:8).

Other Jewish teachings on death include the following:

- Every human soul has its own assignment and has an obligation to fulfill its assignment. If a soul fails, it's reincarnated and given another chance.

- Heaven and hell exist (called **shamayim** and **gehennom,** pronounced shah-*mah*-yeem and geh-*heh*-num). But the Jewish ideas of heaven and hell are quite different from Christian views. Judaism doesn't conceive of hell as a place of eternal torment with fiery pits and desperate loneliness. In Judaism, hell is a more of a waiting room or temporary place where the soul is refined or where it waits before its next incarnation in the body of another person. Jewish tradition also describes hell as somewhere a person can be in this world when he or she is stuck in some unfortunate state of consciousness. (See my book *Kabbalah For Dummies*, published by Wiley, for more on these concepts.)

Burying the patriarchs and matriarchs of Judaism

The practice of burying a corpse is well-established in the Torah, which specifically describes the burials of the three patriarchs — Abraham, Isaac, and Jacob.

- **Abraham:** "These are the days of the years of Abraham's life that he lived, one hundred and seventy-five years. Abraham breathed his last and died in a ripe old age, an old man and satisfied with life; and he was gathered to his people. Then his sons Isaac and Ishmael buried him in the cave of Machpelah, in the field of Ephron the son of Zohar the Hittite, facing Mamre, the field which Abraham purchased from the sons of Heth; there Abraham was buried with Sarah his wife." (Genesis 25:7–10)

- **Isaac:** "Isaac breathed his last and died and was gathered to his people, an old man who was fulfilled; and his sons, Esau and Jacob buried him." (Genesis 35:29)

- **Jacob:** "His sons did for him as he had instructed them; his sons carried him to the land of Canaan and buried him in the cave

of the field of Machpelah facing Mamre, which Abraham had bought along with the field for a burial site from Ephron the Hittite. After he had buried his father, Joseph returned to Egypt, he and his brothers, and all who had gone up with him to bury his father." (Genesis 50:12–14)

The Torah also mentions the burials of two of the four matriarchs. Here's a bit of trivia for you: The burial of Rachel contains the first mention of a gravestone in the Torah.

- **Sarah:** "Abraham buried Sarah his wife in the cave of the field at Machpelah facing Mamre, that is, Hebron, in the land of Canaan. So the field and the cave that is in it, were confirmed as Abraham's as an estate for a burial site by the sons of Heth." (Genesis 23:19–20)

- **Rachel:** "Rachel died, and she was buried on the road to Ephrath, which is Bethlehem. Jacob set up a monument over her grave." (Genesis 35:19–20)

Mourning and burial traditions

The Jewish laws and customs pertaining to death are quite extensive. In fact, Judaism is well-known for the many stages that mourners must go through from the moment of the death of a close relative. Cremation is forbidden by Jewish law. The phrase in the Torah that says, "You must bury the body on the same day" (Deuteronomy 21:23) is the basis of this commandment.

Here are two common Jewish death and mourning customs and their corresponding verses in the Torah:

- When a person learns about the death of a close relative, he must tear his clothing as a symbol of mourning.

  "Then Jacob rent his garments and placed sackcloth on his loins." (Genesis 37:34)

- Jewish law requires that a corpse be buried as soon as possible.

  "You shall surely bury him that day." (Deuteronomy 21:23)

It's a Sign! Surveying Some Well-Known Jewish Symbols

The use of symbols is important in Judaism, and the Torah provides the Jewish people with powerful symbols as reminders of God and God's teachings. Three major symbols of Judaism, as found in the Torah, are:

- **Mezuzah** (a sign on the doorpost of every Jewish home)
- **Tzitzit** (a sign on the corners of clothes that Jews wear)
- **Tefillin** (a sign that literally wraps itself around your head and arm)

Mezuzah: A sign of God on the doorpost of your house

One of the most well-known Jewish symbols is the **mezuzah** (meh-zooz-*ah*). A mezuzah is basically a piece of parchment on which specially selected verses from the Torah are written by a certified scribe (see Chapter 14 for more about scribes). The texts written on the parchment include the verses in the Torah that refer to the mezuzah. The parchment is usually put into a little box and attached to the right side of a doorpost as you walk into a Jewish home (see Figure 12-1). Some people put a mezuzah on each of the doors within a house (with the exception of the bathroom). The mezuzah functions as a reminder that God is everywhere and that the Torah instructs you to speak about God and God's teachings as much as possible.

Figure 12-1:
A mezuzah is attached to a house's doorpost.

Jews recite special blessings when attaching a mezuzah to a doorpost. In addition, there are other rules pertaining to a mezuzah, including exactly where it should be placed (on the doorpost on the right side as you walk into a home or room, about one-third of the way down from the top of the door frame) and the exact style of calligraphy that the trained scribe uses on the parchment inside. The commandment to put up a mezuzah can be found twice in the Torah (note the text not in italics):

> _Hear, O Israel! The LORD is our God, the LORD is one! You shall love the LORD your God with all your heart and with all your soul and with all your might. And these words, which I am commanding you today, shall be on your heart. You shall teach them diligently to your children and you shall talk of them when you sit in your house and when you walk on the way and when you lie down and when you rise up. You shall bind them as a sign on your arm and they shall be ornaments between your eyes._ You shall write them on the doorposts of your house and on your gates.

> Deuteronomy 6:4–9

> _You shall therefore impress these words of mine on your heart and on your soul; and you shall bind them as a sign on your arm, and they shall be an ornament between your eyes. You shall teach them to your children, talking of them when you sit in your house and when you walk along the road and when you lie down and when you rise up._ You shall write them on the doorposts of your house and on your gates, _so that your days and the days of your sons may be multiplied on the land which God swore to your fathers to give them, as long as the heavens remain above the earth._

> Deuteronomy 11:18–21

It's customary among traditional Jews to touch the mezuzah as they pass through the doorway where a mezuzah is attached. Some people touch a hand to their mouths, kiss the hand, and then touch the mezuzah (or vice versa), as though they're kissing the mezuzah itself.

Tzitzit: Strings attached

In the Torah, God instructs the Children of Israel to attach special threads to the four corners of their garments. In Hebrew, the threads are called **tzitzit** (tzee-*tzeet*; fringes). This commandment appears twice in the Torah text:

- ✔ "God also spoke to Moses, saying, 'Speak to the sons of Israel, and tell them that they shall make for themselves tzitzit on the corners of their garments throughout their generations.'" (Numbers 15:37–38)

- ✔ "You shall make yourself tzitzit on the four corners of your garment with which you cover yourself." (Deuteronomy 22:12)

Tzitzit are placed on the corners of garments to serve as a reminder of God and God's commandments. Today, you can see tzitzit on the four corners of a Jewish prayer shawl called a **tallit** (tah-*leet*; prayer shawl); Figure 12-2 shows a shawl with tzitzit. In ancient times, typical clothing had four corners, so the tzitzit were on most pieces of clothing. Today, it's not required to attach tzitzit to all garments; in order to fulfill this commandment, some traditional Jewish men wear something called a **tallit katan** (tah-*leet* kah-*tahn*; little tallit) under their shirts. The tallit katan is a square piece of cloth with a hole in the center for the head and tzitzit on the four corners.

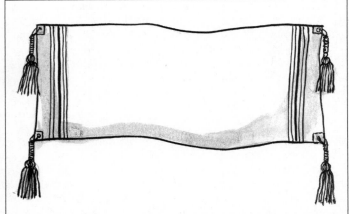

Figure 12-2: Tzitzit on a prayer shawl are reminders of God and God's commandments.

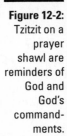

The great Torah commentator, Rashi, points out that the numerical value of the Hebrew letters that make up the word "tzitzit" as it's spelled in the Mishnah is 600. He also points out that for tzitzit to be correct, each corner has 8 threads and 5 knots, which totals 13. 600 plus 13 adds up to 613, which is the number of commandments in the Torah (see Appendixes B and C).

Tefillin: The ties that bind

The two passages that I reproduce in the earlier section "Mezuzah: A sign of God on the doorpost of your house" are the same source for the commandment to put on tefillin. **Tefillin** (teh-fill-*een*) look quite unusual to someone who has never seen them before or who doesn't know what they are. Tefillin are basically two leather boxes containing pieces of parchment on which verses from the Torah (including the verses that refer to tefillin themselves) are written by a trained and qualified scribe. The boxes have leather straps connected to them, which are used to attached the tefillin to the forehead and the arm (next to the heart), as you can see in Figure 12-3.

Figure 12-3:
Tefillin attach to a person's forehead and arm.

The message behind wearing tefillin is simple and clear: Consciousness of God and God's commandments must be in your mind and in your heart. Traditionally, Jewish men wear tefillin on weekdays during the morning prayer service, but the commandment can be fulfilled any time during the day.

There are many aspects to the proper creation and wearing of tefillin. These details are found in the Oral Torah and include:

- The proper way to make tefillin
- The proper materials to be used (for example, the leather must be from a kosher animal, and the sinew used as the thread that sews the tefillin together must also be from a kosher animal)
- The proper texts, their contents, and the way they should be written
- The proper order of the texts within the tefillin
- The proper way to put on tefillin
- The proper blessings to say when putting on tefillin
- The proper way to remove tefillin
- The proper way to store tefillin

But Is It Kosher? Jewish Eating Practices

One of the most distinctive religious practices among the Jewish people involves the kosher laws found in the Torah. The Jewish laws of **kashrut** (kahsh-*root*; kosher) are complex and wide-ranging, but I summarize their major principles in the following sections.

Don't eat the flesh of a beast that died naturally

A part of the laws of kashrut is the prohibition against eating an animal that has died of natural causes (including death by another animal or by disease). In order for an animal to be acceptable, it must be slaughtered in as painless a way as possible (see the next section). Here are two Torah verses that express this requirement:

- "And you shall be holy men unto Me; therefore you shall not eat any flesh that is torn of beasts in the field; you shall cast it to the dogs." (Exodus 22:30)

> ✔ "You shall not eat of any thing that dies of itself; you may give it to the stranger that is within your gates, that he may eat it; or you may sell it to a foreigner; for you are a holy people to the Lord your God." (Deuteronomy 14:21)

Slaughter animals as painlessly as possible

The laws of kosher slaughtering of an animal for food are complex. But all the laws (outlined in detail in the Oral Torah) support the basic goal of minimizing the suffering of the animal. Those who are qualified to slaughter animals for kosher food are highly trained. In addition, they have the sharpest knives (to prevent tearing the flesh) and must kill the animal with one gesture of the knife — again with the goal of minimizing the animal's suffering. The key phrase in the following passage is "as I have commanded you"; this is the phrase that refers to the proper slaughtering technique.

> *If the place which the Lord your God shall choose to put His name there is too far from you, then you shall kill from your own herd and from your own flock, which the Lord has given you, as I have commanded you, and you shall eat within your gates, whatever your soul desires.*

> Deuteronomy 12:21

Cheeseburgers are for never

Jews who observe the kosher laws can't eat cheeseburgers. Nor can they eat a steak with bread and butter. I can give many more examples, but the general rule according to the Torah is that meat and dairy may not be prepared, served, or eaten together. While the details of this law are complex, the Torah verse that alludes to it appears quite simple: "You shall not cook a kid in its mother's milk" (Deuteronomy 14:21).

This brief statement in the Torah reflects a large area of Jewish law, expanded in the Oral Torah, that forms an essential part of the Torah's kosher laws. Jewish tradition has also developed rules regulating how much time you must wait between eating a meat meal and consuming a dairy product. Although this practice varies from place to place, observant Jews wait between three and six hours between eating meat and then eating a dairy product.

Don't stuff yourself

Although not exactly laws about kosher food, Jewish tradition has developed laws known as *sumptuary laws* that are basically prohibitions against waste and overabundance. Throughout Jewish history, leaders of various communities have tried to enforce these laws and have gone to great efforts to minimize wasteful habits. Scholars point to two passages in the Torah that support these efforts:

- ✔ The first is the passage in Genesis when, during seven years of famine, Jacob tells his sons, "Why do you make yourselves so conspicuous?" (Genesis 42:1). The Talmud explains that Jacob said to his sons, "Do not show yourselves to be sated either before Esau or Ishmael in order that you do not arouse their envy against you."

- ✔ The second verse connected to sumptuary laws is, "And they shall say to the elders of his city, 'This, our son, is stubborn and rebellious, he does not listen to our voice; he is a glutton, and a drunkard'" (Deuteronomy 21:20).

Other important kosher laws

Additional kosher laws found in the Torah include the following:

- ✔ Blood must be removed from meat as completely as possible before consumption.

  "And you shall eat no manner of blood, whether it be of fowl or of beast, in any of your dwellings." (Leviticus 7:26)

  "Only be steadfast in not eating the blood; for the blood is the life; and you shall not eat the life with the flesh." (Deuteronomy 12:23)

- ✔ The only mammals permissible as food are those that chew their cud and have split hooves (such as cows, lambs, and buffalos).

  "Nevertheless, these you shall not eat: those that only chew the cud, or those that only have split hooves. The camel, because he chews his cud but does not have split hooves, is unclean to you." (Leviticus 11:4)

- ✔ Only fish with fins and scales are permissible as food (in other words, no shellfish is allowed).

  "These you may eat of all that are in the waters: whatever has fins and scales in the waters, in the seas, and in the rivers, them you may eat." (Leviticus 11:9)

✔ Birds of prey are forbidden as food.

"And these you shall detest among the fowls; they shall not be eaten, they are a detestable thing: the great vulture, and the bearded vulture, and the osprey." (Leviticus 11:13–19)

✔ Do not eat things that creep upon the earth nor a worm found in a fruit.

"And every swarming thing that swarms upon the earth is a detestable thing; it shall not be eaten. Whatever goes upon its belly, and whatever goes upon all fours, or whatever has many feet, even all swarming things that swarm upon the earth, them you shall not eat; for they are a detestable thing." (Leviticus 11:41–42)

✔ Do not eat things that swarm in the water.

"You shall not make yourselves detestable with any swarming thing that swarms, neither shall you make yourselves unclean with them, that you should be defiled thereby." (Leviticus 11:43)

✔ Do not eat any vermin of the earth.

"For I am the Lord your God; sanctify yourselves therefore, and be holy; for I am holy; you shall not defile yourselves with any manner of swarming thing that moves upon the earth." (Leviticus 11:44)

✔ Do not eat winged insects.

"And all winged swarming things are unclean unto you; they shall not be eaten." (Deuteronomy 14:19)

Chapter 13

Walking through the Torah Synagogue Service

*P*eople attend synagogues on Shabbat for many reasons — not all of them so great. Some sit in the back and gossip. Some come just for the refreshments after the services. Still others like to pray among their neighbors.

But the truly compelling reason for attending a synagogue Shabbat service on Saturday morning is to hear the public reading of the Torah. According to Jewish tradition, there's no requirement for prayer to be public; but what *is* required is the public reading from the sacred Torah scroll.

A Torah scroll, found only in a synagogue, is treated with the highest regard; it's the primary sacred object of Jewish life. Every aspect of the care and treatment of a Torah scroll serves to protect the Torah's sanctity. The physical scrolls are treated with the same delicacy shown to a newborn baby.

In most synagogues, the Torah service is breathtakingly dramatic and moving. The most sacred object in Judaism is carried in a procession throughout the synagogue. It's undressed from its elegant wrapping, and a portion of the wisdom it contains is read aloud and listened to carefully by the community of worshipers. In this chapter, I describe a Torah service in its entirety.

Understanding the Basic Customs of Torah Readings

The reading of a Torah scroll on Shabbat has two key characteristics: The reading is public, and it involves only a small portion of text. Given the length of the Torah, if a congregation were to try to read the entire Torah scroll in one sitting, everyone would be at the synagogue for a while! In the following sections, I explain these customs in more details.

Reading the Torah publicly

It's a Jewish custom to read the Torah out loud publicly. In fact, Moses read portions of the Torah to the congregation of Israel. The Torah says, "And he took the book of the covenant, and read it in the hearing of the people; and they said: 'All that the Lord has spoken will we do, and obey'" (Exodus 24:7). Torahs have been read publicly on a weekly basis in Jewish communities and synagogues for thousands of years. It's easy for everyone today to own a copy of the Torah text, but for many centuries, the only way to ensure that everyone heard God's instructions to the Jewish people was to conduct public readings.

Why is the public reading of the Torah so important? Judaism has a basic belief that it's the responsibility of every individual in a community to commit himself or herself to a lifelong habit of learning. And what's contained in the Jewish definition of learning? For thousands of years, it has meant the study of the Torah. Young children study the Torah, teenagers study the Torah, adults study the Torah, and the community elders study the Torah.

The Torah teaches that on a daily basis one should be occupied with the study of the Torah. After all, if the Torah is God's communication through Moses of the truth about reality, why shouldn't there be a preoccupation and dedication to the study of it? In the words of the Torah, "You shall teach them diligently to your children, and shall talk of them when you sit in your house, and when you walk by the way, and when you lie down, and when you rise up" (Deuteronomy 6:7).

Reading a portion of the Torah weekly

Centuries ago, Jewish sages developed a system that allows an individual or a community to read the entire Torah in one year. The system divides the Torah into bite-size, weekly portions, and one portion is read each Shabbat.

Most synagogue congregations throughout the world and throughout history have followed this system. The main purpose of the weekly Torah program, as established by the sages, is to make sure that everyone in the community becomes familiar with the Torah's teachings.

This weekly Torah program can be compared to going to a gym. If you go to a gym once a month for eight hours, you're wasting your time because you don't get into shape and can easily injure yourself. But if you go to the gym every few days and work out for 20 minutes each visit, you can make real progress. It's the same with studying the Torah: Studying one small portion each week allows you to absorb a lot more than you would in a handful of marathon sessions. And within a year, you're back to the beginning again.

In the following sections, I describe the origins of reading the entire Torah in one year and compare it to another tradition: reading the Torah in a three-year cycle. I also explain the importance of dividing the Torah into weekly portions.

Comparing the one-year cycle to the three-year cycle

The annual cycle of Torah study was developed and practiced in ancient Babylonia. (Generally speaking, today this area where a large and important Jewish community existed for centuries is known as Iraq.) But a three-year cycle was used in the ancient Land of Israel. There, the Five Books of Moses was divided into at least 154 sections that took three years to complete. This three-year cycle of Torah study lasted until the 12th century, when it ended because there were too few Jews in the area to maintain the custom.

Today, some liberal congregations prefer to work on a three-year cycle. In most cases, the three-year cycle doesn't divide up the Torah differently from those on an annual cycle but rather a smaller part of the weekly portion is publicly read. So every three years it can be said that the entire Torah from beginning to end was available to be heard publicly. Because liberal congregations tend to have synagogue services that are shorter than those of more traditional congregations, one way to shorten the length of the service is by shortening the public Torah reading.

There are at least two ways to determine the custom of a congregation today. One is simply to ask the rabbi. The other is pay close attention during the Torah reading and follow along to find out whether the whole weekly portion is being read. During the synagogue service, each person has a copy of the text of the Five Books of Moses in book form called a **chumash** (khoo-*mahsh*). Someone announces the portion of the week and its location in the text. If you're following the reading in your personal copy and notice that only a part of the portion is read, the congregation is almost surely on a three-year cycle.

Dividing the Torah into 54 sections

The Torah is divided into five separate parts known as the Five Books of Moses (I discuss these books in Part II). All five books taken together are divided into 54 smaller units. Because there are 52 weeks in a year and sometimes the annual calendar has a slightly different number of Saturdays, there are times when 2 of the 54 portions are studied in the same week so that the entire text can be completed in one annual cycle.

The annual cycle ends and begins on the Jewish holy day of **Simchat Torah** (sim-*kaht* toe-*rah*) each fall (see Chapter 11 for more about this day). On that day, the last verses of the fifth book of the Five Books of Moses (Deuteronomy) are read publicly, followed by the first verses of the first book of the Five Books of Moses (Genesis.)

Each Torah portion has a name generally taken from the first few words of the Torah portion itself. For example, the first Torah portion is known as **Parashat Bereshit** (pahr-ah-*shat* bah-ray-*sheet*; In the beginning) and is about the creation of the world. The second Torah portion is called **Parashat Noakh** (pahr-ah-*shat* noh-akh; Noah) and contains the story of Noah and the Flood. The term "parashat" means "portion." (See Chapter 3 for a complete list of Torah portions and their corresponding verses.)

Connecting with others by reading the same section at the same time

One factor that contributes to the special experience of attending a public reading of the Torah on Shabbat is the knowledge that people all around the world who also attend public Torah readings are focusing their attention on the very same section of the Torah on the same day. People say that the strong emotional element of this custom has surely served the Jewish people well.

Throughout the centuries, the shared focus on a life based on the Torah has been largely responsible for the sustained sense of family among Jewish people throughout the world. The Jewish people aren't a religion, nation, or race; the Jewish people are a *family*. The whole Jewish family, from biblical times to the present, has focused on the Torah, and for centuries the Jewish community has sustained a system whereby Jews throughout the world are, in a sense, all on the same page at the same time.

Preparing for the Torah Service

The Torah contains the sacred words of God and is God's representative in the world. I compare preparing to be in a room with a Torah scroll to preparing to be in a room in which a king is about to enter. In fact, in Jewish tradition, God is sometimes referred to as **melekh malkhay ha'melakhim** (*meh*-lekh *mahl*-khay ha-mehl-*lah*-kheem), which means "the King of King of Kings." If the king of a kingdom were about to arrive, it would seem appropriate for a minimum number of people to be present in order to show the king respect. And one always stands in the presence of a king. So it is with the Torah, as you find out in the following sections.

Having a quorum of ten

In the synagogue, you just don't grab a Torah scroll and read it. First of all, a Torah scroll in a synagogue is only read when a **minyan** (min-*yahn*; quorum) of ten individuals is present. Traditionally, the minyan must consist of ten males who have reached age 13, the age of Bar Mitzvah, the coming-of-age ceremony in Judaism. In recent decades, liberal synagogues throughout the United States have included women in that quorum.

Why is a quorum of ten necessary to read a Torah scroll? It's an ancient Jewish belief that when ten souls come together in one place to worship or to study the Torah, the presence of God is more keenly felt. This special category of God's presence is called the **Shekhinah** (sheh-*khee*-nah).

What happens if in a traditional synagogue there are fewer than ten men present when a prayer service is about to begin? It's common in Jewish neighborhoods for someone to go outside of the synagogue to see if there are men around who would be willing to join the prayer group in order to establish the minyan. In the synagogue of my hometown, there were occasions when someone actually telephoned local Jews asking them if they could come by to complete the quorum.

If nine men are present and no tenth man can be found, in such cases it's permissible to do one of two things:

- ✔ Ask a boy in the congregation to touch a dressed Torah scroll (see more on dressing and undressing a Torah later in this chapter) or hold a Torah text that's printed in book form.
- ✔ Open the holy closet where the Torah scrolls are kept as a symbolic way of completing the minyan. Ordinarily, this holy closet is closed during the reading of the Torah. (I describe this holy closet later in this chapter.)

If fewer than nine men are present but no more can be located to complete the minyan, there's no solution. And without a quorum, the Torah simply can't be read.

Showing respect by standing

According to Jewish law, it's permissible to sit on a seat or chair while the Torah is publicly read, but in some synagogues it's customary to stand during the entire public reading of the Torah (which can take 30 to 45 minutes on a Shabbat morning).

Standing during the reading of a Torah scroll is a gesture of respect both for the Torah and for God. But standing also transforms the Torah service into an even more special experience. Personally, standing for the reading of the Torah has always been my habit. In fact, I prefer to stand during the synagogue service throughout the entire public reading of the Torah. The experience of standing before a Torah scroll while it's being read often prompts me to feel what so many others have felt throughout the centuries: that I am standing at Mount Sinai and listening to the Word of God.

The general rule of thumb is to stand when the Torah is present — that is, from the moment the Torah scroll is taken from its holy closet (see the following section) until it is put back. Some people feel that it's appropriate to sit while the Torah scroll is lying on the table from where it's read. But even with this more relaxed custom, as soon as someone picks up the Torah scroll, it's time to stand again.

Taking the Torah Scroll from Its Holy Closet

A synagogue's Torah scrolls are stored in a special place in the sanctuary. The Jewish people consider the Torah scroll the most sacred object in the world and not to be compared to any other object, but it's useful to think of the Torah's storage place as a fancy china closet in your grandmother's home that contains some beautiful heirloom dishes that your family rarely uses — and only on special occasions. Imagine, for example, a special set of dishes that has been in your family for generations. They're stored carefully and taken out of their storage place gently. Using them inspires deep, emotional feelings. That's how it is with the synagogue's Torah scrolls.

Facing the Ark and Jerusalem

Sacred Torah scrolls are kept in the synagogue sanctuary, which is the room for prayer. The impressive and beautifully decorated holy closet known as the **Aron HaKodesh** (*ah*-rohn ha-*koh*-desh) in which Torah scrolls are kept (most synagogues have more than one Torah scroll) is located in the most honored position in that sacred space. The Aron HaKodesh, which is also referred to simply as the **Aron** (*ah*-rohn; Ark), dominates the synagogue sanctuary, and all seats face it. You can see the layout of a typical synagogue sanctuary in Figure 13-1.

During the prayer service, people who pray according to Jewish custom face the holy city of Jerusalem, which has been a focal point of Jewish history since the time of Moses. In Jewish sanctuaries throughout the world, the Aron HaKodesh is situated so that an individual facing it also faces the Holy Land in general and Jerusalem in particular. For example, in the Western Hemisphere, you look east when facing the Ark in your local Jewish house of prayer; on the other side of the world, the Ark faces in the opposite direction.

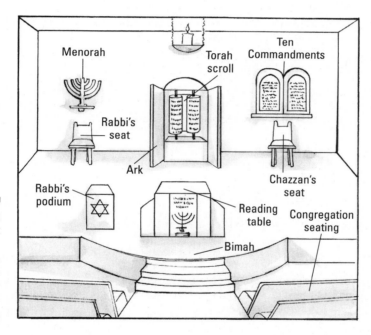

Figure 13-1: The layout of a synagogue, including the holy closet.

Opening the doors

An Aron HaKodesh typically has two doors. In front of the doors is a decorative curtain called a **parochet** (pah-*row*-khet), which is reminiscent of the curtain that was on the original Ark of the Covenant. During the Torah service, it's generally the custom to give an honor to an individual by asking him (or her, in liberal synagogues) to move the parochet to the side and to open each of the two doors (sometimes it's one sliding door) at the beginning of the Torah service. A congregation usually appoints one person whose responsibility it is to give out the various honors. In order to make appropriate selections for honors, this individual is usually well-informed about the members of the congregation and the guests who are present at each Torah service.

Any of the following people may receive the honor of opening the Aron HaKodesh:

- ✔ An honored guest in the synagogue that week
- ✔ A member of the congregation who was ill and absent for a period of time but has returned to services
- ✔ A person celebrating a special occasion like a birthday, anniversary, and so on
- ✔ A person who is in the synagogue to recite a special prayer marking the anniversary of the death of a loved one
- ✔ A person who has made a financial donation to the synagogue and is given an honor as thanks for the gift

Retrieving the scroll and closing the doors

After the doors of the Aron are opened, usually someone else approaches and takes the Torah scroll out. (This role is also considered an honor.) At this stage, the Torah scroll is beautifully dressed in all its detail (I discuss the dressing and undressing of the scroll later in this chapter).

When the Torah is removed from the Aron HaKodesh, the congregation sings lines from the classic Kabbalistic text, the Zohar, and then recites additional prayers and songs. (I go into detail about the Zohar in Chapter 3.)

The individual who takes the Torah out of the Aron HaKodesh hands it off to the **chazzan** (khah-*zahn*; cantor). The chazzan receives the Torah scroll and holds it in his right arm in a way best described as a hug or embrace.

The Aron HaKodesh doors are closed, and the Torah scroll is one step closer to the time and place of its public reading. But first, it must go through a procession, which I cover in the next section.

Following the Torah Scroll Procession

During a synagogue Torah service, the appearance of the Torah scroll outside of the Ark is an emotional moment. Participants stand in awe as the beautifully wrapped Torah scroll makes an appearance in the community during a processional. After all, the Torah scroll is a precise copy of the ancient scrolls believed to be traceable back to Moses, who received the teachings contained in the Torah from God.

The Torah is a beautiful and sacred object and is so much at the core of Judaism that its presence in the sanctuary as the processional winds its way through the people brings a mood of awe — both of the holiness of the Torah scroll and its awesome contents. In the following sections, I describe the phases of this amazing processional.

Moving through the synagogue sanctuary

The person carrying the Torah is usually the chazzan, but it can be the rabbi of the congregation or others. Behind him are other honored individuals who follow as the Torah is carried through the sanctuary and among those present. This processional group may include the rabbi, the chazzan, the leadership of the synagogue, and the individual(s) who received the honor of opening the Ark (see the earlier section "Opening the doors" for more information). The group also may include a young person celebrating a Bar or Bat Mitzvah.

The congregation remains standing and watches the Torah as it makes the rounds. There's no set path for the processional; the winding line of people often goes up and down the aisles of the synagogue sanctuary or uses some other path. The goal is to bring the Torah scroll as close to as many people present as possible so that they have an opportunity to actually kiss the Torah.

Kissing the Torah as the procession passes by

The affection and connection experienced by participants in the Torah service is outwardly expressed by kissing the dressed Torah as the processional passes by. The leader of the processional has the right to stop at any time, but generally the processional moves slowly and people kiss the Torah as it passes by.

Sometimes the processional passes by too quickly for some to make actual physical contact with the Torah. When this happens to me, I simply throw a kiss in the Torah's direction.

In synagogues today, the kissing takes various forms but always involves the mantle covering the Torah. (I describe the mantle in more detail in the later section "Undressing the Torah Scroll.")

- ✔ Some people touch the mantle covering the Torah and then kiss their hands.

- ✔ Others kiss their hands and then touch the Torah's mantle.

- ✔ Some people don't use their hands but rather hold a prayer book or the end of a prayer shawl and touch it to the Torah mantle as it passes by in the processional. Then they kiss the book or shawl.

- ✔ Some kiss the Torah mantle with their lips if they get close enough to the Torah scroll as it passes by.

There's no fixed rule on how to kiss the Torah. The method is one of personal preference and custom.

Regular participants in Torah services confirm that in no way is the processional a form of idolatry. Although physical, even kissing the Torah as it passes by doesn't imply that the Torah scroll is treated like a god. Students of the Torah know that God is beyond all form. The great honor and respect that the Torah scroll receives is really aimed at the Infinite One.

Reaching the reading platform

The processional accompanies the Torah scroll to its reading platform, known as a **bimah** (*bee*-mah). Once the Torah arrives at the bimah, members of the processional return to their places in the sanctuary.

When the person holding the Torah during the processional places the Torah scroll on the bimah, a **ba'al koray** (bah-*ahl koe*-ray; master of the reading), an individual in the community who is skilled at publicly reading the Torah, approaches along with at least one or two others who stand at the sides of the reading stand. These people are assigned the task of making sure the reader makes no mistakes. The **gabbai** (*gah*-bye; attendant), whose job it is to invite and announce each honoree who blesses the Torah, also stands at the bimah. (I describe all these folks in more detail later in this chapter.)

Undressing the Torah Scroll

You can find this verse in the Torah: "This is my God and I will adorn Him" (Exodus 15:2). Over 2,000 years ago, the Jewish sages interpreted this verse as meaning that all Jewish ritual objects should be made as beautiful as possible. The concept is known in Hebrew as **hiddur mitzvah** (hih-*door* mitz-*vah*; beautiful commandment). The sages wrote, "Adorn yourself before Him in the fulfillment of the commandment. Make a beautiful Torah scroll . . . and wrap it with beautiful silk" (Talmud: Tractate Shabbat. 133b).

Torah scrolls are beautifully dressed. The "dress" of the Torah is based on special clothing and ornaments worn by the High Priest in the holy temple in Jerusalem. During a synagogue service, when the dressed Torah scroll arrives at the bimah, it must be undressed; this is done with an attitude of reverence and formality. There are no special words sung during this undressing. Usually a gabbai carefully and reverently removes each of the following items (as shown in Figure 13-2) and sets them aside except for the yad (the pointer), which is used during the Torah reading:

✔ **Keter Torah:** Synagogues that can afford it dress the Torah with a very fancy crown, often made of silver or even gold, on top of the scroll. A Torah crown is known as **Keter Torah** (*keh*-tehr *toe*-rah); in Hebrew, "keter" means "crown."

✔ **Rimmonim:** Ornamental items called **rimmonim** (rih-moe-*neem*; pomegranates) are frequently hung over the wooden poles of the scroll, which are called the **etz chayyim** (aytz khah-*yeem*; the Tree of Life). Shaped like pomegranates with bells attached, the rimmonim usually are made of silver or some other precious metal.

✔ **Yad:** Ancient Jewish tradition forbids people from touching the actual Torah scroll with bare hands, so the Torah reader uses a ritual object known as a **yad** (yahd; hand) to point to each word as he pronounces it out loud. The yad is a small pointer, usually made of metal or wood, that's often ornate and at the end of which is the shape of a pointing hand. A yad generally has a chain attached to it, and it's hung on the mantle or around one of the wooden poles of the Torah scroll.

✔ **Tas:** A decorative breastplate called a **tas** (tahs; shield) hangs from the Torah poles. The use of a tas to decorate the Torah began in the 16th century and recalls the breastplate worn by the High Priest of the Temple. Today, the tas usually is made of silver and is decorated with intricate carvings that may include biblical scenes, two twin columns recalling the ancient Temple, floral designs, lions, and other ornate shapes and images.

✔ **M'eel:** A wound and tied scroll is dressed in a cylindrical mantle known as a **m'eel** (meh-*eel*; robe or mantle) that's constructed out of fabric (most typically plush velvet).

✔ **Wimpel:** A band of cloth known as a **wimpel** (*whim*-pull; cloth) holds together the tightly wrapped Torah scroll.

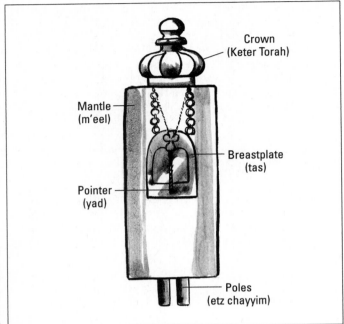

Figure 13-2:
The parts of
a Torah
scroll.

Receiving the Honor of Blessing the Holy Words

Each weekly Torah portion read publicly on Shabbat is divided into seven sections, which allows for seven individuals to receive the great honor of being called to the bimah and to stand before the Torah scroll as it is read. It's one of the most coveted honors in all Jewish life, and the choreography of participating in this highly valued honor has developed with precision over the centuries. An additional honor called the **maftir** (*mahf*-teer) adds an eighth honor. On Shabbat morning, the maftir is a repetition of the last several lines of the Torah portion. The person who recites these lines often also recites a portion from the books of the Prophets. This prophetic reading is called a **haftarah** (hahf-*tah*-rah).

Understanding who can be called

To understand the way in which the eight people are called to the Torah on Shabbat, you need some background. Throughout the centuries, Jews have known, genealogically, which of the following they descend from:

- ✔ **Kohanim** (co-ha-*neem*), the priests of the Temple in Jerusalem
- ✔ **Leviim** (leh-*vee*-eem), the tribe who didn't have land in ancient Israel but were assigned the task of helping in the Temple, mostly singing during the Temple service

A Jewish person who isn't a descendant of the priests or the helpers is in a third general category called **Yisroel** (yis-roe-*ale*; Israel).

With this breakdown in mind, the Jewish sages decided many centuries ago that the first honor of blessing the Torah should go to a Kohan, the second to a Levi, and the rest to anyone else. If no Kohan is present, the first honor goes to a Levi. If both are absent, anyone qualified (meaning a male adult in traditional congregations and a male or female adult in liberal congregations) may be called to bless the Torah.

Announcing the honorees' names

Most synagogues have a **gabbai** (*gah*-bye; attendant), a layperson who is assigned a variety of tasks in the synagogue. These tasks may include

- ✔ Choosing or identifying people to receive the honor of reciting a blessing over the Torah reading
- ✔ Undressing and dressing the Torah
- ✔ Reading from the Torah
- ✔ Standing next to the person who is reading from the Torah in order to check pronunciation and correct any mistakes in the reading

One doesn't approach the Torah without receiving an invitation to do so, and the gabbai issues that invitation. Although there are many customs for how this is done and what the gabbai says, the invitation generally takes the form of an announcement of the person's name in Hebrew. (See the sidebar "What's in a Hebrew name?" for more information about Hebrew names.)

The invitation to come before the Torah is never a surprise. Usually sometime during the early part of the synagogue service, the gabbai approaches each of the seven individuals who are to be called so that they're ready to receive the honor. After the gabbai calls your name, it's customary to go to the bimah quickly and with enthusiasm, using the shortest path from your seat to the bimah.

What's in a Hebrew name?

Most Jews have Hebrew names, most often taken from deceased family members (in the German and Eastern European custom) or living relatives (in the Spanish, Portuguese, North African, and Middle Eastern custom). Sometimes one's Hebrew name comes from that of a revered person, such as a great rabbi, whom parents want to honor.

Names are extremely important in Jewish tradition, and Jewish parents usually take great care and deliberation in making this decision. It's believed that if a Jewish person doesn't like his or her Hebrew name, the parents may have made an error and given the wrong name. In such cases, it's important that the person find his or her "true" name. This idea is based on the belief that every Jewish person has a Hebrew name designated by God. When parents think they're deciding what to name their children,

they're really being inspired by a holy spirit. If the parents aren't in tune with this spirit or consciously avoid the divine inspiration, the baby doesn't get his or her proper name. Hebrew names for both males and females include the name of one's father, and some people also include one's mother's name.

Here's how my name breaks down: My secular name is Arthur Kurzweil, but my Hebrew name, which the gabbai at my synagogue uses to call me to the Torah, is Avraham Abba ben Chaim Shaul.

- ✔ Avraham Abba was one of my great grandfathers.

- ✔ The word "ben" means "son of."

- ✔ Chaim Shaul is my father's first name.

Ascending to the Torah

The honor of being called to stand before the Torah during its public reading is known in Hebrew as **aliyah la-Torah** (ah-lee-*yah* leh-*toe*-rah; ascending to the Torah). The reference to "ascending" has two meanings.

- ✔ On a literal level, the person called to the bimah is going up to a raised platform, so the act involves an actual physical ascent.
- ✔ On a more sublime level, the person called to the Torah is participating in a spiritual ascent, an ascent to see and hear the word of God.

When standing before an open Torah scroll, those who know the significance of the Torah usually experience an amazing and unique sensation. The ancient calligraphy, written precisely as it has been written for centuries, seems to jump off the parchment and reverberate with holiness.

In traditional synagogues and as custom has dictated for centuries, only men are called to the Torah. Today, in liberal synagogues where women are counted in the minyan (quorum), women are also given the honor of participating fully in the Torah service, including the reciting of the blessings. In addition, in liberal communities, when the patriarchs Abraham, Isaac, and Jacob are mentioned, the four matriarchs of Judaism, Sarah, Rebecca, Rachel, and Leah, are also included.

Blessing the Torah before and after each part of the reading

In the biblical book of the prophet Nehemiah, Ezra the Scribe blessed God before he read publicly from the Torah. The blessing recited in synagogues today is referred to in the Talmud as the most supreme of all blessings. (Head to Chapter 3 for more information about the Talmud.)

When the individual who is called to bless the Torah arrives before the open Torah scroll, the gabbai or the person reading the Torah uses the yad to point to the word that will begin the reading (I describe the yad in the earlier section "Undressing the Torah Scroll"). The honoree touches his **tallit** (tah-*leet*; prayer shawl) to the scroll in the place where the reader will begin and then kisses the tallit. (Remember that one's hands never touch the parchment directly; this is forbidden by Jewish law.) The honoree then recites:

> *Blessed be the Lord who is blessed.*

The congregation responds:

> *Blessed be the Lord who is blessed for all eternity.*

The honoree repeats:

> *Blessed be the Lord who is blessed for all eternity.*

The honoree then says:

> *Blessed are You, Lord our God, King of the universe, who has chosen us from among all the nations and given us His holy Torah. Blessed are you, O Lord, who gives the Torah.*

After the section of the Torah has been read (I discuss the actual Torah reading later in this chapter), the honoree once again touches the Torah with his tallit, kisses it, and recites this concluding blessing:

> *Blessed are You, Lord our God, King of the universe, who has given us the Torah of truth and planted eternal life within us. Blessed are You Lord, who gives the Torah.*

Delving deeper into the blessing of the Torah

Two aspects of the honoree's blessing over the Torah prompt a little clarification:

✔ **The reference to the chosen people:** The concept of the chosen people has absolutely nothing to do with any assumed superiority. Judaism doesn't teach that Jews are better than others; rather, the label refers to added requirements and obligations imposed by God upon the Jewish people. As "priests among the nations" (as the Torah states), Jews have

the task of relating to the world as though it's sacred and every detail can be raised to holiness.

✔ **The use of present tense:** It's noteworthy that the blessing is in the present tense, as in "who gives the Torah." Present tense is used because, according to the teachings of Judaism, God is constantly giving the Torah to the world and new understandings are happening all the time.

After the first honoree finishes his concluding blessing, he steps aside and the next honoree is called. It's generally the custom for an honoree to stay on the bimah while the next honoree recites the blessings and the next section of the Torah portion is read; then the previous honoree goes back to his place in the congregation.

Reciting a healing prayer

Customs vary from synagogue to synagogue, but within every Torah-reading service on Shabbat is the recitation of a special prayer for healing. In some congregations, the gabbai recites the prayer seven times, after each of the seven honorees ascend and recite their Torah blessings. In other synagogues, the gabbai recites the prayer once, intending to include all seven honorees as well as all others in need of healing.

The prayer is known as **Mi Sheberakh** (mee sheh-*bay*-rakh; the One who blessed). There are various forms of this prayer. Here is one popular example:

> *He who blessed our forefathers Abraham, Isaac, and Jacob — may He bless [the person's Hebrew name] because he has come to the Torah in honor of the Omnipresent, in honor of the Torah. As a reward for this, may the Holy One, Blessed is He protect him and rescue him from every trouble and distress, from every plague and illness; and may He send blessing and success in his every endeavor together with all Israel, his brethren. Now let us respond: Amen.*

The Big Event: Reading the Torah Out Loud

When the moment arrives for the Torah to be read out loud, there's absolute silence in the sanctuary. Talking and even whispering to a neighbor are forbidden, and failure to obey this custom is considered the utmost disrespect to the Torah and to God. At this point, everyone in the congregation has a copy of the Five Books of Moses in book form in front of them, open to the page for the current week's Torah portion. There's an air of great anticipation throughout the sanctuary because the high point of the service has arrived.

Qualifying as "the master of the reading"

According to Jewish tradition, if you're called to the Torah during the Torah service, it is to recite the proper blessings. But technically, you can recite the blessings *and* read from the Torah. Unfortunately, in most congregations the majority of those present aren't qualified to read. In order to read from the Torah scroll, a person must

✔ Be able to read Hebrew without any vowels or punctuation, because ancient Hebrew has only consonants and no commas or periods

✔ Be able to read from the Torah in a specific style of chanting known as **trop** (trup) used exclusively for public Torah readings

✔ Understand what he's reading

✔ Be able to identify where each of the seven sections of each week's Torah portion begins and ends

✔ Know how to pronounce words with various spellings, because one word may be spelled in different ways in different parts of the Torah

Most congregations have at least one Hebrew expert in their midst. He may be the rabbi of the congregation or may even be a knowledgeable person hired by the congregation to read from the Torah scroll. Regardless of his background, this person is called the **ba'al koray** (bah-*ahl* koh-*ray*; the master of the reading).

Looking at every word — no memorizing!

According to the Jewish law, the ba'al koray (Torah reader) must look at the words while reading. Even if he has the text memorized, he must look at every word as he pronounces it. This rule is based on a verse from the Torah itself: "You shall not add to the word which I am commanding you, nor take away from it, that you may keep the commandments of the Lord your God which I command you" (Deuteronomy 4:2).

By looking carefully at the text as he reads a particular portion of the Torah, the ba'al koray is less likely to add or subtract from the text. In addition, in order for a Torah scroll to be considered acceptable for public reading, it must be letter-perfect (see Chapter 14 for more details). The reader who looks at each word is in a good position to detect errors.

More than once in my life, I've been in a Torah service when the reader suddenly sees a mistake in the text. When this happens, the Torah reading is stopped and another Torah scroll is taken out of the Aron HaKodesh. The ba'al koray continues the reading with the replacement scroll.

Pronouncing every word correctly

It's not unusual for people in a congregation to call out loud when the Torah reader makes an error in pronunciation. And pronunciation errors aren't uncommon given that there aren't any vowels in the Torah.

To use an example from English, assume that a sentence reads, "Th ct st n th flr." With the correct vowels, the sentence is "The cat sat on the floor." But the word "st" may also be pronounced "sit" or "set." Of course, from the context of the other words, interpreting "st" as "sat" makes the most sense. The absence of vowels is why the Torah reader needs to be knowledgeable.

Nevertheless, even the most well-informed Torah reader can make a mistake from time to time. When someone realizes the error and shouts out a correction, the reader isn't insulted. On the contrary, the serious ba'al koray is far more devoted to reading the Torah correctly than to proving that he's perfect.

It's customary for every synagogue to have at least one person standing at the side of the bimah, next to the Torah reader, following along in a printed version of the Torah that has vowels and punctuation. This person may be the gabbai (see the earlier section "Announcing the honorees' names" for more on the gabbai) or someone else who's qualified and asked to take on this responsibility. Sometimes both the gabbai and an additional person participate in carefully following along with the reading. These people can help the reader quietly if he makes any errors.

Concluding the Torah Service

So seven or eight people have blessed each piece of the Torah reading for the week, and you've enjoyed a flawless reading by the reader. What happens next?

A Torah service concludes with lifting the Torah for everyone to see, dressing it, walking through another procession, and returning it to its rightful place in the Ark.

Lifting the Torah for all to see

The Talmud contains a record of an ancient custom of raising the Torah scroll after the reading and showing it to all of those present (see Chapter 3 for more about the Talmud). A new honoree who's strong enough to lift the Torah scroll (which is often quite heavy) grasps each of the two poles, picks up the Torah, and turns it so that at least three columns of the parchment text are visible to the congregation. It's the duty of each member of the congregation to stand and look at the scroll with great affection and devotion. The honor of lifting the Torah in this way and at this time is known as **hagbahah** (*hahg*-bah-ah; lifting); see Figure 13-3.

After the lifting and display of the Torah scroll, another new honoree performs what is known as **gelilah** (geh-*lee*-lah; rolling), when the Torah is dressed.

Figure 13-3:
The lifting of
the Torah
scroll.

Dressing the Torah

Dressing the Torah is the reverse process of undressing it, which I discuss earlier in this chapter. It's usually done by the same person who did the undressing.

1. The scrolls are rolled up and tightened at the place where the week's portion ends so that the scroll is ready for the continuation of the reading the next week.

2. The wimple is wrapped around the scroll to further tighten it, and it's tied securely.

3. The mantle is placed on the scrolls, followed by the breastplate, the crown, and the rimmonim. The yad, which usually has a looped chain on its handle, is placed over one of the poles of the Torah scroll.

When it's fully dressed, the Torah scroll is ready to be returned to the Aron HaKodesh.

Going through another procession (and more kissing!)

Just as there's a procession when the Torah scroll is taken out of the Aron HaKodesh (which I describe earlier in this chapter), a similar procession takes place before the scroll is returned to the Aron. The gabbai or the person who read from the Torah holds the scroll in his right arm and is followed by the rabbi and honored individuals. (These honored individuals include the two people who lifted and dressed the Torah scroll.) The procession winds its way around the sanctuary, again giving everyone an opportunity to kiss the dressed Torah scroll.

Returning the Torah to the Ark

Generally, the honored person who originally took the Torah out of the Aron HaKodesh (as I describe earlier in this chapter) waits in front of the Aron to physically return the scroll back to its place. After that, the doors of the Aron are closed, and the Shabbat prayer service continues.

Chapter 14

The Final Commandment: Writing a Torah Scroll

In This Chapter

▶ Digging into the requirement for all Jews to write a Torah

▶ Choosing to hire a scribe or write a Torah scroll yourself

▶ Discovering the basic rules about writing a Torah scroll

▶ Gathering the necessary writing supplies

▶ Knowing what to do when a Torah needs repair

You can count 613 commandments in the Torah when you start with the beginning of the first book of Moses, the book of Genesis, and work your way through to the last words of the fifth book of Moses, the book of Deuteronomy. (See Part II for more about all five books.) The first of these many commandments is the divine injunction to "be fruitful and multiply" — in other words, to have children (Genesis 1:28). The last commandment is God's directive that each of the Children of Israel "write down this song," interpreted as meaning to write a Torah scroll (Deuteronomy 31:19).

Nobody can actually perform all 613 commandments. Some are for men, and others for women. Some can only be performed in the Holy Land, and others are required of specific people like a priest or a king. But many Torah authorities teach that everyone must write a Torah scroll. In this chapter, I explain the reasoning behind and process of writing a Torah scroll. I also discuss the proper care and repair of handwritten Torah scrolls.

God Said So! The Law behind Writing a Torah Scroll

The Torah used in synagogues today is a precise document. Every letter, every unusual spelling, and every dot is a duplication of the original Torah, handed down from one generation to the next. The original Torah was recorded by Moses, who's considered in Jewish tradition to be the greatest teacher and prophet who ever lived. Moses received the Torah from God during his encounter on Mount Sinai. Moses didn't author the ancient and timeless document called the Five Books of Moses, however; Moses was simply God's secretary or scribe.

In the book of Exodus (see Chapter 5), the Torah explains that Moses gathered all the people who were with him, read the scrolls he was writing as he recorded God's message, and taught God's laws. When Moses read his Torah, the Children of Israel responded in a phrase that reveals an important lesson about how to grasp the Torah's message: "The people all responded with one single voice. . . they said, 'We will do and we will hear'" (Exodus 24:7). In Hebrew, that phrase is **na'aseh v'nishmah** (nah-ah-*seh* vuh-nish-*mah*).

Jewish commentaries on the Torah frequently point out that the Children of Israel didn't say, "We will hear and then we will do." Rather, they said, "We will do and we will hear," meaning that first we will do it and only after we do it will we really hear it. As it says in the Torah, to understand the Torah is to experience it, to participate in it, and to do it. And only by doing the Torah do you come to understand it from the inside.

In addition, near the very end of the Five Books of Moses in the book of Deuteronomy (see Chapter 8), during the final speech that Moses delivered to the Children of Israel, Moses quotes God as saying "Therefore write down this song and teach it to the people of Israel; put it in their mouths, in order that this song may be My witness against the people of Israel" (Deuteronomy 31:19).

In his authoritative code of Jewish laws dealing with the writing of a Torah scroll, the commentator Maimonides writes, "Each and every man of Israel is commanded to write a Torah scroll for himself, as it says 'Therefore write down this song' which means write a Torah scroll. . . ." Commentator Abraham Ibn Ezra teaches that everyone who knows how to write must participate in the activity of writing a Torah, and another Torah commentator known as the Ralbag claims that the reason for this is "so that every person of Israel will be able to study the Torah when he has the opportunity." (See Chapter 16 for more about Torah commentators.)

But not all Jewish sages agree on this point. The great Torah commentator Nachmanides, for example, explains that this verse refers to Moses and Joshua and means that only Moses and Joshua were instructed to write a Torah. In addition, Rav Sa'adiah Gaon, a revered sage who lived around the year 900 and was the leading Torah authority in his generation, doesn't include writing a Torah scroll among his list of the 613 commandments. Despite some disagreement, all the other early authorities list this commandment as the last of the 613, and this is the law.

A dispute about the first Torah scroll

The Talmud (see Chapter 3) contains a well-known disagreement between two famous sages in the rabbinic period (70 to 500 CE), Rabbi Yochanan and Resh Lakish. Rabbi Yochanan was of the opinion that the Torah was given scroll by scroll. However his friend and frequent Torah study partner, Resh Lakish, insisted that the Torah was given in one piece. Then another sage, Rabbi Levi, taught that many lines from Leviticus and Numbers were written before the rest of the Torah. Rashi, the great Bible and Talmud commentator, writes that Resh Lakish didn't mean that the whole Torah was literally given all at once on Mount Sinai; rather, he was implying that Moses wrote down each passage as God told it to him. During the 40 years of wandering in the desert, Moses compiled these passages and sewed them all together into one document.

Decisions, Decisions: Hiring a Scribe versus Completing a Torah Yourself

According to Jewish law, even if you inherit a Torah scroll from your father or mother, you're still commanded to write one for yourself. But obviously not everyone is qualified to do so. Writing a Torah scroll carries many requirements and also involves quite a bit of artistic skill and talent (see the later section "Understanding the Ground Rules of Torah Writing" for more information). Therefore, it has become a custom among Jews to hire a qualified scribe to write a Torah in order to fulfill this commandment. However, it's still possible to fulfill the commandment without hiring a professional Torah writer. I explain both options in the following sections.

Hiring a professional

Writing a Torah is a specialized skill. A person trained and qualified to write a Torah scroll is known as a **sofer** (*sow*-fair; scribe). A sofer must be a spiritual person observant in the laws and customs of Judaism and especially knowledgeable in the laws governing the proper writing of a scroll. Believe it or not, a sofer needs to know more than 4,000 laws in order to be qualified to write a Torah scroll! For example, there are ten laws just concerning the writing of the first letter of the Hebrew alphabet, the aleph.

Tradition suggests that scribes be right-handed, although it's surely not forbidden for a left-handed person who's highly skilled and qualified to be a Torah scribe. The recommendation simply comes from the fact that Jewish tradition is partial to the right side, which is considered to be the side of expansiveness and love whereas the left side is the side of restraint and justice.

If you want to become a Torah scribe, this is usually achieved by becoming an apprentice to someone who is a master of the art and who is completely versed in the thousands of laws pertaining to the writing of a Torah scroll. You don't need to be a rabbi or have a certain degree from a school. But tradition requires that, in addition to all the required technical knowledge and artistic talent, you must be a pious person, observant of Torah law, honest, ethical, and faithful.

To fulfill the commandment to write a Torah scroll, you don't usually hire one person by yourself. Most often a synagogue will arrange to buy a Torah from a qualified scribe or his agent, and members of the congregation participate by sharing the expenses (see the next section). Regardless of the scribe's reputation, nothing replaces examining the Torah itself, and this must be done by someone who knows what he's looking for. Some questions asked include:

- Is the writing beautiful?
- Is the writing legible?
- Is the writing the same throughout? (Sometimes a scribe will have other scribes do parts of the scroll and then have them sewn together. While this is acceptable, it isn't always preferred.)
- Is the parchment clean?

Writing your own Torah

The tradition has evolved that one need not write an entire Torah; it's enough to simply "complete" a Torah scroll. And writing just one letter is thought to actually complete the Torah scroll and fulfill this commandment. This point is codified in the Talmud: "One who corrects even a single letter in a Torah scroll is like one who has written the entire scroll."

So how do you go about completing a Torah scroll in this manner? Here's a common example: When a synagogue purchases a new Torah scroll, the event often is used as a fundraiser. The synagogue announces to the congregation that a Torah scroll is being purchased and then organizes a fundraising effort by selling letters or words to be written to the members of the congregation. In this way, funds are raised to purchase the Torah scroll and everyone who's interested gets the opportunity to participate in its writing.

Here's a bit more about how this process of Torah writing often works: The synagogue purchases an unfinished Torah; often the parts left out include well-known passages like the Ten Commandments or famous prayers and stories. Members of the congregation donate money in order to have the honor of writing these letters or words. A skilled scribe is called in for the occasion, and each donor holds the pen with the scribe as the scribe does the writing. It's only symbolic, but the participants truly feel and know that they're involved in the completion of a 100 percent kosher Torah.

If you aren't able to participate in the purchasing or writing of a Torah scroll, there is, according to many authorities, another way to fulfill this commandment: by simply purchasing books that teach about the Torah and its wisdom. Purchasing this book, *The Torah For Dummies,* can actually be considered a way of fulfilling the commandment of writing a Torah.

Understanding the Ground Rules of Torah Writing

A scribe must adhere to many rules, regulations, and guidelines in writing a Torah; the following sections provide an overview of the general rules entailed in the writing of a Torah.

Undergo a ritual bath before beginning

A **mikvah** (mihk-*vah*) is a pool of water constructed from exact specifications according to Jewish tradition that's used ritually for many reasons in Jewish life. (You can see a mikvah in Figure 14-1). When you go to a mikvah, an essential part of the ritual is being completely covered with water. Immersion in a mikvah is considered to be a symbolic spiritual cleansing. It's an unfortunate myth that entering a mikvah has anything to do with physical impurity or being dirty because the ritual is purely spiritual.

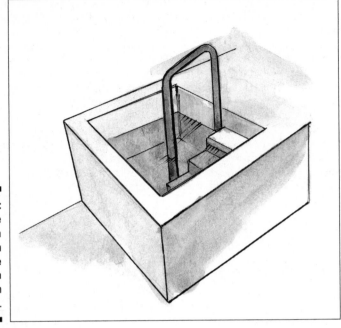

Figure 14-1:
A scribe
visits a
mikvah
before
starting a
new Torah
scroll.

Scribes who write Torah scrolls visit mikvahs for immersion. Some immerse themselves when they begin a new Torah whereas others go at the beginning of each day while they're working on a Torah. I've even heard of scribes who immerse themselves in a mikvah before writing God's name each time. For practical purposes, they usually leave spaces where the names of God appear in the text, visit the mikvah, and then fill in those names.

Test a pen by writing the name of the ultimate villain

The quintessential enemy of the Jewish people is the biblical figure Amalek, who attacked the children of Israel from behind as they left Egypt. The Torah states,

> *Remember what Amalek did to you along the way when you came out from Egypt, how he met you along the way and attacked among you all the stragglers at your rear when you were faint and weary; and he did not fear God. Therefore it shall come about when the Lord your God has given you rest from all your surrounding enemies, in the land which the Lord your God gives you as an inheritance to possess, you shall blot out the memory of Amalek from under heaven; you must not forget.*

Deuteronomy 25:17–19

While it's paradoxical that the Torah says both to blot out Amalek's name and to remember him, this idea is reflected in the way Torah scribes begin the actual writing process. In order to be sure that the ink they're using is both the proper color and flows properly, and that the quill pen distributes the ink in the proper thickness, the scribe tests the pen and ink on some piece of parchment other than the Torah scroll itself. (I discuss all these supplies later in this chapter.)

The test is simple. Each time the scribe sits down to begin his work, he writes the name "Amalek" on the parchment and then crosses it out a number of times. Just like a painter preparing his or her paint on a palette, the scribe is looking for the right color and consistency of the ink and confirmation that it's flowing from the pen to the parchment evenly and smoothly.

Refrain from relying on memory

No matter how many Torah scrolls a scribe has written or how familiar a scribe is with the words of the text being written, it's forbidden by Jewish law for a scribe to write any words of the Torah by memory or by dictation. Even if the scribe is writing a familiar verse of the Torah (or even a phrase of just a few words), the scribe is absolutely obligated to look carefully at a previously written Torah scroll (or an exact facsimile of a Torah scroll). He must use it as a reference, reading each word in the text out loud before writing it down. By working closely with a previously written copy, a scribe ensures that he has the right attitude to write a new Torah and that the new Torah is accurate.

Having the proper attitude

Whether it's prayer, the act of giving charity, the celebration of holy days, or making love with one's partner, there's the physical aspect of the action and the spiritual aspect. One's private inner attitude is considered to be an important part of every religious action. The important Jewish concept of inner intent is called **kavanah** (kah-vah-*nah*).

Writing a Torah scroll is more than the act of copying the text. The inner attitude of the scribe is an essential part of the process. A chef I know once told me that one of the most important ingredients of a dish is the attitude of the chef as he or she prepares it. I've even heard that a person can get sick if he or she eats a dish made by a chef who had a bad attitude while cooking! So it is with the writing of a Torah: It's a holy act and one for which the scribe must be able to maintain a spiritually elevated state of mind and heart.

By not relying on his memory, the scribe is more conscious of the words he's writing. When I was in grade school, we said the Pledge of Allegiance every morning. I remember that it quickly became automatic, and I was able to recite the words without even thinking about them. If the words had been projected in the front of the classroom for me to see, I'm sure that I would have been much more aware of what I was saying.

The Torah's vital statistics

The Torah scroll has been intricately studied since it was received by Moses. Every letter, every word, every space between words, and every dot — in short, every detail — is of interest to students of the Torah and the scribes who write Torah scrolls. One way to protect and ensure the perfection of a Torah scroll is to take inventory of its details. Here are some such Torah statistics:

✔ A Torah scroll has 187 chapters, 5,845 verses, 79,976 words, and 304,805 letters.

✔ The book of Genesis has 1,534 verses.

✔ The book of Exodus has 1,209 verses.

✔ The book of Leviticus has 859 verses.

✔ The book of Numbers has 1,288 verses.

✔ The book of Deuteronomy has 955 verses.

✔ The Hebrew alphabet has 22 letters and 5 final letters.

✔ The most common letter in the Torah is a "yud," which appears 31,530 times.

✔ The least common letter in the Torah is a "tet," which appears 1,802 times.

✔ The most common final letter in the Torah is the Final "Mem," which appears 10,623 times.

✔ The least common final letter in the Torah is the Final "Feh," which appears 834 times.

✔ There are 248 columns in a Torah scroll.

✔ Every column of the Torah scroll has 42 lines.

✔ Every line in the Torah scroll has about 30 letters in it.

Maintaining accuracy

Scribes must look at a copy of the Torah text they're writing for a practical reason as well. Torah scrolls must be perfect and without even the slightest error, so looking at a copy of what he's writing helps the scribe concentrate and be precise. (See the later section "Avoid making an error" for more information.)

For similar reasons, it's strictly forbidden for someone to orally dictate the text of a Torah to a scribe. One obvious reason for this rule is that just as there are various accents spoken in the United States — for example a Southern accent is quite different from a New England accent — so too are there various accents for spoken Hebrew. It would be quite easy for a scribe to make a mistake in writing the text if he were to hear the words spoken with a particular accent rather than read them.

For ten years I lived in the largest and most densely populated religious Jewish neighborhood in America, Boro Park in Brooklyn, New York. In this one neighborhood, different subgroups spoke with radically different accents. For example, in one synagogue people said the word "baruch," which is the first word of every blessing, as "bahw rookh" while another group down the street said "bahw reekh." If a scribe were to hear these two variations, he may write them differently, but in Torah writing, only one would be correct. If the scribe wrote the incorrect one, the Torah would then be imperfect, and he would have to start over again.

Write every word by hand in Hebrew

Torah scrolls aren't printed; according to Jewish law, they must be handwritten in Hebrew.

Figure 14-2 shows the Hebrew alphabet and the English pronunciations of the letters. The form that the letters take is known as **ketav Ashuri** (keh-*tahv* ah-*sure*-ee; Assyrian writing).

Following are the three major styles of writing the Hebrew alphabet for a Torah. They're distinguished from each other in the same way that typefaces are different, with slight differences in the details of how certain letters are formed. Each synagogue selects its Torah scrolls based on the preferences of the community:

- **Beit Yosef** (beyt *yo*-safe; the house of Joseph): This style is named after Rabbi Joseph Karo, the 16th-century author of the **Shulchan Aruch** (shool-*khahn* ah-*rookh;* the Code of Jewish Law). Rabbi Karo codified this style of writing, which is the standard style used by most Ashkenazi (European) Jews.

- **ARI** (ah-*ree*): The 16th-century Kabbalist Rabbi Isaac Luria was known for the acronym of his name, ARI. For Torah writing, ARI refers to the style of writing he instituted. This style is usually used by Chassidim and others who follow Kabbalistic tradition.

- **Sefardi** (seh-far-*dee;* Spanish): Regarding Hebrew writing, Sefardi refers to the style of writing used by Jews of Spanish, Portuguese, and Middle Eastern descent.

Avoid making an error

There are 304,805 letters in a **Sefer Torah** (*say*-fehr toe-*rah;* the book of the Torah). The term "Sefer Torah" is the specific way to identify a Torah scroll as opposed to a printed and bound version of the Torah text. If even one letter is missing or added, the Torah's considered **pasul** (pah-*sewl;* unacceptable or not kosher). It is interesting to note that one letter of the Torah is .000328 percent of the entire Five Books of Moses, but that's all it takes for a Torah scroll to be unacceptable and use of it is forbidden.

The most typical errors found in Torah scrolls are

- The omission of one or two letters that are the same and that follow each other

- The omission of words or phrases that are repeated in a passage near the one being written

- The writing of the same word or letter twice

Letter Name	Pronunciation	Hebrew Letter	The Sound It Makes
aleph	*ah*-lehf	א	makes no sound
bet	beht	ב	makes a "B" sound as in "boat"
vet	veht	ב	makes a "V" sound as in "veterinarian"
gimmel	*gee*-mehl	ג	makes a "G" sound as in "girl"
dalet	*dah*-leht	ד	makes a "D" sound as in "door"
hey	hey	ה	makes a "soft H" sound as in "hello"
vav	vahv	ו	makes a "V" sound as in "video"
zayin	*zah*-een	ז	makes a "Z" sound as in "zipper"
khet	cheht	ח	makes a strong guttural "H" sound
tet	teht	ט	makes a "T" sound as in "teaspoon"
yud	yohd	י	makes a "Y" sound at the begin-ning of a word as in "young." This letter also behaves like a vowel at times.
kaf	kahf	כ	makes a "K" sound as in "kite"
khaf	khahf	כ	makes a strong guttural "H" sound
lamed	*lah*-mehd	ל	makes an "L" sound as in "lemon"
mem	mehm	מ	makes an "M" sound as in "mouse"
nun	noon	נ	makes an "N" sound as in "no"
samekh	*sah*-mehch	ס	makes an "S" sound as in "soda"

Figure 14-2a:
The Hebrew alphabet.

ayin	*ah-*yeen	ע	makes a barely audible guttural sound in the back of the throat (for practical purposes as most nonnative speakers can't make this sound, this letter is a "silent letter.")
pey	*pay*	פּ	makes a "P" sound as in "popsicle"
fey	*fay*	פ	makes an "F" sound as in "fish"
tzadee	*tzah-dee*	צ	makes a hard "Tz" sound as the double zz in "pizza"
koof	*kohf*	ק	makes this "K" sound as in "Kansas"
reish	*raysh*	ר	makes the "R" sound as in "round." This letter is actually a "guttural" letter. Roll it like a Spanish "R," and also pronounce it from the back of the throat.
shin	*sheen*	שׁ	when the dot is on the right side of the letter, it makes a "Sh" sound as in "show"
sin	*seen*	שׂ	when the dot is on the left side of the letter it makes an "S" sound as in "Sam"
tav	*tahv*	ת	makes a "T" sound as in "toe"

Figure 14-2b:
The Hebrew alphabet.

A Torah scroll with an error can be repaired, of course (I discuss the repair of scrolls later in this chapter), but until it's repaired, it's forbidden to read from it publicly. In recent years, computers have helped in the task of proofreading Torahs. Torah scrolls are scanned, and it isn't uncommon to find misspelled words or missing and extra letters even in a Torah that has been read from for many years and is assumed to be perfect.

Recite a blessing every time God's name is written

Many names for God are included in the Torah (see Chapter 2 for a list). When the text calls for the writing of one of God's names, the scribe must raise his pen before writing the last letter of the word immediately preceding the name of God and inspect the tip of the pen to be certain that it isn't defective. The scribe then recites the blessing, "I am now writing this Holy Name in order to sanctify the Divine Name" and finishes writing the name.

There are about 2,000 occurrences of the various versions of God's name in the Torah. If a scribe makes a mistake when writing one of these names, he isn't allowed to erase and correct it as he is permitted to do with other words (see the later section "Discovering errors in a Torah scroll"). Rather, the panel of parchment is put into a **genizah** (geh-*nee*-zah; storage). Destroying anything with God's name on it is strictly forbidden, so sacred texts with errors either are put into permanent storage or buried in a Jewish cemetery. (I discuss Torah storage and burial later in this chapter.)

Using the Right Torah Writing Supplies

Every aspect of writing a Torah scroll is dictated by Jewish tradition, including the scribe's supplies and techniques. The writing of a Torah is like a carefully choreographed dance.

A copy to copy

As I explain earlier in this chapter, scribes must not write a Torah (not even a letter) from memory. Therefore, a **tikkun sofer** (*tee*-koon *sow*-fair) is available to them. A tikkun sofer, sometimes just called a "tikkun," is an exact facsimile of a Torah scroll in book form and is designed as a guide for scribes writing a copy of the Torah. Each and every letter must be copied directly from either a Torah scroll that's known to be letter-perfect or a tikkun sofer. You can see a sample of a tikkun sofer in Figure 14-3.

Before there were printed books, a scribe had to use a perfect Torah scroll as his guide. Today, it's common for scribes to use the book form because it's simply more manageable. In addition, the scribe would rather not run the risk of damaging or staining an actual Torah scroll by copying from it. Although a tikkun sofer sometimes has additional information in it, such as the Torah blessings, it's basically and simply a facsimile of a Written Torah used by scribes to write a new Torah scroll.

בְּרֵאשִׁית בָּרָא אֱלֹהִים אֵת הַשָּׁמַיִם וְאֵת הָאָרֶץ
וְהָאָרֶץ הָיְתָה תֹהוּ וָבֹהוּ וְחשֶׁךְ עַל פְּנֵי תְהוֹם וְרוּחַ
אֱלֹהִים מְרַחֶפֶת עַל פְּנֵי הַמָּיִם וַיֹּאמֶר אֱלֹהִים יְהִי
אוֹר וַיְהִי אוֹר וַיַּרְא אֱלֹהִים אֶת הָאוֹר כִּי טוֹב
וַיַּבְדֵּל אֱלֹהִים בֵּין הָאוֹר וּבֵין הַחשֶׁךְ וַיִּקְרָא
אֱלֹהִים לָאוֹר יוֹם וְלַחשֶׁךְ קָרָא לָיְלָה וַיְהִי עֶרֶב
וַיְהִי בֹקֶר יוֹם אֶחָד
וַיֹּאמֶר אֱלֹהִים יְהִי רָקִיעַ בְּתוֹךְ הַמָּיִם וִיהִי מַבְדִּיל
בֵּין מַיִם לָמָיִם וַיַּעַשׂ אֱלֹהִים אֶת הָרָקִיעַ וַיַּבְדֵּל בֵּין
הַמַּיִם אֲשֶׁר מִתַּחַת לָרָקִיעַ וּבֵין הַמַּיִם אֲשֶׁר
מֵעַל לָרָקִיעַ וַיְהִי כֵן וַיִּקְרָא אֱלֹהִים לָרָקִיעַ שָׁמָיִם
וַיְהִי עֶרֶב וַיְהִי בֹקֶר יוֹם שֵׁנִי
וַיֹּאמֶר אֱלֹהִים יִקָּווּ הַמַּיִם מִתַּחַת הַשָּׁמַיִם אֶל
מָקוֹם אֶחָד וְתֵרָאֶה הַיַּבָּשָׁה וַיְהִי כֵן וַיִּקְרָא
אֱלֹהִים לַיַּבָּשָׁה אֶרֶץ וּלְמִקְוֵה הַמַּיִם קָרָא יַמִּים
וַיַּרְא אֱלֹהִים כִּי טוֹב וַיֹּאמֶר אֱלֹהִים תַּדְשֵׁא הָאָרֶץ
דֶּשֶׁא עֵשֶׂב מַזְרִיעַ זֶרַע עֵץ פְּרִי עֹשֶׂה פְּרִי לְמִינוֹ
אֲשֶׁר זַרְעוֹ בוֹ עַל הָאָרֶץ וַיְהִי כֵן וַתּוֹצֵא הָאָרֶץ
דֶּשֶׁא עֵשֶׂב מַזְרִיעַ זֶרַע לְמִינֵהוּ וְעֵץ עֹשֶׂה פְּרִי
אֲשֶׁר זַרְעוֹ בוֹ לְמִינֵהוּ וַיַּרְא אֱלֹהִים כִּי טוֹב וַיְהִי
עֶרֶב וַיְהִי בֹקֶר יוֹם שְׁלִישִׁי
וַיֹּאמֶר אֱלֹהִים יְהִי מְאֹרֹת בִּרְקִיעַ הַשָּׁמַיִם לְהַבְדִּיל
בֵּין הַיּוֹם וּבֵין הַלָּיְלָה וְהָיוּ לְאֹתֹת וּלְמוֹעֲדִים וּלְיָמִים
וְשָׁנִים וְהָיוּ לִמְאוֹרֹת בִּרְקִיעַ הַשָּׁמַיִם לְהָאִיר עַל
הָאָרֶץ וַיְהִי כֵן וַיַּעַשׂ אֱלֹהִים אֶת שְׁנֵי הַמְּאֹרֹת
הַגְּדֹלִים אֶת הַמָּאוֹר הַגָּדֹל לְמֶמְשֶׁלֶת הַיּוֹם וְאֶת
הַמָּאוֹר הַקָּטֹן לְמֶמְשֶׁלֶת הַלָּיְלָה וְאֵת הַכּוֹכָבִים
וַיִּתֵּן אֹתָם אֱלֹהִים בִּרְקִיעַ הַשָּׁמַיִם לְהָאִיר עַל
הָאָרֶץ וְלִמְשֹׁל בַּיּוֹם וּבַלַּיְלָה וּלְהַבְדִּיל בֵּין הָאוֹר
וּבֵין הַחשֶׁךְ וַיַּרְא אֱלֹהִים כִּי טוֹב וַיְהִי עֶרֶב וַיְהִי
בֹקֶר יוֹם רְבִיעִי
וַיֹּאמֶר אֱלֹהִים יִשְׁרְצוּ הַמַּיִם שֶׁרֶץ נֶפֶשׁ חַיָּה
וְעוֹף יְעוֹפֵף עַל הָאָרֶץ עַל פְּנֵי רְקִיעַ הַשָּׁמַיִם
וַיִּבְרָא אֱלֹהִים אֶת הַתַּנִּינִם הַגְּדֹלִים וְאֵת כָּל נֶפֶשׁ
הַחַיָּה הָרֹמֶשֶׂת אֲשֶׁר שָׁרְצוּ הַמַּיִם לְמִינֵהֶם וְאֵת
כָּל עוֹף כָּנָף לְמִינֵהוּ וַיַּרְא אֱלֹהִים כִּי טוֹב וַיְבָרֶךְ
אֹתָם אֱלֹהִים לֵאמֹר פְּרוּ וּרְבוּ וּמִלְאוּ אֶת הַמַּיִם
בַּיַּמִּים וְהָעוֹף יִרֶב בָּאָרֶץ וַיְהִי עֶרֶב וַיְהִי בֹקֶר יוֹם
חֲמִישִׁי

Figure 14-3:
A sample
from a
tikkun sofer
of a small
part of a
Torah scroll.

WORDS OF WISDOM

The first 13 copies of the Torah

In the fifth of the Five Books of Moses, it says that the Torah was recorded by Moses. In fact, Moses handwrote 13 copies — not just one. Jewish tradition teaches that when Moses knew that he was going to die, he proceeded to write the 13 copies. The Torah also says, "Take this Torah, and put it by the side of the Ark of the Covenant" (Deuteronomy 31:26). With regard to this verse, Talmudic sage Rabbi Yannai teaches, "He wrote out thirteen Torahs; twelve for each of the twelve tribes, and one that he placed in the ark, so that if anyone were to try to misrepresent anything, they would find it in the copy that was in the ark."

Parchment (but not just any old parchment)

A Torah scroll may be written only on parchment from the skin of a kosher animal. Kosher animals are those that have split hooves and chew their cud, like cows and sheep (see Chapter 12 for more about keeping kosher). This parchment is known as a **klaf** (klahf), and a sheet of it is known as a **yeriah** (yeh-*ree*-yah; sheet). Nowadays, the skin is treated by soaking it in limewater and other chemicals and then scraping the hair off; in ancient times (at least 2,000 years ago), the skin was soaked in barley and salt water. Regardless of the initial preparation, when the surface no longer has hair, the scribe or someone who's qualified to make sacred parchment that qualifies for making a Torah scroll stretches the skin, waits for it to dry, and then presses it flat. The skin is then sanded until it becomes smooth and its sheets are prepared for being written upon.

Parchment used for a Torah scroll must be prepared by a Jewish person who's creating the parchment expressly for use as a Torah. It's not permissible to buy parchment from any source. Generally, a scribe who writes a Torah also knows how to make parchment properly. In addition to the necessity of being made of the right materials, the parchment must be made with the proper intention. The supplies needed to write a Torah scroll can be purchased from vendors in Israel as well as in the United States. Because this is an extremely specialized activity, the best way to locate these sources is to ask a qualified scribe.

Although there's a proper way to slaughter an animal for it to be kosher and fit for eating, the animal whose skin is used as parchment need not be slaughtered in a ritually acceptable manner. As long as the animal is qualified as kosher, the parchment can be used for a Torah scroll.

Parchment made of fish skin can't be used for a Torah scroll due to its unpleasant odor. Also, although parchment made from the skin of birds is permissible, it's impractical because it's so thin and is liable to have holes in it.

A quill from a turkey or a goose

Quills for writing a Torah come from kosher birds, like a goose or turkey. The turkey quill is more commonly used because the points of turkey quills last longer than others. A scribe prepares his quill by shaving the thick end of the feather and then slitting the end. Most traditional scribes make their own quills, but quills are also available commercially from supply houses that sell quills and special ink for Torahs and other sacred scrolls. There are no special rituals regarding the quill, but as with every other aspect of writing a Torah scroll, the proper intention is always essential.

Permanent black ink

According to Jewish tradition, only black ink is acceptable for Torah writing, and ink of any other color is not kosher for a Torah scroll. The Talmud contains a story describing a Torah scroll used in ancient Alexandria in which God's name was written in gold ink each time it appeared. The sages declared the Torah scroll to be unusable, reasoning that the gold was reminiscent of the gold used to make the Golden Calf (see Chapter 5 for more about this story).

According to Jewish law and tradition, the ink must also be permanent, not erasable.

Torah scribes prepare their ink in very small quantities in order to keep it fresh. Today, the ink used for Torahs is made from a mixture of gum arabic, gallnut or tannic acid, copper sulfate, and water; centuries ago, Torah ink was made from soot, honey, wax, gum, gallnut, and water.

A Little TLC: Proper Torah Care, Repair, and Burial

All sacred Jewish texts that contain God's name, including Torah scrolls, receive special treatment. If a Torah scroll is disqualified for use for one reason or another, it's not thrown away (God forbid!) but is repaired, placed in a genizah, or buried properly in a Jewish cemetery.

Taking good care of a Torah scroll

Various recommendations are made regarding the proper care of a Torah scroll. Here are the general rules of good Torah scroll care:

- ✔ The **Aron HaKodesh** (*ah*-rohn ha-*koh*-desh; Holy Ark) where the Torah scrolls are kept in a synagogue must be moisture-free and well-ventilated to prevent mold growth on the Torah.

- ✔ If a Torah scroll needs to be transported, extreme care must be taken to avoid humidity, rain, or excessive bumps — all of which can cause damage to the Torah scroll.

- ✔ Each time the Torah is unrolled to be read publicly (see Chapter 13), it needs to be rolled again carefully and not too tightly before being put back in the Aron HaKodesh. Parchment is easily crushed or even ripped if one isn't careful, and if a Torah scroll is rolled tightly, letters may rub together and be worn away or the parchment may crack.

- ✔ It's crucial that a Torah scroll gets enough air. Even if it's not being unrolled for public reading, the scroll should be rolled from one end to the other from time to time to prevent molding and drying out.

- ✔ The Torah reader as well as those people who receive the honor of offering a blessing before the open Torah scroll must never touch the parchment directly. Even when the Torah is read with a yad (pointer), the reader must not to touch the letters with the pointer because of the risk of scratching the parchment and damaging the letters.

Discovering errors in a Torah scroll

There are many possible reasons for declaring a Torah scroll unfit for use. Some examples include:

- ✔ A word is missing or misspelled.
- ✔ A letter is missing or improperly written.
- ✔ A name of God is misspelled.
- ✔ Two letters are touching each other.

Sometimes an error in the text is discovered during a public reading of the Torah. If the error is significant, such as a missing word or a misspelling of one of God's names, the Torah is immediately set aside and the reading proceeds with another Torah scroll. If there are no other Torah scrolls available, the Torah reading must stop, as if there are no Torah scrolls present at all.

But it also may happen during a reading that the reader thinks a word is mis-spelled but the error is less obvious, such as a letter looking somewhat unclear because it's slightly smudged or was written sloppily. This can easily happen because some letters in Hebrew are remarkably similar; for example, the three letters "vav," "zayin," and "nun" aren't all that different (refer to Figure 14-2). One way to determine the status of such a letter is to ask a child who knows the Hebrew alphabet to approach the Torah and identify the letter. If the child says the wrong letter, the Torah is set aside. If the child says the correct letter, the reading goes on. In either case, after the reading, arrangements are made to try to repair or clarify the letter so that there's no doubt about its identity. After all, Torahs must be perfect!

An error found in a Torah scroll can be considered minor or major.

✔ Minor errors are correctable. For example, if a thin letter (such as the Hebrew letter "vav," which is simply a thin vertical line) is missing, there's usually enough space for the scribe to fit it in.

✔ Major errors are generally not correctable. For example:

- When a thick letter is found to be missing, there usually isn't enough space to make a repair. Even if there's enough room, inserting a letter is often aesthetically unpleasing and not acceptable.

- In the case of a name of God being misspelled, there's no choice but to place that sheet of parchment in a genizah. According to Jewish law and tradition, erasing the written form of any of God's names is strictly forbidden.

Repairing a Torah scroll

Even with the most careful treatment, periodically most Torahs need some kind of maintenance or repair. The most common problems that need a skilled scribe's attention are:

✔ **Some of the letters need sharpening or fixing, or broken letters need repair.** If spelling errors or calligraphy errors are small, the scribe can scrape out the text in error with a sharp blade or piece of glass and then rewrite it. If possible, an incorrect letter can be altered. Some Hebrew letters are easily turned into other letters by adding a stroke (similar to changing a "P" into a "B" by adding one curved line). If a spelling error is significant, the entire sheet of parchment must be replaced. If two Torahs have errors and are the same size, it's permissible to remove a sheet of parchment with an error from one Torah and replace it with a perfect sheet from the Torah. The incomplete Torah is then either repaired or put in a genizah.

- ✔ **Some of the sheets of parchment need resewn.** When a sheet of parchment is torn, the tear may be sewn up if it extends into two lines of text on an old Torah. If the tear extends to the third line of text of a newer Torah, it also may be sewn up. However, larger tears require the sheet to be replaced.

- ✔ **The parchment needs cleaning.** A qualified scribe can clean a Torah without damaging it. Sometimes the parchment needs to be scraped, but appropriate cleaning solutions can also be used by someone with experience.

If a Torah needs repair because of an error in the writing, it must be repaired within 30 days or else it must be put in a genizah.

Storing or burying a Torah scroll when it's beyond repair

A genizah is the storage place for old and seriously worn sacred books and scrolls that will no longer be used. Usually books and scrolls that are no longer usable are held in a genizah before burial, but there are also genizahs that simply store unusable sacred scrolls and books forever, and no further burial occurs. Sacred Jewish books are put in a genizah or buried in a Jewish cemetery because anything containing any one of the several forms of God's name in Hebrew is considered too holy to throw away or dispose of in any way other than proper burial.

Chapter 15

Always Up for Discussion: Analyzing the Torah

The Torah isn't a book that you can read, finish, and then say that you understand. Even if you reread the Torah a second time, a third time, or even a hundred times, you can't say that you really know it. Not fully. Serious students of the Torah know that studying the work is an endless process because the Torah is said to be infinite in its depth.

Even if you spend a lifetime studying the Torah, memorizing it, understanding it, and mastering every commentary that has ever been written on the Torah, you still could not say that you now know it completely. This is because, by definition, everyone understands the Torah in his or her own way.

In this chapter, I introduce you to the basics of Torah analysis. I explain that the Torah has endless possibilities for interpretation and that you can read the Torah on four general levels, from the most literal to the most hidden. I also touch on the idea of codes and numbers in understanding the Torah. For details on using different translations and commentaries to help you study the Torah, head to Chapter 16.

Grasping the Infinite Possibilities of Interpreting the Torah

I often watch Christian preachers on Sunday morning television, and I get the impression that they generally believe that the Torah (the first five books of the Christian Bible) should be understood literally. They read a verse and understand it just as it's written. I also get the impression that they believe that only one "accepted" interpretation is allowed. The Jewish people relate to the Torah in a very different way.

In principle, the Torah has an infinite number of levels of meaning. Because of this, it's a document that requires careful analysis as well as the aid of commentaries. It's the responsibility of all Jews everywhere to establish a relationship with the Torah and to participate and struggle while exploring its myriad of levels.

The fact that the Torah has so many levels of meaning doesn't mean that any and every interpretation is always correct. The ancient tradition of the study of the Torah includes limits and parameters. One of my teachers uses the analogy of a game of chess to explain this fact. Chess is a game with well-established rules. For example, a pawn is permitted to make certain moves on the chess board; you may want the pawn to move like a queen, but the rules dictate that it simply can't make that move. A pawn moves like a pawn, and a queen moves like a queen. Nevertheless, countless chess games are played by millions of people every day and for centuries past, and there seems to be no end to the creativity and diversity that can be expressed on the 8-x-8-inch playing board. Similarly, Torah interpretation has its rules, as described in the Oral Torah, but within those rules there are infinite possibilities for creativity and individual participation.

In the following sections, I explain some basics about understanding the nature of both the Torah and Torah interpretation, such as the multiple facets of the Torah, the idea that the Torah contains everything, the concept of everyone being on a different level of Torah understanding, and the possibility of finding your identity in the Torah.

Just like a diamond: Studying the Torah's 70 facets

The number 70 appears frequently in Jewish life and lore. Some commentators point out that the number 70 is the result of multiplying 7, which is a profound number in Judaism (the 7 days of creation), with 10, which is also a profound number (10 commandments, 10 essences of existence according to Jewish theology, and 10 fingers). Seventy, some sages point out, is a number that implies completeness. Following are just a handful of examples of its prominence:

- ✔ Seventy nations existed in the world of the Torah.
- ✔ Seventy Jewish souls from Jacob's family went down to Egypt.
- ✔ Moses chose 70 elders.
- ✔ Seventy sages make up the Jewish supreme court, the Sanhedrin.

> ✔ Seventy words make up the original Kiddush, the special prayer sanctifying Shabbat.
>
> ✔ The numerical value of the Hebrew word for wine is 70.
>
> ✔ The numerical value of the Hebrew word **sod** meaning "secret" is 70.
>
> ✔ Noah had 70 descendants.
>
> ✔ A line in the **Midrash** (*mid*-rahsh; rabbinic commentary on the Torah; see Chapter 3) says, "The Holy One Blessed be He has seventy names; Israel has seventy names; the Torah has seventy names; Jerusalem has seventy names (Numbers Rabbah 14:12)."
>
> ✔ Jewish tradition speaks of the 70 faces of the divine **Shekhinah** (sheh-*khee*-nah; God's presence in the world). Tradition teaches that it's possible for individuals to participate in bringing God's presence into the world.

The tradition of Torah study includes the idea that the Torah has 70 facets, and like a diamond, these facets help to make the Torah shine in one's eyes. **Shiv'im panim laTorah** (shih-*veem* pah-*neem* lah-toe-*rah*) is an ancient Hebrew phrase that means "there are 70 faces in the Torah."

Even though the Torah text is exact and never changes, your understanding of each word, sentence, story, and detail is never limited to its literal meaning (I discuss the literal meaning of the Torah in the later section "Just the facts, ma'am: The literal level"). Rather, by looking at the Torah from various angles, every detail shines and twinkles like a star. Stars are like diamonds in the sky, and the image of a diamond with 70 facets has become a way in which students of the Torah understand a part of its nature.

What a great teacher teaches tomorrow is Torah: Finding everything in the Torah

As I describe in Chapter 1, it's difficult to define the word "Torah." It's used to refer to the Five Books of Moses, but "Torah" also has a broad meaning that transcends any specific document or collection of documents. Yes, the Torah is the Five Books of Moses, and yes, the Holy Scriptures of the Jewish people begin with the Five Books of Moses and then continue with the books of the Prophets and other holy writings. But the term "Torah" transcends the definition that includes all the sacred books of Jewish literature throughout the centuries.

Torah transcends time and what can be contained within finite letters on finite pages. It may sound outrageous that Torah includes the notion that what a great teacher teaches *tomorrow* is Torah, but this is precisely how serious students see the Torah.

But students of the Torah encounter an important paradox (and acknowledge that they need to embrace it): On the one hand, the Torah is infinite and therefore can't be contained in any finite document or body of literature. On the other hand, the Five Books of Moses, the document most well-known as the Torah of the Jewish people, contains everything — past, present, and future.

When looked at through the right lens at the right time and on the proper spiritual level, everything can be found in the Torah. The Torah scroll and its contents are multidimensional to the infinite degree. It has been said that whereas many religious traditions conceive that Scripture comes from heaven, the Jewish tradition conceives of the Torah *as* heaven. In Jewish tradition, involving oneself in the analysis and interpretation of the Torah is considered an act of participating with God in the creation of the universe.

Recognizing that everyone's on a different level of understanding

In traditional circles, where Torah is studied daily and intensely, there's a general assumption that each person understands the Torah on his or her own individual level. Everyone seeks their own level. The Torah is conceived of as so vast that it can easily contain all these levels, from the level of the simplest child to the level of the greatest genius.

Traditional Jewish life contains the notion of the **maggid** (*mah*-geed). This term is often translated as "storyteller" or "preacher," but it actually refers to a very specific kind of teacher — one who can speak to a group of students who are all on different levels and make them feel as if they're being addressed individually. The greatest of Torah teachers can be said to do two things simultaneously: speak to each student on his or her own level, and raise each student to a higher level.

It would be irresponsible of me to give the impression that Torah study is some kind of free-for-all, where everything goes, every point of view is acceptable, and no one can make a mistake. That simply isn't true. What is true is that everything is up for discussion. Questions are not only permissible but are a required part of the process of Torah study.

One can even go as far as saying that if it weren't for questions, the traditional Jewish process of Torah study couldn't happen. Traditional Torah study is never a process of one person insisting to everyone else that "this is the way it is." Rather, a student of the Torah can express a point of view that should and often does get challenged by another student. As my teacher put it, "Every question is permissible; not every answer."

Every person is a letter: Using the Torah to discover your identity

One popular image used among the community of Torah students throughout the ages that also reflects the view that each person understands the Torah on his or her own level is that of each student of the Torah finding his or her "letter" in the Torah. One of the meanings contained in this image is that it's not one's task to mimic others.

A well-known story from Jewish tradition talks about Rabbi Zusya (*zoo*-sha), who was a student of the great master the Maggid of Mezeritch (*mah*-geed of *mehz*-rich). Rabbi Zusya taught that when his soul arrives in heaven, he won't be asked why he wasn't Moses but rather why he was not Zusya. Each student must become an individual, not some rubber stamp of someone else. Finding one's letter in the Torah, therefore, is finding one's own identity.

It's widely acknowledged among Torah students that each tends to be drawn to his or her own part of the Torah. For many people, certain verses resonate deeply. Some traditional Jews even acknowledge the fact that they have their own **pasuk** (pah-*sook*; line of text in the Torah). For example, each of my three children wears a silver bracelet or ring engraved with specific lines from the Torah that resonate with them.

I once did a project in which I asked a number of leading Jewish educators the following question: Where do you suggest that someone who's just beginning to get involved in Jewish life begin? Each gave me the exact same answer: Find one mitzvah (one divine commandment from the Torah), and do it forever. Become an expert on that one mitzvah by learning all its facets, its history, and its details.

Each of those teachers knew that the Torah is like a hologram in that every tiny part actually contains the whole. Students of the Torah know that by focusing on one sentence, or by delving into one mitzvah, or even by locating and exploring one single letter of the Torah, the process will lead to studying the Torah in its entirety.

Entering the Garden of Torah Interpretation

The English word "paradise" comes from the Hebrew word for garden or orchard. Because Hebrew vowels aren't part of the Hebrew alphabet and usually aren't used in ancient texts, the four letters *p-r-d-s* are pronounced par-*des*. The image of the student of Torah entering the **pardes** of Torah, the garden of Torah, is an ancient one.

Centuries of Torah students have confirmed that the process of Torah study is profoundly pleasurable. Some students study Torah for hours each day, spending every spare moment studying the Torah. It's common to see traditional Jews carrying at least one book around with them at all times; the book is usually a traditional text that focuses on one aspect of the Torah. The practice of carrying the book allows constant access to the most pleasurable experience of entering the plush and beautiful garden of Torah.

The garden of Torah contains all levels of meaning. It's considered dangerous to your spiritual and psychological health to go beyond the level for which you're ready (see the sidebar "Rabbi Akiva and a tale of four rabbis" for an example). Four general levels are represented by each of the Hebrew letters for the word "orchard," PaRDeS:

- ✔ P for **p'shat** (literal)
- ✔ R for **remez** (the hint)
- ✔ D for **d'rash** (the moral)
- ✔ S for **sod** (the secret)

I explore each of these levels in the following sections.

Torah study can be quite demanding. Traditional students of Torah often engage in deep and profound analysis of the text that requires high levels of concentration and the ability to understand and work with abstract ideas. Sometimes the Torah challenges a person on a deeply emotional and personal level and cuts to the very core of his soul. Sometimes, Torah study lays a person bare as he confronts the most personal of spiritual issues. Nevertheless, entering the process of Torah study is entering paradise, the absolutely beautiful and perfect garden.

Interpreting the Torah on different levels is similar to the way you perceive any art form. A poem can have many meanings, as can a film, a sculpture, and all other creative efforts. The difference is that with art, you're free to have any interpretation you want; it's completely personal. Interpreting the Torah has its boundaries, and it's essential to have a qualified teacher who can help guide your understanding of the Torah text and help to make sure that you don't *misinterpret* the Torah in a way that's incompatible with Jewish tradition.

There's still room for unprecedented interpretations that have never before been taught. The term for a new interpretation of the Torah is **chidush** (*khih-doosh*; new development). But a new insight into the meaning of the Torah must be tested over time by learned individuals to make sure that it's in harmony with the teachings of the sages and the oral tradition.

Rabbi Akiva and a tale of four rabbis

Every student of Torah sooner or later falls in love with Rabbi Akiva (ah-*key*-vah) (c. 50 CE–c. 135 CE). Rabbi Akiva was one of the greatest rabbis of all time and perhaps the greatest rabbi in the entire rabbinic period of Jewish history.

One of the remarkable parts of his personal story is that that he didn't know the ABC's of Hebrew until he was 40 years old. According to the Talmud, before he was 40, Rabbi Akiva was an ignorant shepherd who was hostile toward religion in general and Jewish tradition in particular. But as the story goes, a young woman named Rachel saw Akiva the shepherd and detected his great potential. Rachel said to Akiva that she would marry him if he would promise to dedicate himself to learning Torah. The insight that Rachel had into Akiva's character, abilities, and potential was accurate.

Rabbi Akiva is clearly the great hero for all who decide late in life to return to the spiritual path. Rabbi Akiva also started late in life and grew to the very pinnacle of spiritual development.

He appears hundreds and hundreds of times in rabbinic literature and is known as one of the great spiritual masters of Jewish history and tradition. In fact, a story that every Kabbalist is familiar with tells of Rabbi Akiva's greatness when describing four rabbis who entered an orchard.

Four great rabbis — Ben Azzai, Ben Zoma, Elisha ben Abuya, and Rabbi Akiva — entered the pardes, the orchard or garden of Torah study. These four rabbis explored the Torah to the greatest depth and encountered the most sublime, esoteric, and profound teachings.

The story of the four rabbis indicates the dangers of studying on a level you're not prepared for. Ben Azzai entered the most profound depths of Torah study and died. Ben Zoma entered and went crazy. Elisha ben Abuya entered and became a heretic. Only Rabbi Akiva, as the text indicates, "Entered in peace and left in peace."

Just the facts, ma'am: The literal level

The Hebrew letter with the sound of a "p" in the word **prds** stands for the Hebrew word **p'shat** (puh-*shot*). P'shat asks for the literal meaning of words. One general area of Torah study includes a search for the basic meaning of the text itself. An example of a literal interpretation of a verse in the Torah is the very first commandment found in Genesis. When the Torah says, "Be fruitful and multiply" (Genesis 1:28), it means just that: Have children!

Just because the text says something literally doesn't mean that you're only supposed to understand it literally. Instead, you may see another meaning in the verse on your own, or you may read a commentary that suggests another level of meaning. Torah commentators throughout the ages have earned reputations regarding the various levels of Torah interpretation. Some mainly focus on the literal meaning; others are more inclined to write or teach on the homiletic level or mystical level. Serious students of the Torah find that they become partial to certain commentators because the students are personally inclined to see things on the same general level as the commentators. The best example is a well-known phrase from the Torah, "an eye for an eye, a tooth for a tooth"(Exodus 21:23). Read literally, it means that equal retaliation is appropriate; literally, it means that if you poke my eye out, I can poke your eye out. *Jewish tradition and law absolutely forbids this kind of retaliation.* Jewish tradition has a far more humane approach to subjects of retribution and reconciliation, so this literal interpretation is false. The Oral Torah teaches that monetary compensation is paid to the injured person (Talmud, Tractate Bava Kamma 83b).

What exactly are you implying? The hint

When you read a book or a poem, or when you watch a movie, a TV show, or a play, it's obvious that not every detail is said explicitly; some things are implied. For example, if you watch a movie about New York City and the camera pans the skyline, the presence or absence of the World Trade Center Twin Towers can help you determine when the movie takes place and perhaps even the mood of the urban setting. By gathering other clues and by close examination of the facts, all sorts of conclusions can be drawn that aren't explicit.

Similarly, there is a level of understanding and study of the Torah called **remez** (*reh*-mehz; the hint) that points to an effort to read the Torah text and to reveal what's implied but not stated explicitly. For example, the Torah doesn't say that divorce is permissible (at least it doesn't come out and say it directly). But the Torah does lay out what a couple must do to get divorced, implying that divorce is in fact permissible. The text offers hints and implications that allow you to make certain assumptions about facts that aren't revealed through specific words.

When a commentator on the Torah or any student of the Torah comes up with a hint or remez, it's open to severe analysis because of how easy it is to jump to conclusions and convince yourself that something is being hinted at when in fact it isn't. For instance, do you remember the magician David Copperfield's magic trick of making the Statue of Liberty disappear? Obviously, he didn't make the Statue of Liberty actually disappear. If he had those powers, he wouldn't be an entertainer but would use his powers for all kinds of other important things. David Copperfield created the illusion of the disappearance. In the same way, the student of Torah has to be cautious when jumping to conclusions about the Torah text — what seems to be there may be an illusion.

So, what's the point? The moral

One core aspect of the Torah is its focus on deeds and human experiences in the world. Yes, the Torah deals with eternal ideas and spiritual concepts such as the soul, miracles, and faith, but it's largely a document teaching proper behavior and healthy attitudes.

One of the four general levels of Torah explication is **d'rash** (duh'*rahsh*). This level signifies the homiletic, the ethical message, the inspiration for more refined behavior, the adage that can change your life, or simply put, the moral of the story.

When a student of the Torah reads and studies the text, he or she is often looking for guidance for living life. That guidance can be quite concrete, such as in the area of good business practices, or it can be more spiritual in nature, like how and when to pray and deepen one's relationship to God. The Jewish view of both spiritual and physical acts is that they are *both* spiritual. The d'rash level of Torah interpretation usually provides practical teachings that nourish the student.

For example, the Torah and the great texts of Jewish tradition contain the story of Abraham leaving his family home to begin his journey. Students can learn an inspiring amount from the results of a major life decision like Abraham's.

The word "Torah" comes from the same root as the Hebrew word for instruction. And you can find much of the instruction contained in the Torah when pursuing the d'rash of the text. I devote Part III to the behavior lessons found in the Torah.

Do you want to know a secret? The deepest level

A central image of the Jewish tradition is one of God looking into the Torah and creating the world. One of the implications of this image is that everything is contained in the Torah, or as the great rabbinic sages put it, the Torah is the blueprint for the world. The **sod** (sohwd; secret level) of Torah interpretation is the pursuit of the deepest spiritual ideas and most sublime revelations.

For thousands of years, Jews of all ages and at all levels of understanding have pursued the secrets of the Torah. The Five Books of Moses in the form of a Torah scroll isn't just one more document among the great collection of sacred texts of the world. Rather, in Jewish tradition the Torah is considered to be part of the root structure of the world. Every letter, every space between every letter, and indeed every aspect of the Torah is filled with divine revelation.

The greatest Torah commentators throughout the centuries have done the following and found profound meaning:

 ✔ Counted letters

 ✔ Given letters numerical values

 ✔ Reversed letters

✔ Found inconsistent spellings of the same word and discovered important lessons in these inconsistencies

✔ Found some letters written larger or smaller in the Torah scroll and taught the meaning of these differences

Many other details of the Torah have infinite potential to reveal the deepest secrets that God has revealed. One example of how a word can have deeper meaning than you may think about at first glance is the Hebrew word **tzibbur** (*tzee*-boor; community). It consists of three Hebrew consonants that, when seen together, the great Torah sages consider an acronym for a basic spiritual concept having to do with three types of individuals on the spiritual path:

✔ The "tz" sound, called a **tzadee** (*tzah*-dee), is connected with the perfect saint known as the **tzadik** (tzah-*deek*). There are people in the world who are at such a high level of purity that they don't even know what temptation feels like.

✔ The "b" sound, which is made by the Hebrew letter **bet,** the second letter of the Hebrew alphabet, is connected to the **beinoni** (bay-no-*nee*), the intermediate individual on the spiritual path (the level in which most people find themselves). Unlike the tzadik, the beinoni knows temptation but is able to resist it. The constant tension of that struggle is the level at which the beinoni lives his life.

✔ The "r" sound, which is called the **resh** (raysh), is connected with the **rasha** (*rah*-shah; the evil individual). At the root of his being, the rasha has a point of view about life that's a major distortion of the way it should be. The evil individual is wicked through and through.

In other words, the simple Hebrew word for community, tzibbur, is far richer in meaning than just a combination of letters that signifies one concept of community. Rather, those three letters point to the essence of the human soul in the world, where the student of Torah asks the question "Who am I?"

Analysis of the word "tzibbur" reveals that human beings are souls in constant struggle. Inner urges and elements of the soul are at odds with each other, and one of the primary activities of life is the struggling with these various forces in the soul in order to be able to choose and reject the urges properly, at the right time and the right place. The close analysis of the word "tzibbur" is an example of the sod, the secret hidden in the Torah and waiting to be revealed.

Although anyone can potentially have a deep, mystical insight into the hidden meaning of a verse or verses in the Torah at any time, the sod level of Torah interpretation generally comes after years of experience and scholarship. As with any personal interpretation, it's always advised that a Torah student have a qualified teacher with whom he can test new ideas.

A twist on understanding the Zohar

One of the classic books of Torah literature that has achieved the status of a sacred text among the Jews is the **Zohar** (see Chapter 3 for full details on this text). The Zohar is often referred to as a commentary on the Torah containing the sod (in other words containing many of the secrets hidden within the Torah). Some say that the Five Books of Moses is the p'shat (the literal) and the Zohar is the sod (the mystical or secret).

My teacher teaches an interesting twist on the Zohar that's actually the opposite of that point and that offers a profound insight into the Five Books of Moses itself. My teacher teaches that

the Zohar is the p'shat and the Torah is the sod. In other words, when one reads the Zohar, the mystical concepts are there for the taking; they're explained and explored rather explicitly. In contrast, in the Five Books of Moses, the deepest and most profound ideas aren't on the surface but rather are embedded in the text. So the Torah student is like a miner looking for diamonds. Like diamonds, the ideas aren't always visible but nonetheless exist deep within the text and are accessible to the student who's diligent and invests time in the pursuit of Torah wisdom.

Examining the "Bible Codes": Are They Legit?

Trying to pierce through the Torah text to locate secret or hidden messages has always been a part of legitimate Torah study. But it's not always easy to separate tried-and-true methods that have stood the test of time and are based on solid Torah scholarship from faddish approaches using questionable methods. One such highly questionable approach is generally known as the Bible Codes.

The meaning of hidden codes

In 1997, a former reporter for the *Washington Post* and the *Wall Street Journal* wrote the bestseller *The Bible Code* (Touchstone). In his book, Michael Drosnin expresses what many people have speculated about the Torah: that it's actually a secret code and the proper approach can reveal its secrets.

According to Drosnin, a number of techniques can be used to reveal the Torah's messages, including counting letters in certain arithmetic sequences. For instance, if you take the first letter of each word in a sequence of words, those letters may create another word. For example, the first letter of each of the words in the phrase "great out doors" spell out GOD.

The best-known example in Drosnin's book reveals through a sequencing method that the Torah seems to predict the assassination of the former prime minister of Israel Yitzhak Rabin. The words "Yitzhak Rabin" and the phrase "assassin that will assassinate" intersect when Drosnin applies a certain method of counting in sequences.

People may ask, "Are these calculations mere coincidences, or can secrets of the Torah actually be revealed by recognizing the text as a secret code?" Many critiques of *The Bible Code* reveal deep skepticism and even scorn at Drosnin's techniques. One critic, for example, applied Drosnin's methodology to *Moby Dick* and found that the book references the assassinations of Prime Minister Indira Gandhi, Soviet exile Leon Trotsky, Reverend Martin Luther King, Jr., John F. Kennedy, Princess Diana, and Abraham Lincoln. This critic's intent is simply to show that finding so-called "hidden" messages is coincidence and that the messages aren't legitimate messages imbedded into the texts by their authors.

But whether Drosnin is right or not, one good lesson that comes from *The Bible Code* is that the approach is consistent in one significant way with the traditional way Torah scholars have been relating to the text since time immemorial. The basic assumption is that the Torah contains far more than a simple narration of stories and laws from ancient times. If the *Bible Code* phenomenon does nothing else but inspire people to look at the Torah more carefully, it's my opinion that it has done some good in the world.

An example of how a coincidence can seem to make sense is the interesting phenomenon in the 46th Psalm of the King James Version of the Bible. If you count to the 46th word of Psalm 46, and if you count 46 words from the last word of Psalm 46, the two words put together spell "Shakespeare." It's said that Shakespeare was 46 years old when the King James Version of the Bible was published. Is this a coincidence? Or did the author deliberately put this into the translation of the book of Psalms? I have my opinion: I think it's a fantastic coincidence.

The significance of numbers

Unlike the Bible Codes, which use methods not sanctioned by Jewish tradition, there are traditionally accepted methods of analyzing the Torah as a hidden code through the system known as **gematria** (geh-*mah*-tree-yah; Aramaic for "numerology" with a connection to the Greek word "geometry"). An ancient and accepted approach to exploring the depths of the Torah, gematria is based on the fact that each letter in the Hebrew alphabet has a numerical value. The system calculates the numerical values of letters, words, or phrases and thereby gains insight into the text.

The assumption in gematria is that the numerical values aren't coincidental but rather are part of God's intention. For example, if two words have the same numerical value, scholars say that there's a connection between them that needs to be revealed.

Following are three of a number of ways Jewish tradition determines the numerical value of each letter (see Figure 15-1):

- ✔ **Absolute value:** Absolute value means that each letter has an accepted numerical equivalent. For example, the first letter of the Hebrew alphabet, **aleph,** equals 1, the second letter, **vet,** equals 2, and so on through **yud,** which has the value of 10. After the yud, the next several letters are increased by 10 until the last three letters, which are increased by 100. These values are traditionally accepted as one way of using Hebrew letters to represent numbers.

- ✔ **Ordinal value:** Ordinal value calculates each of the 22 letters of the Hebrew alphabet differently and assigns consecutive numbers from 1 to 22 to each letter. For example, aleph equals 1, khaf equals 11, tav equals 22. (Some Hebrew letters have final forms; you can see all the values for final letters in Figure 15-1.)

- ✔ **Reduced value:** Reduced value reduces each letter to a figure of one digit. For example, aleph (which equals 1), yud (which equals 10), and kuf (which equals 100) all have a numerical value of 1. Similarly, bet (2), khaf (20), and reish (200) all have a numerical value of 2. In this method, the letters have only nine equivalents rather than 22.

Related to reduced value is integral reduced value, in which the numerical value of an entire word is reduced to one number. If the sum of the numbers in one word is more than nine, the numbers are added together until one digit remains.

Hebrew Letter	Letter Name	Absolute Value	Ordinal Value	Reduced Value
א	aleph	1 or 1000	1	1
ב	vet	2	2	2
ג	gimmel	3	3	3
ד	dalet	4	4	4
ה	hey	5	5	5
ו	vav	6	6	6
ז	zayin	7	7	7
ח	khet	8	8	8
ט	tet	9	9	9
י	yud	10	10	1
כ	khaf	20	11	2
ל	lamed	30	12	3
מ	mem	40	13	4
נ	nun	50	14	5
ס	samekh	60	15	6
ע	ayin	70	16	7
פ	fey	80	17	8
צ	tzadee	90	18	9
ק	koof	100	19	1
ר	reish	200	20	2
ש	shin	300	21	3
ת	tav	400	22	4
ך	final khaf	500	23	5
ם	final mem	600	24	6
ן	final nun	700	25	7
ף	final fey	800	26	8
ץ	final tzadee	900	27	9

Figure 15-1:
The different values of the letters of the Hebrew alphabet (including final letters).

The divine name **Elohim** is a simple example of gematria: The name has the same absolute value (86) as the Hebrew word **hateva** (hah-*teh*-vah; nature). The name of God "Elohim" refers to that part of God who can be seen as the Creator and expresses Himself in nature. Here's how the Hebrew spellings of the two words add up:

> Elohim = aleph-lamed-hey-yud-mem = 1 + 30 + 5 + 10 + 40 = 86
>
> Hateva = hey-tet-bait-ayin = 5 + 9 + 2 + 70 = 86

Are you interested in finding out more about gematria? You can uncover a good amount of gematria in the Torah commentaries of Rabbi Judah Loew ben Bezalel (1525–1609). He's generally known among scholars as the Maharal of Prague or simply the Maharal. Another great Torah commentator, Rabbi Isaiah Horowitz (who happens to be a direct ancestor of mine), also uses gematria frequently in his masterpiece of Kabbalah, *The Two Tablets of the Covenant*. A good book to help you begin to explore this subject in more detail is *The Wisdom of the Hebrew Alphabet* by Michael L. Munk (Artscroll Mesorah).

Chapter 16

Studying the Torah with Translations, Commentaries, and Other Resources

The original language of the Torah is Hebrew, and it is best if you can read the original for the same reason it's best to read any work of literature in its original language: Every translation is itself a commentary and must, by definition, reflect the bias of the translator. However, most people, including most Jews, can't read Hebrew. Luckily, many translations of the Torah are available, along with many commentaries and additional tools to help you to understand the text. In this chapter, I start you on the road to deeper Torah study with information on translations, commentaries, and other helpful resources. Turn to Chapter 15 for basics on analyzing the Torah.

Reading a Translation of the Torah

If you want to read or study the Torah (the Five Books of Moses) and can't do so in its original Hebrew, turn to a translation. Most English translations of the Torah include additional commentaries, which either are written by contemporary writers or are translations of classical commentaries. (I discuss commentators in more detail later in this chapter in the section "Getting Help from Great Classic and Contemporary Commentators.")

A Torah commentary is usually a word-by-word, phrase-by-phrase, or line-by-line explanation of the meaning of a text offered by some Torah authority. Torah commentaries may include

- Additional information that helps the reader understand the text

- Definitions of terms

- A comparison of one verse to similar language in a different verse

- Answers to anticipated questions or problems that a Torah student may have

- Expansion of ideas contained in the text

- Indication that a verse is actually a commandment

- Help relating the text to contemporary life

Figure 16-1 shows translated Torah text surrounded by commentary.

In the following sections, I introduce you to several popular Torah translations and help you choose the best translation for your needs.

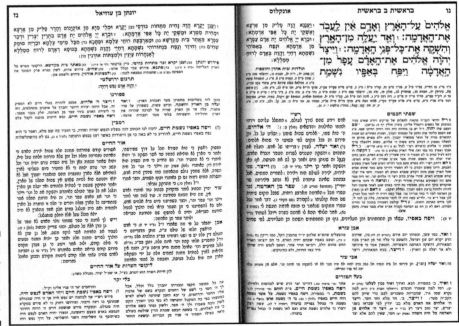

Figure 16-1:
Commentary
surrounding
a Torah
translation.

Surveying translations used by different Jewish movements

Different movements within the American Jewish community usually favor one or two translations of the Torah over others. While every synagogue selects the translations it wants to use — as well as all other Jewish practices — the following list runs down who generally reads what:

- **Chassidic:** Chassidic Judaism, which is based on the original teachings of the **Baal Shem Tov** (bah-*ahl* shem towv; master of the Good Name), contains many subgroups. Three of the largest groups are Satmar, Lubavitch, and Bobov. The synagogues of each of these groups generally use editions of the Torah in Hebrew. The most well-known Chassidic group is Lubavitch; the teachings of this group's leaders and revered teachers from past generations can be found in the Gutnick edition of the Torah.

- **Orthodox:** The Orthodox movement in America is divided into modern Orthodox and **haredi** (khah-*ray*-dee; one who is in awe of God), sometimes known as ultra-Orthodox. In Orthodox synagogues that have English translations of the Torah, the one most commonly found is *The Chumash: The Stone Edition.* I've also known some Orthodox synagogues to use *The Living Torah.*

- **Conservative:** There are some Conservative synagogues where you can find equal participation among men and women in all rituals, while other Conservative synagogues continue to follow the traditional divisions between male and female roles. (Check out Chapter 13 for more about the Torah synagogue service.) The authorized Conservative Torah translation and commentary is *Etz Chayyim.*

- **Reform:** The Reform movement, like the other movements listed previously, isn't monolithic in synagogues' practices. Some are more traditional than others. For example, some Reform houses of worship use no Hebrew, and some actually refuse to allow their rabbis to wear a **kippah** (key-*pah*; skullcap), while other Reform synagogues are more traditional. The Reform movement uses an authorized Torah translation and commentary called *The Torah: A Modern Commentary;* it's commonly referred to as "Plaut" after the surname of its major translator and commentator.

- **Reconstructionist and Renewal:** Neither the Reconstructionist movement (the first movement to have begun in North America) nor the Renewal movement (a relatively new movement that considers itself transdenominational) has its own official Torah translation and commentary, and the resources used vary widely among the synagogues and prayer groups of both movements.

The following sections summarize (in order of my most to least favorite) the most popular translations of the Five Books of Moses currently available in English.

The Living Torah

The Living Torah, written by the late Rabbi Aryeh Kaplan, was published in 1981. It's probably the most clear and readable English edition of the Five Books of Moses that exists.

One of the most important features of this edition is Rabbi Kaplan's footnotes, in which he explains and justifies his decisions regarding the translation of difficult words and concepts. It's important to be aware of the fact that *The Living Torah* isn't always a literal translation; rather, it's a translation based on the accepted rabbinic commentaries and Jewish laws that are a part of authentic Jewish practice and belief. As far as Torah translations go, *The Living Torah* by Rabbi Aryeh Kaplan is my personal favorite.

The Chumash: The Gutnick Edition

The Gutnick Edition by Rabbi Chaim Miller is a noteworthy Torah translation because it's written in modern English, but despite its contemporary sound, it's quite faithful to traditional Jewish commentaries and understandings of the text.

In addition to a translation of the Torah text, *The Gutnick Edition* contains lots of supplementary material to aid and nourish the reader. You get translations of classic commentaries and running commentary based on the oral teachings of the greatest rabbi and Jewish leader of the 20th century, Rabbi Menachem Mendel Schneerson, also known as the Lubavitcher Rebbe. And if that weren't enough, throughout each volume of this translation are hundreds of additional insights from Jewish tradition to further enlighten the Torah text. The book also contains many diagrams and tables to help you get a firm grasp of the text.

The Chumash: The Stone Edition

The Stone Edition of the Five Books of Moses is a beautiful volume with a contemporary-sounding English translation. It's also well-known in traditional Jewish circles as being faithful to the classic commentators.

Of particular note in *The Stone Edition* is the contemporary commentary produced by a team of scholars under the direction of Rabbi Nosson Scherman. This commentary draws upon classic biblical commentaries, Talmudic insight, and contributions from contemporary scholars. This Torah translation also includes an excellent index.

Meam Loez

The English edition of *Meam Loez* (meh-*ahm* low-*ez*; people of a foreign tongue) is a 20-volume set that's well worth the investment. The original edition of this Torah translation was written by Rabbi Yaakov Culi and published in 1730. *Meam Loez* was originally written in Ladino (lah-*dee*-no), a language that's a synthesis of Hebrew and Spanish, and is often considered to be the greatest publication to ever to appear in that language. It became a major classic among Jews in the entire Mediterranean region and has remained an important publication within the Jewish world. Although this translation and commentary is in no way connected with a movement within Judaism, the content is based on traditional teachings.

This edition is really much more than a translation and commentary on the Torah. It's a rich Jewish education in itself, filled with background information, history, customs, laws, and thorough explanations of holidays and rituals.

The Pentateuch and Haftaroth: The Hertz Edition

With a running commentary that moves phrase-by-phrase throughout the translation, the English translation in *The Hertz Edition* comes from the first Jewish Publication Society translation and was completed in 1917. Although an out-of-date and often difficult translation to understand, *The Hertz Edition* of the Five Books of Moses was surely the most popular edition used in American synagogues in the 20th century. In my opinion, this translation is generally uninspired. Many American synagogues continue to use *The Hertz Edition,* but it's rapidly being replaced with the many better alternatives. I predict that it will soon completely disappear, but it was the accepted translation for the last few generations. Because of its widespread use, most American Jews over the last several decades, regardless of their movement affiliation, are familiar with *The Hertz Edition.*

The Chumash: The Hirsch Edition

Nineteenth-century German Rabbi Samson Raphael Hirsch had a significant influence on Modern Orthodox Judaism, and his commentary on the Five Books of Moses remains quite popular (as does his German translation of the Torah). The English version of *The Chumash: The Hirsch Edition* contains translations of Rabbi Hirsch's selected commentary, which draws upon rabbinic commentaries as well as includes Hirsch's own insights. Some people feel that even though it was published in the 19th century, *The Hirsch Edition* has a strikingly modern feel to it. It's not widely used but is highly regarded and certainly worth using due to the fine reputation of its author.

Etz Hayim

Produced by the Conservative movement in the United States, *Etz Hayim* (aytz khah-*yeem*; the tree of life) is a modern translation of and commentary on the Torah. Although it's growing in popularity among nontraditional Jews, *Etz Hayim* has received fierce criticism from the traditional Jewish community, particularly for some of the 40 topical essays written by scholars within the Conservative movement.

Unfortunately, when you read the commentary and essays closely, you may get the sense that a number of the individuals involved in the translation and commentary are skeptical at best about the divine nature of the Torah. The commentaries are more firmly based on historical speculation, cross-cultural analysis, and archaeology than on Jewish spiritual tradition. The commentary is surprisingly literal; its editors seem to completely avoid traditional Jewish theology and are more preoccupied with contemporary academic scholarship. Simply put, the translation and commentary have strange priorities, looking at the Torah more as a historical document than a spiritual one.

The Torah: A Modern Commentary

This volume, popular among liberal synagogue congregations, is basically a gender-sensitive version of a Jewish Publication Society translation, with largely gender-neutral God language and a new translation of the book of Genesis. The commentary by W. Gunther Plaut, a leading Reform rabbi, combines modern and classical sources.

Although *A Modern Commentary* is used widely, its heavy reliance on modern points of view that haven't stood the test of time and that often contradict some basic views of traditional Judaism make it questionable as a reliable source for discovering what the classical commentators have to say about the Torah.

It's Greek to me: The Septuagint

When the Second Temple was completed in Jerusalem in 516 BCE, the Jewish people lived under Persian rule. When the Persian Empire fell apart in 330 BCE, the Jewish people found themselves under Greek rule. Around 313 BCE, the Greek king Ptolemy ordered the Jewish sages to translate the Torah into Greek. The story of what happened is recorded in the Talmud (see Chapter 3 for more about the Talmud):

> "King Ptolemy once gathered 72 sages. He placed them in 72 chambers, each of them in a separate one, without revealing to them why they were summoned. He entered each one's room and said: 'Write for me the Torah of Moshe, your teacher.' God put it in the heart of each one to translate identically as all the others did." (Tractate Megillah 9)

Jewish legend records that Ptolemy discovered all the translations to be exactly the same. Even though the identical translations are considered to be a miracle, the Talmud says, "On the 8th of Tevet, the Torah was rendered into Greek during the days of King Ptolemy, and darkness descended upon the world for three days." The day the sages finished their Greek translations of the Torah is considered to be a sad one on the Jewish calendar because of the view that the Torah would be neither understood nor easily misunderstood as long as it remained in Hebrew. The thinking was that a person who was knowledgeable in Hebrew was also probably knowledgeable about how the Torah was to be understood. But if the Torah were to appear in another language, people without the proper understanding of how it's to be read and grasped could easily distort its message. After all, the Torah was given to Moses along with the methodologies for cracking it open.

Although 72 Jewish sages participated in the translation, the Greek translation of the Torah is known as the *Septuagint,* which means the number 70, thus rounding the number of sages involved down from 72 to 70.

Selecting the right translation for your needs

Be careful when you select a translation of any book, especially the Torah. Often the translator, publisher, or committee supervising the translation has a bias that comes through in the text — either subtly or obviously. You may find that one translation is too stiff and almost incomprehensible, whereas another is warm, down-to-earth, and reader-friendly. For example, many people are used to the King James Version of the Bible, whose language has crept into our culture, but it's difficult to imagine Moses using Old English phraseology or God using words like "hath" and "shalt."

It's important to keep in mind that every translation *is* a commentary, which means that the translator's choice of words can differ vastly from one book to another. You can see a good example of this in a comparison of two of the more popular English translations of the Five Books of Moses: the Jewish Publication Society edition and *The Living Torah*. In an incident recorded in the Torah about a person named Dina, the Jewish Publication Society translation (*Tanakh — The Holy Scriptures,* Jewish Publication Society) says he "saw her, and took her and lay with her by force." In contrast, *The Living Torah* says he "seduced her, slept with her, and then raped her." Clearly, there's an emotional difference between the words "saw" and "seduced" and even more of a difference between the phrases "lay with her by force" and "slept with her and raped her." Both translations communicate what happened, but by using the word "raped" rather than "lay with her by force" *The Living Torah* is using blunt, modern language that doesn't sanitize the event for today's reader. When I read "lay with her by force," I surely don't get the same sense of the violence of the act as I do when I hear the word "raped."

The selection of a translation should be based not only on the language used in the translation but also on the additional materials included in the volume. Some Torah translations are simply translations, whereas others include additional commentaries and other aids to support the reader.

If you're looking for a translation and commentary that accurately represents what Jewish tradition has taught for centuries and that's based on ideas firmly rooted in Jewish tradition, I strongly suggest *The Living Torah, The Chumash: The Gutnick Edition,* or *The Chumash: The Stone Edition*. If you want to see what mainstream Conservative congregations are using, *Etz Hayim* is the one for you. If you want to see what most Reform congregations are using, go with *The Torah: A Modern Commentary*. My suggestion is to focus on the traditional editions so that you can see what Jews have been studying for centuries and so that you can familiarize yourself with classical Jewish tradition and fundamental ideas of Judaism. It's much like seriously learning how to dance: You first learn the basic, classical dance steps and techniques, and then you can consider modern improvisations and new approaches.

The best place to shop for any of these editions is a good Jewish bookstore. Most major cities in the United States have at least one Jewish bookstore with helpful staff members. You can also find many Jewish book sites online. Just type "Jewish books" into your favorite search engine to find what you're looking for.

Getting Help from Great Classic and Contemporary Commentators

Throughout Jewish history, thousands of Torah commentaries have been written. Most of these commentaries don't accompany complete translations of the Torah text; rather, they're essays or books on selected details of the Torah. There also are books containing commentaries on the various Jewish holy days, on specific commandments appearing in the Torah, and on countless other topics from the Torah. As with Torah translations, I suggest that you visit a good Jewish bookstore in order to build your library. You'll be amazed at the vast number of books on just about every possible subject relating to topics found in the Torah. Remember, the Jewish people have been known for centuries as "the people of the book."

Writing your own Torah commentary

I used to be a regular visitor to Biegeleisen's, a bookshop in New York City. It was a cramped, multilevel shop with thousands of used Jewish books piled high to the ceiling and so many piles that it was almost impossible to walk around. When flipping through old Hebrew books that were once owned by students, I could always see the margin notes written by the individuals who had owned the volumes. From a cross-reference in the margin to the place where a particular Torah verse or a similar one appears again to some clarification of a difficult phrase or definition of some difficult vocabulary word, these notes by book owners are Torah commentaries.

It's the obligation of every student of the Torah to write his or her own commentary. I'm not referring to a commentary that's worthy of being published. Rather, it's totally appropriate for every Torah student to record insights, questions, and points of clarification in the margins of their Jewish books, including the chumash. This practice is comparable to highlighting and making notes in college textbooks.

In the case of Torah study, active participation and involvement by the student of the Torah is essential. Remember that the blessing said before beginning to study the Torah is a statement of thanks to God for requiring that you **la'asok b'divrei Torah** (la-ah-*soak* b'*div*-ray toe-*rah*; get involved with the words of Torah).

Over the centuries, certain Jewish teachers and their teachings have attracted great numbers of admirers. A handful of Torah commentators have risen above all the others and have developed a strong authority by virtue of the great numbers of people who use their commentaries and the influential individuals who endorse them. In the following sections, I discuss five absolute superstars in the world of Torah commentary. (The first three are great sages from the past, and the last two are contemporary masters.)

Open and frequent disagreement exists among even the greatest of commentators. You don't have to look hard to find differences of opinion among the greatest sages in Jewish history. Jewish tradition honors, encourages, and respects diversity of opinion. Jewish tradition also considers the ability to contain diverse points of view a virtue.

Rashi: You can't read the Torah without him

Rabbi Shlomo Yitzchaki (1040–1105), known as **Rashi** (*rah*-she), was an 11th-century rabbi who lived in France. His commentaries on the Five Books of Moses and the Talmud (see Chapter 3) have both been elevated to the highest possible status: Throughout the generations, editions of the Five Books of Moses produced by religious publishers have invariably contained at least one commentary, and that commentary has generally been that of Rashi.

Many publications over the centuries have been referred to as "Chumash with Rashi," meaning the Five Books of Moses with Rashi's brilliant commentary. Today, if you go into a Jewish bookstore and ask for a "Chumash with Rashi," you'll be offered several editions of this classic work of Jewish literature.

Rashi's commentary is actually his selection of comments from rabbinic literature that reveal some of the most fundamental concepts in the Torah. Rashi has a way of getting quickly to the point and anticipating common questions that most typical Torah students have, clarifying just about every possible question about the meaning of the text. He has a rare and uncanny ability to make profound points and offer deep insights in simple, direct, and down-to-earth language. Some say that Rashi provides the most basic and simplest Torah commentary, whereas others insist that Rashi's commentary is the deepest and most profound. Still others recognize it as a wonderful guide through the Torah.

Name that Torah commentator!

In the world of Torah commentators, many of the greatest superstars are known by names created as acronyms. Here are a few examples:

- **Raavad:** Rabbi Avraham ben David
- **Ram:** Rabbi Meir ben Samuel

- **Rambam:** Rabbi Moses ben Maimon
- **Ran:** Rabbi Nissim ben Reuven
- **Riban:** Rabbi Judah ben Nathan
- **Rif:** Rabbi Isaac ben Jacob Alfasi
- **Rosh:** Rabbi Asher ben Jeheil

Abraham Ibn Ezra: A 12th-century master commentator

Rabbi Abraham ben Meir Ibn Ezra (c. 1089–c. 1164) was a poet, philosopher, grammarian, and biblical commentator during the Golden Age of Muslim Spain.

Ibn Ezra's commentary on the Five Books of Moses is based largely on his vast knowledge of Hebrew grammar and literature. It's interesting to note that Ibn Ezra often expressed skepticism of some traditional beliefs and anticipated some of the conclusions of modern scholarship. Several volumes of Ibn Ezra's commentary have been translated and published in English.

The Ramban: The Kabbalistic commentator

Thirteenth-century Rabbi Moses ben Nakhman Gerondi (1194–c. 1270), usually referred to as the **Ramban** (rahm-*bahn*), is often referred to as a mystic known for his profound grasp of Kabbalah. His Torah commentary is decidedly spiritual and has earned a reputation as one of the most inspiring and beloved of all Torah commentaries. A multivolume English translation of the Ramban's commentary is available in Jewish bookstores and Web sites. A new edition, called *The Torah: The Ramban's Commentary* is a projected multivolume edition that's new on the market. *Ramban: Commentary on the Torah* is a five-volume translation that is complete, but the translation isn't as clear as *The Torah: The Ramban's Commentary.*

The Ramban's Torah commentary deals in great detail with every aspect of the Torah, from simple explanations about details of the text to mystical insights. In his commentary, the Ramban often discusses and disagrees with the commentaries of Rashi (see the earlier section) and Ibn Ezra (see the preceding section).

The Ramban's commentary is an early example of a commentary that includes the teachings of Kabbalah. He includes a number of Kabbalistic interpretations, generally beginning them with the phrase "according to the way of truth." (If you would like to find out more about Kabbalah, be sure to check out my book *Kabbalah For Dummies,* published by Wiley.)

Elie Wiesel: An inspirational modern commentator

Most people know Elie Wiesel for his Nobel Peace Prize; his best-selling memoir, *Night;* or his appearances in the mass media. Many have no idea that this gifted writer and teacher has had a lifelong passion for Torah study and is the author of a contemporary Torah commentary that has inspired many.

For many years in New York City, Elie Wiesel has delivered a series of lectures that, in part, take a close look at the Five Books of Moses. *Messengers of God: Biblical Portraits and Legends* (Random House) is a collection of edited transcripts of Wiesel's discourses on the Torah. It's a moving and profound volume available in most major bookstores. It's also worthwhile to explore the many other books by Elie Wiesel. His writing is beautiful, his passion for his subjects is legendary, and his love for and knowledge of the Torah is evident in most of his books.

Rabbi Adin Steinsaltz: A contemporary genius

Rabbi Adin Steinsaltz of Jerusalem is considered one of the most influential and brilliant rabbis alive today. He travels the world teaching when he's not writing one of his many profound books and commentaries. His Talmud commentary is almost universally considered a work of genius within the Jewish world, and many are confident that it will live on for centuries if not forever.

Rabbi Steinsaltz's genius is evident in all his books. He's able to express deep and profound ideas through contemporary examples and analogies. He also can contain many worlds within himself, and he displays this on every page of his writings: He's a man of God and a scientist, a master of the Talmud and a master of Kabbalah, a man of faith and a skeptic, knowledgeable about the most modern things and steeped in ancient tradition, often very funny and deadly serious about life. Recently, 70 of the leading traditional rabbis in Israel identified Rabbi Steinsaltz as the wisest rabbi of our time.

Rabbi Steinsaltz has also written specifically on individual personalities in the Torah and the issues that their lives and stories provoke. For example, his remarks on the matriarch Sarah go far beyond the biblical narrative and look at Sarah in a timeless way as the quintessential partner. His series of radio lectures about biblical personalities exists in a collection called *Biblical Images*. These lucid essays lead the reader to many of the revelations to be found in the Torah. Another of his books specifically about aspects of the Five Books of Moses is *In the Beginning: Discourses on Hasidic Thought*. In this work, Rabbi Steinsaltz focuses on a number of episodes and issues in the book of Genesis. If you wanted to explore the work of only one contemporary Torah authority alive today, Rabbi Adin Steinsaltz would be your best choice.

Using Other Resources to Study the Torah

A serious student of the Torah needs guidance from commentators who are familiar with the ways of understanding the Torah and open it up to reveal its wisdom. (I introduce you to several major commentators earlier in this chapter.) A helpful way to begin studying the Torah is to focus on a small portion of it at one time.

The Five Books of Moses is divided into 54 sections that correspond to the weeks of the year (for some weeks, there are two Torah portions). Each week, the corresponding Torah portion is read publicly in synagogues throughout the world (see Chapter 13 for more about the Torah synagogue service). This division of the Torah into 54 portions allows you to easily review the entire Five Books of Moses within the cycle of one year. The individual who attends a synagogue on Shabbat or follows the weekly divisions accumulates years of Torah study as time passes. For example, I began to pay attention to the Torah portion of the week approximately 30 years ago, so in a real sense I've been through the entire Five Books of Moses at least 30 times.

Focusing on the Torah portion of the week is such a common practice among Jews that I receive e-mails from individuals who are simply collecting their thoughts on the Torah portion and offering their own synthesis and insights to friends and colleagues studying the same portion.

I give you some guidance on studying the Torah in small doses with the help of the resources in the following sections.

Surfing the Web

Many Web sites offer Torah commentaries on the portion of the week, and some will even e-mail you once a week with a commentary or lesson based on that week's Torah portion. Some of the best ones to check out are

- ✔ Aish HaTorah: www.aish.com/torahportion
- ✔ Chabad Lubavitch: www.chabad.org/parshah/default.asp
- ✔ Ohr Torah Stone: www.ohrtorahstone.org.il/parsha/index.htm
- ✔ Rabbi Berel Wein: www.rabbiwein.com
- ✔ Simon Jacobson: www.meaningfullife.com/torah/parsha
- ✔ Torah.org: www.torah.org
- ✔ Union for Reform Judaism: urj.org/Torah
- ✔ United Synagogue: www.uscj.org/Divrei_Torah_Around_7027.html
- ✔ Yeshiva University: www.torahweb.org
- ✔ Yeshivat Har Etzion: www.vbm-torah.org

Checking out Jewish newspapers

There are dozens of Jewish newspapers available throughout the United States and the world. For American readers, a visit to the American Jewish Press Association Web site at ajpa.org reveals information on all the Jewish newspapers in the country, most of which are published weekly and include at least one column by a rabbi or teacher deriving lessons from the Torah portion of the week. All these Jewish newspapers are available by subscription through the mail.

Listening to the local rabbi's sermon

Though not always the case, it's often true that rabbis deliver sermons based on the weekly Torah portion in their synagogues on Friday night and more often on Saturday morning. Such a sermon is generally known as a **d'var Torah** (d'*vahr toe*-rah; words of Torah) and consists simply of taking a word, verse, or theme from the Torah text and looking at it closely. In the d'var Torah, the rabbi usually tries to apply the wisdom of the verse to contemporary life.

During the Shabbat morning prayer service, the Torah portion is read publicly in the synagogue sanctuary and the rabbi offers his remarks immediately afterward. Some rabbis even make a practice of coming down from the pulpit into the congregation and continuing the discussion by asking for questions and comments on the Torah portion from members of the congregation.

Part V
The Part of Tens

The 5th Wave

By Rich Tennant

SARAH – Upon learning she was pregnant at the age of 90, becomes the Mother of Israel and coins the term "Oy!" on the same day.

© RICHTENNANT

I'm what...?

In this part . . .

Every *For Dummies* book has a Part of Tens, and there's perhaps no better known "list of ten" than the Ten Commandments. To start out this part, I review the Ten Commandments for you, showing you that there are two slightly different versions in the Torah and that different Christian denominations actually count the Ten Commandments differently than Judaism does. In addition to the Ten Commandments, many verses in the Torah have become part of common knowledge; in this part, I quote from and explore ten different verses that are often known by nonexperts but that are also commonly misunderstood.

Chapter 17

The Ten Commandments According to the Torah

Although the Ten Commandments are probably the most well-known part of the Torah, you may not know an interesting fact about them: Two versions of the list are in the Torah itself — one in the book of Exodus (see Chapter 5) and one in the book of Deuteronomy (see Chapter 8) — and differences exist between the two lists. In principle, there are no redundancies in the Torah, so when the great sages look at the Torah and see two different versions, they assume that the repetition is for a deliberate reason. In the case of the Ten Commandments, the sages teach that both versions were heard at the same time (like two different audio speakers in a stereo system). Each of the differences has been carefully studied and analyzed in the Oral Torah.

In addition, different Christian denominations count the commandments differently from the traditional Jewish count. Here's how it all shakes out:

✔ Roman Catholics, Lutherans, and Anglicans combine the first and second commandments into one commandment, and they divide the tenth into two commandments.

✔ Eastern Orthodox Christians combine the first commandment and the first part of the second commandment into one commandment, leaving the second part of the second commandment by itself. The rest of the commandments are the same as those followed by Jews.

✔ Some Protestant groups don't recognize the first commandment, and they divide the second commandment into two (one being "You shall have no other gods before Me" and the other "You shall not make for yourself an idol").

In this chapter, I present the two different versions of each commandment in the Torah (some are identical while others are different), explain what they mean, and explode some myths about them. But before I get into the details, I want to review some basic facts about the Torah's Ten Commandments that will help you to understand their place in Jewish tradition.

- In Hebrew, there's no term that means "the ten commandments." Instead, the Hebrew phrase **aseret hadibrot** (ah-*ser*-et hah-*dib*-rote; the ten utterances) is used to refer to the commandments. The significance of using "utterances" rather than "commandments" is based on the mystical teaching that God sustains the world at all times through divine speech and that this speech, or utterances, consists of ten fundamental forces that constantly create the world. On one level, these utterances form the Ten Commandments, and on another level, they form the ten forces that are the basis of all existence.

- The Ten Commandments are counted as part of the Torah's 613 commandments. Some sages teach that the Ten Commandments actually contain all 613, whereas others organize the 613 commandments into ten groups corresponding to the Ten Commandments.

- Some sages teach that all the 248 positive commandments (see Appendix B) are part of the first commandment ("I am the Lord your God") and that all the 365 negative commandments (see Appendix C) are part of the second commandment ("You shall have no other gods before Me").

- The first four commandments are between God and humans. The last six commandments are between people.

- According to Jewish law, the Ten Commandments in the Torah only apply to Jews. According to the Torah, there are seven commandments (some of which are the same as the Ten Commandments) that apply to all people. (Chapter 4 covers these seven universal commandments called the Noahide Laws.)

"I Am the Lord Your God . . ."

I am the Lord your God, who brought you out of the land of Egypt, from the house of slavery.

Exodus 20:2

I am the Lord your God who brought you out of the land of Egypt, out of the house of slavery.

Deuteronomy 5:6

This first commandment doesn't even sound like a commandment, but it's the most important one. The Torah sages understand this commandment to mean that it's essential that you have a relationship with the Creator. As the great Jewish philosopher Maimonides writes as the very first line of his 14-book masterpiece, the Mishneh Torah, "The foundation of all foundations and the pillar of all wisdom is to know God." (Turn to Chapter 2 for more information about getting to know God.)

"You Shall Not Recognize Other Gods before Me . . ."

> You shall not recognize other gods before Me. You shall not make for yourself a carved image, or any likeness of what is in heaven above or on the earth beneath or in the water under the earth. You shall not prostrate yourself to them or serve them; for I, the Lord your God, am a jealous God, visiting the iniquity of the fathers on the children, on the third and the fourth generations for My enemies but showing loving kindness for thousands of generations, to those who love Me and keep My commandments.
>
> Exodus 20:3–6

> You shall have no other gods before Me. You shall not make for yourself an idol, or any likeness of what is in heaven above or on the earth beneath or in the water under the earth. You shall not worship them or serve them; for I, the Lord your God, am a jealous God, visiting the iniquity of the fathers on the children, and on the third and the fourth generations of those who hate Me, but showing loving kindness to thousands, to those who love Me and keep My commandments.
>
> Deuteronomy 5:7–10

Jewish tradition understands the commandment as urging people not to limit their conception of God in any way. God is beyond all conceptions and can't be represented, even symbolically, by an object. As one of my teachers said, "If you think you grasp God, one thing is certain: You're wrong."

"You Shall Not Take the Name of the Lord Your God in Vain . . ."

> You shall not take the name of the Lord your God in vain, for the Lord will not leave him unpunished who takes His name in vain.
>
> Exodus 20:7 and Deuteronomy 5:11

Jewish tradition views the spoken word with the utmost seriousness. For example, Jewish law considers embarrassing someone in public with your words equal to murder (see Chapter 9 for more details). An oath or a promise is a reality in the world and shouldn't be taken lightly. Therefore, using God's name in an oath or promise that goes unfulfilled is a serious error.

"Remember the Sabbath Day, to Keep It Holy . . ."

Remember the Sabbath day, to keep it holy. Six days you shall labor and do all your work, but the seventh day is a Sabbath to the Lord your God; you shall not do any work, you or your son or your daughter, your male or your female servant, your animal or your stranger within your gates. For in six days the Lord made the heavens and the earth, the sea and all that is in them, and He rested on the seventh day; therefore the Lord blessed the Sabbath day and made it holy.

Exodus 20:8–11

Guard the Sabbath day to keep it holy, as the Lord your God commanded you. Six days you shall labor and do all your work, but the seventh day is a Sabbath of the Lord your God; in it you shall not do any work, you or your son or your daughter or your male servant or your female servant or your ox or your donkey or any of your cattle or your sojourner who stays with you, so that your male servant and your female servant may rest as well as you. You shall remember that you were a slave in the land of Egypt, and the Lord your God brought you out of there by a mighty hand and by an outstretched arm; therefore the Lord your God commanded you to observe the Sabbath day.

Deuteronomy 5:12–15

The most obvious difference between the two versions of the Ten Commandments shows up in this commandment. One version tells you to remember the Sabbath, and the other tells you to guard it. Some sages reconcile the difference by teaching that God spoke both words at the same time. There's a Jewish custom of lighting at least two candles to usher in Shabbat: one for the word "remember" and the other for the word "guard."

In Jewish life, the two words have very different meanings.

- ✔ On the Sabbath, Jews *remember* the Sabbath by lighting candles and saying a blessing over a glass of wine on Friday night.

- ✔ All the laws that help Jews to preserve the Sabbath as a day of rest (like not spending money on the Sabbath and not taking a ride in a car) are ways of *guarding* the Sabbath.

See Chapter 11 for more about this important day.

"Honor Your Father and Your Mother . . ."

Honor your father and your mother, so that your days may be prolonged in the land which the Lord your God gives you.

Exodus 20:12

Honor your father and your mother, as the Lord your God has commanded you, that your days may be prolonged and that it may go well with you on the land which the Lord your God gives you.

Deuteronomy 5:16

Honoring your parents doesn't mean obeying your parents. Instead, the great rabbinic sages say that grown children should make sure that their parents are provided for and treated with respect. As for decisions about your life, you can disobey your parents and still honor them. How? One example is that if your parents tell you to do something that's forbidden by Jewish law, you must not obey your parents. The two words "honor" and "obey" simply have different meaning in Jewish life. This is similar to the advice I've always given my children about their relationships with their schoolteachers: Feel free to disagree with them, but always do it with respect. In the same way, you can honor your parents, treating them with care and kindness, without having to obey them.

"You Shall Not Murder"

You shall not murder.

Exodus 20:13 and Deuteronomy 5:17

This commandment is often mistranslated as "You shall not kill." But there are many reasons to kill, including killing in self-defense and killing in the context of war. According to Jewish law, if someone is about to kill you, you have an obligation to stop them and perhaps kill them first. "You shall not murder," on the other hand, refers to killing as an act of violence.

The potential murderer is called a **rodef** (*row*-deaf; pursuer). Jewish law insists that a pursuer can be stopped by killing him first. According to Jewish law, the act of killing someone who is about to murder you isn't considered murder.

"You Shall Not Commit Adultery"

You shall not commit adultery.

Exodus 20:13 and Deuteronomy 5:17

In biblical times, polygamy was permitted, so the classic interpretation of this commandment defines adultery as a married woman having sexual relations with a man other than her husband. When the great rabbis outlawed polygamy among European Jews, the definition of adultery was also broadened to include a married man who has sexual relations with a woman other than his wife.

"You Shall Not Steal"

You shall not steal.

Exodus 20:13 and Deuteronomy 5:17

In the original context of the Ten Commandments, stealing means stealing people, commonly known as kidnapping. Of course it's also forbidden to take what's not yours, but the traditional definition was kidnapping. Today, it includes robbery and even extends to dishonest business practices.

"You Shall Not Bear False Witness Against Your Neighbor"

You shall not bear false witness against your neighbor.

Exodus 20:13 and Deuteronomy 5:17

"Bearing false witness" sounds much fancier than it is. Basically, it means that you shouldn't lie, in a court or out of it. The exception is the minor, white lie — the Jewish sages who interpreted the Ten Commandments understood that sometimes a white lie is necessary to protect a person's feelings. For example, the Oral Torah (see Chapter 3) teaches that if you don't think a bride is beautiful, you should tell her that she is anyway. Similarly, if you visit a dying person in the hospital, you shouldn't say, "You look terrible" even if that's the case.

"You Shall Not Covet Your Neighbor's House . . ."

You shall not covet your neighbor's house; you shall not covet your neighbor's wife or his male servant or his female servant or his ox or his donkey or anything that belongs to your neighbor.

Exodus 20:14

You shall not covet your neighbor's wife, and you shall not desire your neighbor's house, his field or his male servant or his female servant, his ox or his donkey or anything that belongs to your neighbor.

Deuteronomy 5:18

One good ground rule for envy, according to the Torah, is this: If you envy someone and covet something that he has, imagine that you would have to trade places with the person in *every* aspect of his life. Don't just stop at imagining having another person's money or good looks; imagine that if you had his money, you would also have his body, parents, occupation, *and* problems.

Chapter 18

Ten Frequently Misunderstood Quotes from the Torah

In This Chapter
▶ Discovering some misunderstandings about the Torah
▶ Understanding the real meanings of some famous Torah verses

*T*here's no question that the Torah has been misquoted, misunderstood, and slandered over the centuries. There are many reasons for this:

✔ Anti-Semites looking for ways to justify their hatred and prejudice take the easy route of quoting something out of context in order to distort its meaning.

✔ People generally don't know how to approach the Torah, which isn't just another book. Rather, Jews view the Torah as God's instruction book that contains the most profound ideas and sublime secrets of existence. Because the Torah is written and constructed in a unique way, only a serious student who's willing to learn how the book works can truly pierce through its layers.

✔ Many people can't get past the fact that, in principle, there are many levels of meaning to every letter, every word, every sentence, and every story in the Torah. People think that if a text says something, then that's what it means, pure and simple. In reality, the Torah may be pure, but it certainly isn't simple.

The ten quotes in this chapter are among the most misunderstood in the Five Books of Moses. By seeing how these verses have been misunderstood, you can begin to understand just how the Torah needs to be read — with caution and with the aid of highly regarded commentators whose observations have stood the test of time. Chapter 15 has more information on analyzing the Torah; Chapter 16 introduces you to well-known Torah commentators.

"And God Said, Let Us Make Man in Our Image, after Our Likeness"

Confusion about this Torah verse from Genesis 1:26 arises from two points:

- ✔ God is not physical, so any literal understanding of this verse is simply incorrect. God isn't a person and has no physicality.
- ✔ The verse says, "Let us" but doesn't say who the "us" refers to.

Many Torah commentators have explained that the one way in which humans are made in God's image is through the human power of free will, the power to create and destroy. Every other creature, large and small, is part of the stage on which the one actor with freedom — humans — act. Humans weren't created to look like God (Who has no physical appearance); rather, free will is how they're made in God's image.

The Oral Torah (see Chapter 3) addresses why the verse says "Let us make man. . . ." When Moses wrote the Torah as dictated by God, Moses said to God, "Why are you giving people an opportunity, with Your use of the plural 'us,' to claim that there is more than one God?" God responded to Moses by saying, "Keep writing. Whoever wishes to make that mistake will make it. Those who want to make the effort will come to understand that it is with the ministering angels that God has consulted."

The Jewish sages teach that this response by God contained two lessons:

- ✔ When considering a major project, it's wise to consult with others.
- ✔ There will always be people who want to distort the text. People who want to understand the Torah will pursue it and will understand it, whereas those who want to distort the Torah will always be able to find a way if that's what they truly want to do.

Another explanation of this quote is connected with the idea that humans are a microcosm of the universe. The Oral Torah teaches that each person is a whole world. When God created humans, He brought together aspects of everything, so each person contains an aspect of every element in the universe.

"Am I My Brother's Keeper?"

Many people think that the answer to the question, "Am I my brother's keeper?" is "no." I once heard someone say, "Leave me alone. I don't want to get involved. Am I my brother's keeper?" If fact, the Torah says that the opposite is true.

The first murder in human history is recorded in the first book of the Torah, the book of Genesis. In Genesis 4:9, the Torah records that Adam and Eve had a number of children, Cain and Abel being the first two. Cain murdered Abel, and the Torah says that God asked, "Where is your brother Abel?"

Cain responded to the question by asking, "Am I my brother's keeper?," which in Hebrew is, "Ha shomer achi anokhi?" Cain chose a strange word for "I": **anokhi** (ah-no-*khee*). The great Torah sages explain that the word "anokhi" is the same word for "I" that God used to refer to Himself at the beginning of the Ten Commandments. In other words, Cain was really saying, "Isn't God Abel's keeper?"

God asked about Abel's whereabouts in order to give Cain an opportunity to confess, and Cain failed to do so. Jewish tradition is emphatic about the answer to the question: Am I my brother's keeper? Am I responsible for other Jews, all of whom are family members? The answer is simple: Yes!

"Two by Two They Came to Noah into the Ark, Male and Female"

It's a commonly held belief that Noah built an ark and gathered two of each animal onto it. But the Torah doesn't say as much. The Torah says that Noah first gathered two of each animal, one male and one female. But Noah also gathered seven pairs of "clean" animals — that is, animals that were permissible to be offered as a sacrifice on the holy altar. As the Torah says, "You shall take with you of every clean animal by sevens, a male and his female; and of the animals that are not clean two, a male and his female" (Genesis 7:2). The unclean animals came two by two into the ark in Genesis 7:9.

"God Is a Man of War"

One of the great myths and distortions regarding the Torah is the idea that the God of the Torah is a vengeful God, whereas the God of the New Testament is a God of love. Quotes like "God is a man of war," from Exodus 15:3, seem to reinforce this profoundly incorrect idea.

A fundamental idea within Jewish thought is that there's no hierarchy of emotions. All emotions, like love, hate, pride, generosity, and so on, are on the same level and are considered good or bad not by what they are but rather by how they're used. Emotions are like medicine in that timing and dosage are all that keep a medication from being a poison.

According to the tradition of the Torah, sometimes love is exactly what a situation calls for, but at other times, love is absolutely inappropriate. Similarly, sometimes hate is wrong, and sometimes hate is just what's needed.

The idea that everything God does is for the best, even when you can't see it, is a basic point of Jewish theology. God as a "man" of war isn't a bad thing because God knows what every situation calls for and provides just what's necessary.

"An Eye for Eye, a Tooth for Tooth . . ."

The full verse from Exodus 21:24–25 is

> *An eye for eye, a tooth for tooth, a hand for hand, a foot for foot, a burn for burn, a wound for wound, a bruise for a bruise.*

This verse from the Torah is possibly the most misquoted and misunderstood verse in the entire Five Books of Moses, and it's the best example I know of how you simply can't understand the Torah without a commentary. Jewish justice *never* takes this verse literally, and no Jewish court in the long history of the Jewish people ever made a ruling based on a literal grasp of this verse.

According to the Oral Torah, this verse actually means that monetary compensation is required for damages. Of course a person must also confess and express regret to God, but the way to be compensated by someone who injures you is not to injure them. Rather, you take the case to court, and if the court agrees, the person who did the damage must pay you as compensation.

"You Shall Not Lie with a Man as with a Woman: It Is an Abomination"

This verse from the Torah (Leviticus 18:22) is a controversial one and is cited as proof that homosexuality is forbidden according to Jewish law. Of course, two men can love one another, touch one another, embrace, kiss, hold hands, and express verbal affection without being homosexual.

Although many commentators use this verse to condemn homosexuality, some commentators point out that the verse is a specific reference to anal intercourse. According to the sages, the bias against homosexuality is based on the fact that two males can't participate in the sacred act of creating life. My Torah teachers have taught me to avoid transgressions but not to hate those who transgress.

"You Shall Love Your Neighbor as Yourself"

The Talmudic sage Rabbi Akiva went from being an ignorant and illiterate shepherd to becoming one of the greatest teachers and visionaries of Jewish history. Rabbi Akiva said that this verse in Leviticus 19:18 was the essence of the Torah. This quote is often attributed to Jesus of Nazareth, but its appearance in the Torah means that it pre-dates Jesus. Of course, Jesus was a Jew and was presumably quite familiar with the verse and therefore knew its importance among the great Torah sages.

The famous Golden Rule, which states "Do unto others as you would have others do unto you," is a twist on a well-known statement that predates Jesus. An early Jewish sage called Hillel (born 70 BCE) said, "What is hateful to you, do not do to your neighbor. This is the essence of the Torah. The rest is commentary."

The New Testament in general and Jesus in particular quote from the Torah dozens of times. Over the centuries, many people have gotten the impression that these verses are exclusively from Christian scriptures and are unaware of the fact that they're actually from the Torah.

"For the Lord Thy God Is a Jealous God"

In the Torah, God often is given human attributes, both physical and emotional. For example, the Torah says that God stretched out His arm, that His eye looked at the world, and that He was jealous. Of course none of these references should be taken literally. God has no physical form, nor does God have an emotional life that's in any way similar to humans'.

A basic principle of Torah study found in the Oral Torah says, "The Torah speaks in the language of man." In other words, no number of words, no eloquent vocabulary, and no human effort can possibly grasp God or describe God. As one of my teachers points out, if you think you grasp God, then one thing is true: You are wrong.

When the Torah uses "human" words like "jealous" in this verse from Deuteronomy 6:15, it's trying to express something in human terms because there's simply no better way. As I say many times in this book, the person who reads the Torah and just takes it literally is doing it wrong!

"For You Are a People Holy to the Lord Your God . . ."

The full verse from Deuteronomy 7:6 is

> *For you are a people holy to the Lord your God; the Lord your God has chosen you to be for Him a treasured people above all the peoples that are on the face of the earth.*

One of the most misunderstood ideas in all Jewish history has to do with the "chosen people." This notion has absolutely nothing to do with superiority. Nothing!

Jewish writings explain the label "chosen people" as follows: God selected the Children of Israel to take on an extra burden of observing the 613 commandments and relating to the world as a priesthood. Think of the chosen people like this: You have several children and select one of them to do a lot more work and to accept more responsibilitiy than the others — not because that one child is better or a favorite but because of some other reasons that only you know.

With so many added responsibilities, the possibility for failure is much greater, and the Jewish people have often largely failed at the assignment. Only when Jews are permitted and able to accept their assignment and succeed will God's plan for the world come to pass. It's as though the Jewish people are one vital organ in the body of the peoples of the world; if that one organ is unable to perform its function in a healthy way, the rest of the body also suffers.

"You Must Not Make Your Brother Pay Interest . . ."

The full verse from Deuteronomy 23:20–21 is

> *You must not make your brother pay interest, interest on money, interest on food, interest on anything on which one may claim interest. You may make a foreigner [Gentile] pay interest but your brother [fellow Jew] you must not make pay interest.*

I have heard it said many times that the Torah forbids lending money and charging interest. But a careful reading of both verses indicates that not charging interest only pertains to people within the Jewish family. While this may seem offensive and prejudicial at first glance, a full understanding of the Torah as a document for the Jewish people helps to clarify the situation.

As I point out many times in this book, the Jewish people aren't a religion or a race. The Jewish people are a family. As the Torah explains, this family, all of whom descend from Abraham, began as 70 people who went to Egypt and ultimately grew into a nation of millions.

Certainly each person relates to family members differently than he or she does to strangers. For example, I'm much more apt to lend money without interest to my cousin than to someone I don't know. Of course, I can choose whether to lend money without interest to a non–family member, but the Torah says that when it comes to family members I have no choice. Families must support one another. The highest form of charity in Jewish tradition is lending money to help someone to be able to help himself.

Part VI
Appendixes

"Okay, but this remains between the three of us — right?"

In this part . . .

Still can't get enough of the Torah? Appendix A provides you with a basic Torah vocabulary of essential terms and concepts that every student of the Torah needs to know. Appendixes B and C contain lists of the 613 commandments in the Torah: the 248 positive commandments (things to do) and the 365 negative commandments (things not to do).

Appendix A

A Glossary of Torah Terms and Names

*I*n this book, I define each Hebrew or foreign term the first time I introduce it. Because it isn't practical to define every Hebrew term each time it's used, I've selected the most important concepts, terms, and people for this glossary to help you as you read *The Torah For Dummies*.

Aaron: Older brother of Moses; the first High Priest

Abraham: First of the three Patriarchs of Judaism

Abraham Ibn Ezra: A 12th-century master commentator on the Torah

Aggadah: Homiletic, non-legal parts of the Oral Torah

Akiva: One of the greatest rabbis in the Talmud

Aliyah: The honor of reading or reciting a blessing over the Torah during the synagogue service; literally "going up"

Aron HaKodesh: The cabinet where Torah scrolls are kept in the synagogue sanctuary; literally "holy closet"

Asseret HaDibrot: Hebrew term for the Ten Commandments; literally "ten utterances"

Bamidbar: Hebrew name for the book of Numbers; literally "in the wilderness"

Bat Kol: A heavenly voice

Berakhah: A blessing

Bereshit: Hebrew name for the book of Genesis; literally "In the beginning"

Bikkur cholim: Visiting the sick

Bimah: The lectern on which the Torah scrolls are placed when they're being read aloud in the synagogue

Birkat HaMazon: Grace after meals; literally "blessing of the food"

Bitachon: Trust in God

Brit: Covenant

Brit Milah: The ritual circumcision of a male Jewish infant or of a male convert to Judaism; literally "covenant of circumcision"

Caro, Rabbi Joseph: Kabbalist and author/compiler of the *Shulchan Arukh,* the code of Jewish law

Chassidism: Contemporary Jewish spiritual revival movement that began in the early 1700s

Chazzan: Cantor; the person who leads a congregation in prayer

Children of Israel: The Jewish people; descendants of the Patriarch Jacob, who was also known as Israel

Chukim: Laws in the Torah whose reasons are hidden and not given explicitly in the text

Chumash: The Five Books of Moses; literally "five"

Devarim: Hebrew name for the book of Deuteronomy; literally "the words"

D'rash: Homiletic interpretation of something in the Torah

D'var Torah: A (usually) brief lesson or sermon; literally "words of Torah"

D'veykut: Clinging or attachment to God

Eidot: A Torah law that commemorates an event; literally "testimonials"

Emunah: Faith in God

Esau: Son of Isaac; older twin brother of Jacob

Etz chayyim: The wooden poles of a Torah scroll

Gabbai: The person who performs various duties in the synagogue and particularly in connection with the Torah service.

Gemara: Part of the Oral Torah, structured as commentaries on the Mishnah; the Mishnah and Gemara together are the Talmud

Gematria: A system for finding meanings based on the numerical value of letters and words

Gemilut chasadim: Acts of lovingkindness

Hachnasat orchim: Welcoming guests into your home

Hagbahah: The honor of lifting the Torah for all to see during the weekly Torah synagogue service

Halachah: Jewish law; the body of practices that Jews are bound to follow, including biblical commandments, commandments instituted by the rabbis, and binding customs; literally "the path that one walks"

HaShem: Informally used in place of one of the sacred names of God; literally "the name"

Hashgachah Pratit: Divine providence over all the details of life

Hebrew: The language of the Torah

Isaac: Son of Abraham; one of the three Patriarchs of Judaism

Ishmael: Firstborn son of Abraham by Sarah's Egyptian maidservant, Hagar; according to both Muslim and Jewish tradition, he's the ancestor of the Arab people

Israel: The name given to Jacob; also the land that God promised to Abraham and his descendants

Jacob: Son of Isaac; one of the three Patriarchs of Judaism

Joseph: Son of Jacob; sold into slavery by his jealous brothers and became powerful in Egypt, paving the way for his family's settlement there

Judah HaNasi: Compiler of the Mishnah

Kabbalah: The theology of the Jewish people, as found in books like the Zohar and Chasidic writings and teachings

Kashrut: Kosher; Jewish dietary laws; from a root meaning "correct"

Kavanah: Inner intention during prayer and the performance of divine commandments

Keter Torah: A very fancy crown, often made of silver or even gold, on top of a fully dressed Torah scroll

Kibbud Av v'Em: One of the Ten Commandments; literally "honor your father and mother"

Kodosh hakodashim: The most sacred place in the Holy Temple; literally "Holy of Holies"

Kohen: Priest; a descendant of Aaron, charged with performing various rites in the Temple; the plural form is "Kohanim"

Korban: A sacrifice or offering; from a root meaning "to draw near"

Kovod: Honor

Lashon hara: Sins committed by speech, such as defamation; literally "the evil tongue"

Leah: Wife of Jacob and mother of six of his sons; the sister of Rachel; one of the Matriarchs of Judaism

Levites: Descendants of Levi; performed various functions in the Mishkan and Holy Temple

Ma'ariv: Evening prayer service

Ma'asim tovim: The general term for good actions and attitudes

Maimonides: Rabbi Moshe ben Maimon, one of the greatest Jewish scholars in history; commonly referred to by the acronym "Rambam"

Matriarchs: Sarah, Rebecca, Rachel, and Leah; the four foremothers of Judaism

Matzah: Unleavened bread traditionally served during Passover; the plural form is "matzot"

M'eel: A cylindrical mantle or robe constructed out of fabric used to dress a Torah scroll

Melachah: Work prohibited on Shabbat and certain holidays; literally "work"

Menorah: A candelabrum; usually refers to the seven-branched candelabrum used in the Holy Temple

Mezuzah: A case containing a scroll with passages of scripture written on it that's attached to the doorposts of Jewish homes; literally "doorpost"

Middot: Character traits; literally "measures"

Midrash: Stories elaborating on episodes in the Torah that derive a principle of Jewish law or provide a moral lesson; from the Hebrew root meaning "to seek out" or "to investigate"

Mikvah: A ritual bath

Minchah: Afternoon prayer services

Minyan: The quorum necessary to recite certain prayers; traditionally consisting of ten adult Jewish men

Miriam: A prophetess who was the older sister of Moses and Aaron

Mishkan: The Tabernacle; the moveable focal point of worship and sacrifices in the desert

Mishnah: The written compilation of the Oral Torah; forms the basis of the Talmud

Mishneh Torah: A code of Jewish law written by Maimonides

Mishpatim: Ethical commandments in the Torah for which reasons are known; see *Chukim*

Mitzvah: Any of the commandments that Jews are obligated to observe; can also refer to any Jewish religious obligation and generally to any good deed; literally "commandment"; the plural form is "mitzvot"

Moses: The greatest of all the prophets and liberator of the Children of Israel from Egypt; the Hebrew form is Moshe

Nachmanides: Rabbi Moshe ben Nachman; one of the greatest medieval Jewish scholars; commonly referred to by the acronym "Ramban"

Neder: A sacred vow

Noahide Laws: Seven commandments given to Noah after the Flood that are universally binding on all people

Oral Torah: Jewish teachings mainly explaining and elaborating on the Written Torah that were handed down orally until the second century CE, when they were written down and ultimately became the Talmud

Parasha: A weekly Torah portion read in the synagogue

Pardes: The garden of Torah study and interpretation

Pasul: Unacceptable or not kosher

Patriarchs: Abraham, Isaac, and Jacob, the forefathers of Judaism

Pesach: One of the three Jewish pilgrimage festivals; a holiday commemorating the Exodus from Egypt; known in English as Passover

Promised Land: The land of Israel, which God promised to Abraham and his descendants

P'shat: The literal meaning of the Torah text

Rabbi: A person authorized to make decisions on issues of Jewish law; literally "my teacher"

Rachel: Favorite wife of Jacob; one of the Matriarchs of Judaism

Ramban: Rabbi Moshe ben Nachman; one of the greatest Torah scholars in history; also known as Nachmanides

Rashi: Rabbi Shlomo Yitzchaki; one of the greatest Jewish scholars in history, best known for his commentaries on the Torah and Talmud

Rebecca: Wife of Isaac and mother of Jacob and Esau; one of the Matriarchs of Judaism

Remez: Interpreting the Torah text by what the words imply; literally "hint"

Rimmonim: Ornamental items frequently hung over the wooden poles of a fully dressed Torah scroll, shaped like pomegranates with bells attached and usually made of silver or some other precious metal

Rosh Chodesh: The first day of a month on which the first sliver of the new moon appears; literally "head of the month"

Rosh Hashanah: The new year for the purpose of counting years; literally "head of the year"

Sacrifice: A practice of symbolic offerings that hasn't been done since the Holy Temple was destroyed

Sages: The greatest Jewish teachers in history, in particular from the rabbinic period

Sarah: Wife of Abraham and mother of Isaac; one of the Matriarchs of Judaism

Seder: The family home ritual celebrating the holiday of Passover; literally "order"

Semikhah: A rabbinical degree that authorizes a person to answer questions and resolve disputes regarding Jewish law

Shabbat: The Sabbath; the day of rest

Shacharit: Morning prayer services

Shavuot: One of the three Jewish pilgrimage festivals; commemorates the giving of the Torah; literally "weeks"

Shechinah: The indwelling Divine Presence as experienced in the world

Shema: A central Jewish prayer recited three times during each day: morning, evening, and just before going to sleep

Shemot: Hebrew name for the book of Exodus; literally "the names"

Shulchan Arukh: The code of Jewish law written by Rabbi Joseph Caro in the 16th century; literally "the prepared table"

Simchat Torah: The holiday celebrating the Torah and marking the end and beginning of the annual cycle of weekly Torah readings; literally "rejoicing in the law"

Sod: The hidden, Kabbalistic interpretation of the Torah; literally "secret"

Sofer: A trained Torah scribe

Sukkah: The temporary dwellings built during the holiday of Sukkot; literally "booth"

Sukkot: One of the three Jewish pilgrimage festivals; commemorates the wandering in the desert by the Children of Israel; literally "booths"

Synagogue: Widely accepted term for a Jewish house of worship; from a Greek root meaning "assembly"

Tallit: Prayer shawl worn during morning services

Talmud: The most significant collection of teachings from the Oral Torah

Tanakh: The Hebrew Scriptures; often inappropriately called the Old Testament; acronym of Torah (Law), Nevi'im (Prophets), and Ketuvim (Writings)

Taryag Mitzvot: The 613 commandments in the Written Torah

Tas: A decorative breastplate that hangs from the poles of a fully dressed Torah, usually made of silver and decorated with intricate carvings

Tefillin: Phylacteries; leather pouches containing scrolls with passages from the Torah that are used to fulfill the Torah commandment to bind the commandments to your hands and between your eyes

Temple: The central place of worship in ancient Jerusalem where sacrifices were offered; the first Temple was destroyed in 586 BCE; the second Temple was destroyed in 70 CE

Tetragrammaton: The most sacred name for God, consisting of four letters; never pronounced except when the Holy Temple stood and then once a year, on Yom Kippur, when the High Priest spoke this name of God in the Holy of Holies

Torah: In its narrowest sense, the first five books of the Jewish Holy Scriptures; in its broadest sense, the entire body of Jewish teachings; sometimes called the Pentateuch

Tzedakah: Generally refers to charity; literally "righteousness"

Tzitzit: Fringes attached to the corners of some garments as a reminder of the commandments

Vayikra: Hebrew name for the book of Leviticus; literally "and He called"

Wimpel: A band of cloth that holds together a tightly wrapped Torah scroll when it's fully dressed

Yad: The hand-shaped pointer used while reading from Torah scrolls; literally "hand"

Yom Kippur: A day set aside for fasting, depriving oneself of pleasures, and repenting from the sins of the previous year; literally "day of atonement"

Zohar: A mystical commentary on the Torah; the most important Kabbalistic work in Judaism

Appendix B

The 248 Positive Commandments in the Torah

• •

*T*he Oral Torah teaches that the Five Books of Moses contain 613 commandments; that number consists of 248 positive commandments and 365 negative commandments. In other words, the list in this appendix summarizes the actions that the Torah *wants* you to do, and in Appendix C, you can find those things the Torah wants to make sure you *don't* do.

There are several things you need to know about these two lists:

- ✔ Various Torah sages throughout history have disagreed as to precisely what these 613 commandments are. There's no definitive list. My list generally follows the list of Rabbi Moses ben Maimon, known as Maimonides.

- ✔ Judaism 101 (www.jewfaq.org), a wonderful Web site maintained by scholar and law librarian Tracey R. Rich, provides an extremely useful and educational way of breaking down the commandments into general topics. I've based my list on this terrific way of organizing the Torah's commandments.

- ✔ I don't quote the Torah word for word in these appendixes; rather, I paraphrase the verses in the interest of space.

- ✔ You may notice that the Torah verses in my lists often aren't in chapter and verse order. Instead, the order of the commandments in these lists flows from topic to topic in the way that I think makes the most sense. Even though the verses sometimes seem to be out of order, the fact is that the Torah doesn't present the commandments in any apparent order (nor are events recorded in the Torah in chronological order).

- ✔ If you were to look at the actual verses, you may wonder why they don't seem to always *say* what I've indicated. This is because I provide you with the interpretations of these verses by the great Torah sages throughout history — not necessarily the literal meaning.

Relating to God

1. Know that God exists. Exodus 20:2

2. Enhance the reputation of God's name and God's Torah. Leviticus 22:32

3. Know that God is One, a complete Unity. Deuteronomy 6:4

4. Love God. Deuteronomy 6:5

5. Revere God because God is as awesome as it gets. Deuteronomy 6:13

6. Strive to imitate God's good and upright ways. Deuteronomy 28:9

The Torah

7. Appreciate, acknowledge, and honor the old and the wise. Leviticus 19:32

8. Learn the Torah and teach it. (Reading this book is a great start!) Deuteronomy 6:7

9. Connect with scholars and Jewish teachers, and stay close to them. Deuteronomy 10:20

10. Write a Torah scroll for yourself (and yes, penmanship counts!). Deuteronomy 31:19

The Symbols and Signs of Judaism

11. Circumcise newborn males — but be very, very careful! Genesis 17:12

12. Put tzitzit (fringes) on the corners of your clothing. Numbers 15:38

13. Put tefillin on your head. Deuteronomy 6:8

14. Wrap tefillin around your arm. Deuteronomy 6:8

15. Affix a mezuzah to the doorposts and gates of your house. Deuteronomy 6:9

Prayers

16. Worship God with prayer. Exodus 23:25 and Deuteronomy 6:13

17. Say the Shema affirmation of God's unity in the morning and at night. Deuteronomy 6:7

18. Thank God for your food (even in less than adequate restaurants). Deuteronomy 8:10

Love and Human Relations

19. Love your fellow and sister Jews. Leviticus 19:18

20. Rebuke the sinner, but don't be self-righteous about it. Leviticus 19:17

21. If you see your neighbor carrying something, help him with his load. Exodus 23:5

22. If the load falls off your neighbor's beast, help raise it. Deuteronomy 22:4

The Poor and Unfortunate

23. Leave an unreaped corner of your field or orchard for the poor. Leviticus 19:9

24. Leave leftover crops that have not been gathered for the poor. Leviticus 19:9

25. Leave the imperfect clusters for the poor. Leviticus 19:10

26. Leave the single grapes of your vineyard for — you guessed it — the poor. Leviticus 19:10

27. If you have forgotten any bundles of the harvest you've reaped, don't go back and get them. Instead, leave them for the poor. Deuteronomy 24:19–20

28. Give charity according to your means. Deuteronomy 15: 11

The Treatment of Non–Family Members

29. Love the stranger. Deuteronomy 10:19

30. During the sabbatical year, you may collect on the debt of people outside the family. Deuteronomy 15:3

31. It's okay to lend with interest to non–family members. Deuteronomy 23:21

Marriage, Divorce, and Family

32. Honor your father and mother (and give them a call more often). Exodus 20:12

33. Treat your father and mother with respect and reverence. Leviticus 19:3

34. Go make babies. (It will make your parents happy.) Genesis 1:28

35. There's a holy way to establish a permanent relationship with a person of the opposite sex — the sacrament of marriage. Deuteronomy 24:1

36. A newly married man shall be free for one year to rejoice with his wife. (His employer's view may vary.) Deuteronomy 24:5

37. There's a special way to deal with any woman suspected of adultery, and it's in Numbers 5:30.

38. One who falsely accuses his wife of being unchaste before marriage must live with her all his lifetime. (See where your paranoia gets you!) Deuteronomy 22:19

39. Jewish divorce requires a formal written document. Deuteronomy 24:1

40. If you're a man and your married brother dies and his widow is childless, you must marry her (unless properly released from this obligation). Deuteronomy 25:5

41. The widow must formally release her brother-in-law if he refuses to marry her. Deuteronomy 25:7–9

Holy Days, Times, and Seasons

42. The beginning of each month on the lunar calendar is especially holy, and the months and years shall be calculated solely by the Supreme Court. Exodus 12:2

43. Make the Sabbath holy. Exodus 20:7–8

44. Rest on the Sabbath. (What, six days of work each week isn't enough for you?) Exodus 23:12 and Exodus 34:21

45. Celebrate the "Big Three Festivals" (Passover, Shavuot, and Sukkot). Exodus 23:14

46. Rejoice on the festivals. Deuteronomy 16:14

47. Go to the Holy Temple on the festivals. Deuteronomy 16:16

48. Make your home free of leavened products before Passover. Exodus 12:15

49. Rest on the first day of Passover. Exodus 12:16

50. Rest on the seventh day of Passover. Exodus 12:16

51. Eat lots of matzah on the first night of Passover. Exodus 12:18

52. Discuss the Exodus on the first night of Passover. Exodus 13:8

53. Count the 49 days from the time of the cutting of the Omer (first sheaves of the barley harvest). Start counting on the second night of Passover. Leviticus 23:15

54. Rest on Shavuot. It is, for you, another special Jewish holiday. Leviticus 23:21

55. Rest on Rosh Hashanah. Leviticus 23:24

56. Listen to the sound of the shofar (ram's horn) on Rosh Hashanah. Numbers 29:1

57. Fast on Yom Kippur. Leviticus 23:27

58. Rest on Yom Kippur. Leviticus 23:32

59. Rest on the first day of Sukkot. Leviticus 23:35

60. Rest on the eighth day of Sukkot (Shemini Atzeret). Leviticus 23:36

61. Shake the four species (palm branch, etrog fruit, myrtle, and willow) in six directions during Sukkot. Leviticus 23:40

62. Dwell in booths for seven days during Sukkot. Leviticus 23:42

Dietary Laws

63. Examine animals carefully so that you don't eat the ones the Torah forbids. Leviticus 11:3

64. Examine fish carefully so that you don't eat the ones the Torah forbids. Leviticus 11:9

65. Examine birds carefully so that you don't eat the ones the Torah forbids. Deuteronomy 14:11

66. Examine insects carefully so that you don't eat the ones the Torah forbids. Leviticus 11:21

67. Slaughter cattle, deer, and fowl as tradition details. Deuteronomy 12:21

68. If you take a bird's nest, set the mother-bird free. Deuteronomy 22:6–7

69. Cover the blood of undomesticated animals and fowl that have been killed. Leviticus 17:13

Business Practices

70. Lend to a poor person. Exodus 22:24

71. Make sure to return a security deposit to its owner. Deuteronomy 24:13

72. Make sure your scales and weights are accurate. Leviticus 19:36

The Treatment of Employees, Servants, and Slaves

73. Let your hired help eat from the produce they reap. (Free coffee also wouldn't be such a bad idea.) Deuteronomy 23:25–26

74. Pay wages to your workers when they're due. Deuteronomy 24:15

75. Deal with the Hebrew bondsman in accordance with the laws pertaining to him. Exodus 21:2–6

76. Give generous gifts to Jewish servants at the end of their terms of service. Deuteronomy 15:14

77. If a man doesn't want to marry his maidservant, she should be released from working for him. Exodus 21:8

78. If a man wants to marry his Jewish maidservant, he can marry her. Exodus 21:8–9

79. You may keep your Canaanite slaves permanently, but you must treat them well. Leviticus 25:46

Promises, Vows, and Oaths

80. Keep your word. Deuteronomy 23:24

81. Adhere to the special rules about how vows may be annulled. Numbers 30:4–17

82. Swear truly by God's name. Deuteronomy 10:20

The Sabbatical and Jubilee Years

83. Let the land lie fallow in the Sabbatical year. (Let's hear it for Torah ecology!) Exodus 23:11

84. Perform no tree work in the Sabbatical year. Exodus 23:11 and Leviticus 25:2

85. Sound the shofar (ram's horn) to proclaim the Sabbatical year. Leviticus 25:9

86. Release creditors from their debts in the Sabbatical year. Deuteronomy 15:2

87. Gather all the people to hear the Torah read aloud at the close of the seventh year. Deuteronomy 31:12

88. Calculate the years of the Jubilee by years and by cycles of seven years. Leviticus 25:8

89. Keep the Jubilee year holy by resting and letting the land rest. (That is, give yourself and the planet a break.) Leviticus 25:10

90. Grant redemption to the land in the Jubilee year. Leviticus 25:24

The Courts and Court Procedures

91. Make sure that every community has judges and officers. (It's the law to have a legal system.) Deuteronomy 16:18

92. Adjudicate cases of purchase and sale. (It beats less-civilized remedies.) Leviticus 25:14

93. Judge cases of liability of a paid custodian under whose watch the guarded property was damaged. Exodus 22:9

94. Judge cases of loss for which borrowed property was damaged. Exodus 22:13–14

95. Judge cases of inheritance. Numbers 27:8–11

96. Judge cases of damage caused by leaving a pit uncovered. Exodus 21:33–34

97. Judge cases of injuries caused by beasts. Exodus 21:35–36

98. Judge cases of damage caused by trespassing of cattle. (Forgiving cattle their trespasses isn't a Jewish concept.) Exodus 22:4

99. Judge cases of fire-related damage. Exodus 22:5

100. Judge cases of damage caused by giving something to someone to safe-guard and then having that property damaged or lost. Exodus 22:6–7

101. Judge other cases between a plaintiff and a defendant. Ex.22:8

102. If you have evidence that's relevant to any case, you should testify. Leviticus 5:1

103. Examine witnesses. Deuteronomy 13:15

104. Decide cases according to the majority of the judges when there's a difference of opinion. Exodus 23:2

105. Treat both parties in litigation with equal impartiality. Leviticus 19:15

106. Accept the decisions of every Jewish Supreme Court. Deuteronomy 17:11

Injuries and Damages

107. Make a parapet (low railing or wall) for your roof. (Who knows what can happen?) Deuteronomy 22:8

108. If someone is attacking another person with deadly intent, anyone witnessing this must maim or kill the assailant to save the victim. Deuteronomy 25:12

Property and Related Rights

109. Any houses sold within a walled city may be redeemed within a year. Leviticus 25:29

110. If you steal something, give it back. Leviticus 5:23

111. Return lost property. Deuteronomy 22:1

Punishment and Restitution

112. The Court has the power to sentence someone to death by decapitation with the sword. Exodus 21:20 and Leviticus 26:25

113. The Court has the power to sentence someone to death by strangulation. Leviticus 20:10

114. The Court has the power to sentence someone to death by burning with fire. Leviticus 20:14

115. The Court has the power to sentence someone to death by stoning. Deuteronomy 22:24

116. The Court has the power to hang the dead body of someone who has incurred that penalty. Deuteronomy 21:22

117. Bury executed criminals on the day of their execution. Deuteronomy 21:23

118. Exile anyone who commits an accidental homicide. Numbers 35:25

119. Establish six cities of refuge for those who commit accidental homicide. Deuteronomy 19:3

120. Decapitate a heifer in the manner prescribed in order to expiate a murder on the road for which the perpetrator is unknown. Deuteronomy 21:4

121. Make a thief or kidnapper pay compensation — or, in certain cases, pay with his life. Exodus 21:16, Exodus 21:37, and Exodus 22:1

122. Pay monetary compensation for any bodily injury you inflict. Exodus 21:18–19

123. A man who seduces an unbetrothed virgin shall be fined 50 shekels. Exodus 22:15–16

124. A man who has sex with an unbetrothed virgin can be forced to marry her. Deuteronomy 22:28–29

125. Chastise the wicked by whipping or beating them. Deuteronomy 25:2

126. Do to false witnesses as they had plotted to do to the accused. Deuteronomy 19:19

Prophecy

127. Heed the call of every true prophet in each generation, provided that he doesn't change the Torah. Deuteronomy 18:15

Idolatry

128. Destroy idolatry and its accessories. Deuteronomy 12:2–3

129. Kill the inhabitants of a city that has become idolatrous, and burn that city. Deuteronomy 13:16–17

Agriculture

130. The fourth-year fruit of a tree shall be sacred and eaten in Jerusalem. Leviticus 19:24

The Firstborn

131. Pay the priesthood a symbolic amount when a firstborn boy is born. Numbers 18:15

132. Pay the priesthood a symbolic amount for the firstborn offspring of an ass (the animal, not someone you think is a jerk). Exodus 13:13 and Exodus 34:20

133. Break the neck of an ass's firstborn if the ass is not redeemed. Exodus 13:13 and Exodus 34:20

The Priesthood and Holy Temple Workers

134. All kohanim (priests) must wear the priestly vestments for the service. Exodus 28:2

135. Priests are allowed to become ritually impure by attending the burial of their deceased relatives. Leviticus 21:1–3 and Exodus 28:2

136. Show the proper honor to a priest by giving him precedence in all things that are holy. Leviticus 21:8

137. The High Priest must marry a virgin. Leviticus 21:13

138. Send unclean people out of the Sanctuary. Numbers 5:2

139. The priests should bless Israel. Numbers 6:23

140. Reserve a portion of the dough for the priests. Numbers 15:20

141. Levites shall serve in the Sanctuary. Numbers 18:23

142. Give the Levites cities to dwell in. These should also be used as cities of refuge. Numbers 35:2

143. Levites should serve in the Sanctuary in different teams, but on festivals, all priests should serve together. Deuteronomy 18:6–8

Tithes and Taxes

144. Give half a shekel every year to help maintain the Sanctuary. Exodus 30:13

145. Set aside the tithe of the produce for the Levites. Leviticus 27:30 and Numbers 18:24

146. Make sure to tithe your cattle. Leviticus 27:32

147. Levites must reserve one-tenth of the tithes and give it to the priests. Numbers 18:26

148. The second tithe must be set aside in the first, second, fourth, and fifth years of the sabbatical cycle to be eaten by its owner in Jerusalem. Deuteronomy 14:22

149. Set aside the second tithe in the third and sixth year of the sabbatical cycle for the poor. Deuteronomy 14:28–29

150. Give priests their due portions of the carcasses of cattle. Deuteronomy 18:3

151. Give priests the first of the fleece. Deuteronomy 18:4

152. Set aside the great heave-offering (a small portion of the grain, wine, and oil) for the priests. Deuteronomy 18:4

153. Make the prescribed declaration when you bring the second tithe to the Sanctuary. Deuteronomy 26:13 and Numbers 18:11

The Temple, the Sanctuary, and Sacred Objects

154. Build the Sanctuary. Exodus 25:8

155. Set out the showbread and the frankincense every Shabbat. Exodus 25:30

156. Kindle the lights in the Sanctuary. Exodus 27:21

157. Offer up incense twice each day. Exodus 30:7

158. Priests must wash their hands and feet at the time of service. Exodus 30:19

159. Prepare the oil of anointment as instructed, and use it to anoint High Priests and kings. Exodus 30:31

160. If you use sacred things by mistake, you shall make restitution plus 20 percent. Leviticus 5:16

161. Remove the ashes from the altar. Leviticus 6:3

162. Keep the fire on the altar of the burnt-offering ever-burning. Leviticus 6:6

163. Revere the Sanctuary. Leviticus 19:30

164. Whenever the Ark is carried, it should be carried on one's shoulder. Numbers 7:9

165. Observe the second Passover. (No seder necessary.) Numbers 9:11

166. On the second Passover, you should eat the flesh of the Paschal lamb with unleavened bread and bitter herbs. Numbers 9:11

167. Sound the trumpets at the offering of sacrifices and in times of trouble. Numbers 10:9–10

168. Watch over the edifice continually. Numbers 18:1–2

169. Bring a guilt-offering if you have unintentionally committed a trespass against sacred things, or robbed, or lain carnally with a bondmaid betrothed to a man, or denied what was deposited with you and swore falsely to support your denial. Leviticus 7:1

Offerings and Sacrifices

170. Reserve the firstborn of clean cattle for a sacrifice. Exodus 13:2

171. Slay the Paschal lamb. Exodus 12:6

172. Eat the meat of the Paschal sacrifice on the night of Passover. Exodus 12:8

173. Bring your first fruits to the Sanctuary. Exodus 23:19

174. Meat from sin-offerings and guilt-offerings shall be eaten. Exodus 29:33

175. Follow the procedure of the burnt-offering. (Check your local Talmud for details.) Leviticus 1:3

176. Follow the procedure of the meal-offering. Leviticus 2:1

177. Every sacrifice should be salted. Leviticus 2:13

178. If the Court of Judgment makes a bad decision, it should offer up a sacrifice. Leviticus 4:13–14

179. If you sin in error (as regards a transgression punishable by excision), you should offer a sin-offering. Leviticus 4:27–28

180. The value of what you offer for sacrifice should be in accordance with your means. Leviticus 5:7

181. If you're in doubt as to whether you've committed a sin for which one must bring a sin-offering, bring a guilt-offering just to be safe. Leviticus 5:17–19

182. Eat the remainder of meal offerings. Leviticus 6:9

183. The High Priest should make a daily meal offering. Leviticus 6:13

184. Strictly observe the procedure of the sin-offering. Leviticus 6:18

185. Strictly observe the procedure of the guilt-offering. Leviticus 7:1

186. Strictly observe the procedure of the peace-offering. Leviticus 7:11

187. Burn any remaining meat from the holy sacrifice. Leviticus 7:17

188. Burn the meat of the holy sacrifice that has become unclean. Leviticus 7:19

189. A woman who has given birth should bring an offering. Leviticus 12:6

190. A leper should bring a sacrifice after he's cleansed. Leviticus 14:10

191. A man having a physical discharge should bring a sacrifice after he's cleansed. Leviticus 15:13–15

192. A woman with a physical discharge should bring a sacrifice after she's cleansed. Leviticus 15:28–30

193. Observe the special sacrificial service of Yom Kippur. Leviticus 16:3–34

194. Every animal offered for sacrifice shall be without blemish. Leviticus 22:21

195. Cattle must be at least 8 days old before they may be sacrificed. Leviticus 22:27

196. Offer the correct measure for a meal-offering on the second day of Passover together with one lamb. Leviticus 23:10–12

197. On Shavuot, bring loaves of bread together with the prescribed sacrifices to be offered. Leviticus 23:17–20

198. Offer an additional sacrifice on Passover. Leviticus 23:26

199. If you vow to God the monetary value of a person, you shall pay the amount prescribed in the Torah. Leviticus 27:2

200. If an animal is exchanged for one set aside to be sacrificed, both animals become sacred. Leviticus 27:10

201. If you vow to God the monetary value of an unclean beast, you shall pay its value. Leviticus 27:11–13

202. If you vow the value of your house, you shall pay according to the priest's appraisal. Leviticus 27:14–15

203. If you sanctify a portion of your field, you shall pay according to the estimation as delineated in the Torah. Leviticus 27:16

204. Decide which dedicated property is sacred to the Lord and which belongs to the Priest. Leviticus 27:28

205. Confess your sins before God when bringing a sacrifice as well as at other times. Numbers 5:6–7

206. Offer up the regular sacrifices daily. (Take two lambs and call God in the morning.) Numbers 28:3

207. Offer up an additional sacrifice on Shabbat (two lambs, of course). Numbers 28:9

208. Offer an extra sacrifice every New Moon. Numbers 28:11

209. Bring an additional offering on Shavuot. Numbers 28:26–27

210. . . . and on Rosh Hashanah. Numbers 29:2–6

211. . . . and on Yom Kippur. Numbers 29:7–8

212. . . . and on Sukkot. Numbers 29:12–34

213. Make an additional sacrifice on Shemini Atzeret. Numbers 29:35–38

214. Bring all offerings, whether obligatory or of free will, on the first festival after they were incurred (in other words, as soon as possible). Deuteronomy 12:5–6

215. Be sure to offer all sacrifices in the Temple. Deuteronomy 12:14

216. Pay the priesthood a symbolic amount for cattle that were set apart for sacrifices but then became blemished (and thus disqualified). By doing so, these cattle may be eaten by anyone. Deuteronomy 12:15

217. Make an effort to bring sacrifices from places outside of Israel. Deuteronomy 12:26

218. Read the prescribed Torah portion when bringing the first fruits. Deuteronomy 26:5–10

Ritual Purity and Impurity

219. Eight species of creeping things will defile you on contact. Leviticus 11:29–30

220. Food becomes defiled by contact with unclean things. Leviticus 11:34

221. If you touch the carcass of a beast that died by itself, you become ritually unclean. Leviticus 11:39

222. A woman who has just given birth is ritually unclean. Leviticus 12:2–5

223. A leper is unclean and will defile you on contact. Leviticus 13:2–46

224. You can recognize a leper by the prescribed marks. Leviticus 13:45

225. A leper's clothes are unclean and defiling. Leviticus 13:47–49

226. Ditto for a leper's house. Leviticus 14:34–46

227. A man who has had a seminal discharge (outside of intercourse) defiles. Leviticus 15:1–15

228. Semen defiles. Leviticus 15:16

229. To remedy any type of defilement, you need to immerse yourself in a mikvah. Leviticus 15:16

230. A menstruating woman is ritually unclean and defiles others. Leviticus 15:19–24

231. A woman with a flowing discharge is ritually unclean. Leviticus 15:25–27

232. Carry out the ordinance of the Red Heifer so that its ashes will always be available. Numbers 19:9

233. A corpse defiles. Numbers 19:11–16

234. The waters of separation purify one from being unclean by coming in contact with a corpse. Paradoxically, they also defile one who is already clean. Numbers 19:19–22

Lepers and Leprosy

235. Use the leprosy cleansing process as prescribed. It requires cedar wood, hyssop, scarlet thread, two birds, and running water. Leviticus 14:2–7

236. Lepers must shave their heads. Leviticus 14:9

The King

237. Appoint a king. Deuteronomy 17:15

238. The king shall write a scroll of the Torah for himself (in addition to the one that every Jew should write). Deuteronomy 17:18

Nazarites

239. Nazarites must allow their hair to grow. Numbers 6:5

240. At the completion of the Nazarite period, a man shall shave his hair and bring offerings. Numbers 6:9

Wars

241. Anoint a special priest to speak to the soldiers. (Paging Chaplain Cohen!) Deuteronomy 20:2

242. In nonobligatory wars, observe the procedure prescribed in the Torah. Deuteronomy 20:10

243. Expel the seven Canaanite nations from the land of Israel. Deuteronomy 7:1 and Deuteronomy 20:17

244. Deal appropriately with a beautiful woman taken captive in war. Deuteronomy 21:10–14

245. Designate a place outside the camp for sanitary purposes. Deuteronomy 23:13

246. Keep that place sanitary. Deuteronomy 23:14–15

247. Always remember what Amalek did to the Jewish people. Deuteronomy 25:17

248. Destroy all Amalekites. Deuteronomy 25:19

Appendix C

The 365 Negative Commandments in the Torah

● ●

*T*he Five Books of Moses contains 365 negative commandments. Each one describes a belief or an action that's forbidden. I paraphrase these commandments in this appendix. The Torah also contains 248 positive commandments, which are actions that you're supposed to take; see Appendix B for details. Appendix B also contains some noteworthy points about my presentation of the Torah's commandments.

Relating to God

1. Don't entertain the idea that there's any god but the Eternal God. Exodus 20:3

2. Don't curse God. Exodus 22:27

3. Don't be dirty, vulgar, or crude with God's name. Leviticus 22:32

4. Don't test God's word. (When God says something, God means it!) Deuteronomy 6:16

5. Don't edit or revise the Torah. (If it ain't broke, don't fix it!) Deuteronomy 13:1

6. Don't diminish or devalue any of the Torah's commandments. Deuteronomy 13:1

Prayers

7. Don't pray to stone idols or pillars. Leviticus 26:1

Love and Human Relations

8. Don't stay on the sidelines when a life is in danger. Leviticus 19:16

9. Don't hurt or damage anyone with your speech. Leviticus 25:17

10. Don't tell tales out of school — or in! Leviticus 19:16

11. Don't let resentment eat away at your heart. Leviticus 19:17

12. Don't take revenge, no matter how well-deserved you feel it may be. Leviticus 19:18

13. Don't bear a grudge. Human beings aren't that spiritually strong. Leviticus 19:18

14. Don't embarrass people. Leviticus 19:17

15. Don't curse people. Leviticus 19:14

16. Don't put obstacles in people's way that may trip them up, either physically or spiritually. Leviticus 19:14

17. If you see a beast that has fallen down beneath its burden, don't just stand there — help out. Deuteronomy 22:4

The Poor and Unfortunate

18. Don't afflict an orphan or a widow — they have it bad enough. Exodus 22:21

19. Don't reap the entire field. Leviticus 19:9

20. Don't gather gleanings (food that has fallen to the ground while being harvested). Leviticus 19:9

21. Don't gather imperfect clusters from your vineyard (and certainly not from anyone else's!) Leviticus 19:10

22. Don't gather grapes that have fallen to the ground. Leviticus 19:10

23. If you forgot a sheaf in the field, don't return to take it. Deuteronomy 24:19

24. Never refrain from helping a poor person in any way you can. Deuteronomy 15:7

The Treatment of Non–Family Members

25. Don't hurt or wrong strangers by anything you do or say. Exodus 22:20

26. Don't hurt or wrong strangers through any business transaction. Exodus 22:20

27. If you're Jewish, don't marry someone who isn't Jewish. Deuteronomy 7:3

Marriage, Divorce, and Family

28. Don't hit your father or mother. Exodus 21:15

29. No cursing them either! Exodus 21:17

30. Eunuchs shouldn't marry Jewish women. Deuteronomy 23:2

31. Bastards (children of illegitimate relationships) can't marry Jewish women. Deuteronomy 23:3

32. Ammonites or Moabites can't marry Jewish women. Deuteronomy 23:4

33. Don't exclude a descendant of Esau from the community of Israel after two generations. Deuteronomy 23:8–9

34. Ditto for Egyptians. Deuteronomy 23:8–9

35. Premarital sex for women who have never been married is prohibited. (No one said this was going to be easy.) Deuteronomy 23:18

36. A bridegroom shall be exempt for a whole year from taking part in any public labor, such as military service, guarding the wall, and similar duties. Deuteronomy 24:5

37. Don't withhold food, clothing, or conjugal rights from a wife. (Things just get ugly if you do.) Exodus 21:10

38. If a man has made public statements about his wife's unchastity before marriage, he can't divorce her. Deuteronomy 22:19

39. If you divorce your wife and she then marries someone, you can't remarry her. Deuteronomy 24:4

40. A widow whose husband died childless must not be married to anyone but her deceased husband's brother unless the man is not interested. Deuteronomy 25:5

Forbidden Sexual Relations

41. Don't be inappropriately intimate with relatives — it can lead to major trouble. Leviticus 18:6

42. Don't have sex with your mother. Leviticus 18:7

43. No sodomy with Dad. Leviticus 18:7

44. Don't mess around with Dad's wife, even if she isn't your mom. Leviticus 18:8

45. Don't even think about your sister *that way.* Leviticus 18:9

46. No fooling around with your father's wife's daughter. Leviticus 18:11

47. No fooling around with your son's daughter. Leviticus 18:10

48. . . . or your daughter's daughter. (Are you beginning to get the picture?) Leviticus 18:10

49. No sex with your daughter. Leviticus 18:6

50. Don't get physical with your father's sister. Leviticus 18:12

51. . . . or your mother's sister. Leviticus 18:13

52. . . . or your father's brother's wife. Leviticus 18:14

53. No sodomy with Dad's brother. Leviticus 18:14

54. No sex with your son's wife. Leviticus 18:15

55. No incest with your brother's wife. Leviticus 18:16

56. No incest with any of your wife's daughters. Leviticus 18:17

57. No incest with any daughter of your wife's son. Leviticus 18:17

58. . . . or the daughter of your wife's daughter. Leviticus 18:17

59. Sex with your wife's sister? Don't ask! Leviticus 18:18

60. No sex with a menstruating woman. Leviticus 18:19

61. No sex with another man's wife. Leviticus 18:20

62. No male sodomy. Leviticus 18:22

63. No sex whatsoever outside your species. Leviticus 18:23

64. And that goes for women too! Leviticus 18:23

65. No castration of men, animals, or fowl. Leviticus 22:24

Holy Days, Times, and Seasons

66. Don't travel on the Sabbath beyond the limits of your town. Exodus 16:29

67. Don't work on the Sabbath. Exodus 20:9

68. Don't work on the first day of Passover. Exodus 12:16

69. Don't work on the seventh day of Passover. Exodus 12:16

70. Don't have any chametz (leavened products) in your possession during Passover. Exodus 12:19

71. Don't eat any food mixtures containing chametz on Passover. Exodus 12:20

72. Don't eat chametz on Passover. Exodus 13:3

73. Don't even let chametz be seen in your home during Passover. Exodus 13:7

74. Don't eat chametz after midday on the fourteenth of Nissan (the day before Passover). Deuteronomy 16:3

75. Don't work on Shavuot. Leviticus 23:21

76. Don't work on Rosh Hashanah. Leviticus 23:25

77. No food or drink on Yom Kippur. Leviticus 23:29

78. Don't work on Yom Kippur. (Fasting and praying are hard enough.) Leviticus 23:31

79. Don't work on the first day of Sukkot. Leviticus 23:35

80. Don't work on the eighth day of Sukkot (Shemini Atzeret). Leviticus 23:36

Dietary Laws

81. Don't eat meat from unclean animals. Leviticus 11:4

82. Don't eat unclean fish. Leviticus 11:11

83. Don't eat unclean fowl. Leviticus 11:13

84. Don't eat any worms found in a fruit (at least not on purpose). Leviticus 11:41

85. If it creeps on the earth (like insects), don't eat it. Leviticus 11:41–42

86. Don't eat vermin. (Rats!) Leviticus 11:44

87. Don't eat things that swarm in the water. Leviticus 11:43

88. Don't eat winged insects (even though some of them may eat you). Deuteronomy 14:19

89. Don't eat meat that has been torn from an animal. Exodus 22:30

90. Don't eat meat from an animal that died of natural causes. Deuteronomy 14:21

91. Don't eat a limb torn from a living beast. Deuteronomy 12:23

92. Don't slaughter an animal and its young on the same day. (In other words, have some sensitivity for the circle of life.) Leviticus 22:28

93. Don't capture the mother-bird with her young. Deuteronomy 22:6

94. Don't eat the flesh of an ox that was sentenced to be stoned. Exodus 21:28

95. Don't boil meat with milk. Exodus 23:19

96. Don't eat meat with dairy products. (This is also known as the No Cheeseburger Law.) Exodus 23:19

97. Don't eat a certain thigh vein (not to be confused with taking the Lord's name in vain). Genesis 32:33

98. Don't eat tallow fat. (Trans fats also aren't so good for you, but that's a topic for another book.) Leviticus 7:23

99. Don't eat blood. (Vampires take note.) Leviticus 7:26

100. Don't overdo it with food or alcohol. Leviticus 19:26

Business Practices

101. Don't do anything wrong in buying or selling. Leviticus 25:14

102. Don't charge interest on loans to family members. Leviticus 25:37

103. Don't borrow money from family members if they charge interest. Deuteronomy 23:20

104. Don't be a part of any forbidden transaction with interest (as a witness, guarantor, or anything else). Exodus 22:24

105. If you know that a poor creditor can't repay his debt, don't pester him about it. Exodus 22:24

106. Don't take food preparation utensils as collateral. Deuteronomy 24:6

107. Don't exact a pledge from a debtor by force. Deuteronomy 24:10

108. Don't keep a creditor's collateral at the time he or she needs it. Deuteronomy 24:12

109. Don't take a pledge from a widow. Deuteronomy 24:17

110. Don't be fraudulent in measuring items or quantities for sale. Leviticus 19:35

111. Don't possess inaccurate measures and weights. Deuteronomy 25:13–14

The Treatment of Employees, Servants, and Slaves

112. Don't delay payment of a worker's wages. Leviticus 19:13

113. The hired help shouldn't take more than they can eat (so maybe free doughnuts aren't such a good idea). Deuteronomy 23:25

114. A hired laborer shall not eat produce that isn't being harvested. Deuteronomy 23:26

115. Don't force a Jewish servant to do the work of a slave. Leviticus 25:39

116. Don't sell a Jewish servant as a slave. Leviticus 25:42

117. Don't treat a Jewish servant harshly. Leviticus 25:43

118. Don't permit a non-Jew to treat a Jewish servant sold to him harshly. Leviticus 25:53

119. Don't send away a Jewish servant empty-handed when he's freed from service. Deuteronomy 15:13

120. Don't sell Jewish maidservants to anyone. Exodus 21:8

121. Don't surrender a slave who has fled to the land of Israel if his owner lives outside the country. Deuteronomy 23:16

122. Don't wrong such a slave. Deuteronomy 23:17

123. Don't muzzle any beast while it's working among produce that it can eat and enjoy. Deuteronomy 25:4

Promises, Vows, and Oaths

124. For crying out loud, don't swear needlessly. Exodus 20:7

125. Don't violate an oath or swear that something is true when it isn't. Leviticus 19:12

126. Don't break a vow. (If you break it, you'll pay for it!) Numbers 30:3

127. Don't dawdle when it comes to fulfilling your vows or bringing vowed or free-will offerings. Deuteronomy 23:22

The Sabbatical and Jubilee Years

128. Don't till the land in the Sabbatical year. Leviticus 25:4

129. Don't work the land in any way during the Sabbatical year. (That means no weeding, mulching, or pesticides.) Leviticus 25:4

130. Don't reap things that grow in the Sabbatical year as you would reap them in other years. Leviticus 25:5

131. Don't gather fruit of the tree in the Sabbatical year as you would in other years. Leviticus 25:5

132. And don't think you can ask for your money back after the Sabbatical year has passed. Deuteronomy 15:2

133. Don't refrain from making a loan to a poor man because of the "loans forgiven" rule in the Sabbatical year. Deuteronomy 15:9

134. Don't cultivate the soil or do any work on the trees in the Jubilee Year. Leviticus 25:11

135. Don't reap anything that grew by itself in the Jubilee Year, at least not in the same way as you would in other years. Leviticus 25:11

136. Don't gather fruit in the Jubilee Year, at least not in the same way as you would in other years. Leviticus 25:11

The Courts and Court Procedures

137. Don't appoint incompetent or unlearned people as judges (gratuitous political quip deleted). Deuteronomy 1:13

138. Don't curse a judge. Exodus 22:27

139. Don't testify falsely. Exodus 20:13

140. If you testify in a capital case, you can't judge it. Numbers 35:30

141. Sinners shall not testify. (It's too bad this doesn't apply to jury duty.) Exodus 23:1

142. In matters of capital punishment, close relatives of the defendant may not testify. Deuteronomy 24:16

143. Judges may not hear one of the parties to a suit in the absence of the other party. (So much for video testimonies.) Exodus 23:1

144. Never decide a case on the evidence of a single witness. Deuteronomy 19:15

145. In capital cases, don't go by the majority view if only one vote makes the majority in favor of finding the defendant guilty. Exodus 23:2

146. One who has argued in a capital case for acquittal shall not later argue for condemnation. (Thou shalt not be capricious.) Exodus 23:2

147. Don't make wicked decisions. Leviticus 19:15

148. Don't favor the rich and powerful when trying a case. Leviticus 19:15

149. Taking a bribe is a definite no-no. Exodus 23:8

150. Don't be intimidated by a nasty person when trying a case. Deuteronomy 1:17

151. Don't let the poverty of one of the parties affect your judgment. Exodus 23:3

152. Don't be prejudiced when judging strangers or orphans. Deuteronomy 24:17

153. Don't be prejudiced against people even if they have a bad reputation. Exodus 23:6

154. Don't impose a death penalty based on circumstantial evidence or if anyone still has some evidence in favor of the accused. Exodus 23:7

155. Never execute someone accused of a capital offense before he or she has stood trial. Numbers 35:12

156. Don't flout or act against the orders of the Court. Deuteronomy 17:11

Injuries and Damages

157. Don't leave something that may cause hurt. (Life is risky enough without your help!) Deuteronomy 22:8

158. Don't spare a pursuer, but maim or kill him before he reaches the pursued and slays or otherwise assaults him or her. Deuteronomy 25:12

Property and Related Rights

159. Don't make a permanent sale of your field in the land of Israel. Leviticus 25:23

160. Don't change the character of the open land in the area of the Levites or of their fields. Also, don't sell this land permanently. Leviticus 25:34

161. Don't remove landmarks. (Not everyone can afford a fancy-shmancy GPS tracker.) Deuteronomy 19:14

162. Don't deny another person's property rights. Leviticus 19:11

163. Don't swear to deny another person's property rights. Leviticus 19:11

164. No settling in the land of Egypt. Deuteronomy 17:16

165. Don't steal. Leviticus 19:11

166. Don't lie about not finding lost property so as to avoid the obligation to return it. Deuteronomy 22:3

Criminal Laws

167. Don't commit murder. Exodus 20:13

168. No kidnapping. Exodus 20:13

169. Don't rob by violence. Leviticus 19:13

170. Don't defraud. Leviticus 19:13

171. Don't covet whatever belongs to someone else. Exodus 20:14

172. Don't crave whatever belongs to someone else. Deuteronomy 5:18

173. Don't indulge in evil thoughts and sights. Numbers 15:39

Punishment and Restitution

174. Don't allow the dead body of an executed criminal to remain hanging overnight. Deuteronomy 21:23

175. Don't accept ransom from a murderer. Numbers 35:31

176. Don't accept ransom from a perpetrator of accidental homicide so as to relieve him from exile. Numbers 35:32

177. Don't plow or sow the rough valley in which a heifer's neck was broken. Deuteronomy 21:4

178. If you rape a maiden and then (in accordance with the law) marry her, you may not divorce her. Deuteronomy 22:29

179. No punishment may be inflicted on Shabbat. Exodus 35:3

180. Don't exceed the statutory number of times a person who has incurred the punishment of whipping is whipped. Deuteronomy 25:3

181. Don't spare the offender when it comes to imposing the prescribed penalties for causing damage. Deuteronomy 19:13

182. Don't punish someone who has committed an offense under duress. Deuteronomy 22:26

Prophecy

183. Don't make false prophecies. Deuteronomy 18:20

184. Don't hesitate to put a false prophet to death — and don't fear him. Deuteronomy 18:22

Idolatry

185. Don't make a human effigy or contract out to have one made by others. Exodus 20:4

186. Don't make any anatomically accurate three-dimensional human figures for ornament, even if they're not worshiped. Exodus 20:20

187. Don't make idols, meaning an object to be worshiped — not even for others. Exodus 34:17

188. It's forbidden to use the ornament of any object of idolatrous worship. Deuteronomy 7:25

189. Don't make use of an idol or its accessory objects, offerings, or libations. Deuteronomy 7:26

190. Don't drink the wine of idolaters (even if it's on the house). Deuteronomy 32:38

191. Don't worship an idol in the typical way. (Worshiping idols in atypical ways is also forbidden.) Exodus 20:5

192. Never bow down to an idol. Exodus 20:5

193. Don't prophesy in the name of an idol. Exodus 23:13 and Deuteronomy 18:20

194. Don't listen to anyone who does prophesize in the name of an idol. Deuteronomy 13:4

195. Don't lead other Jews astray to idolatry. (It's bad enough if you go astray; you shouldn't take others down with you!) Exodus 23:13

196. Don't entice an Israelite to idolatry. Deuteronomy 13:12

197. Don't love people who entice others to idolatry. Deuteronomy 13:9

198. Don't stop hating such enticers. Deuteronomy 13:9

199. Don't try to save idolatry enticers from capital punishment. Deuteronomy 13:9

200. The target of an idolatry enticer shouldn't plead for his acquittal. Deuteronomy 13:9

201. The target of an idolatry enticer should not refrain from testifying against him. Deuteronomy 13:9

202. Don't swear by an idol to its worshipers. In fact, don't cause *anyone* to swear by it. Exodus 23:13

203. Don't even think about idolatry! Leviticus 19:4

204. Don't adopt the customs and practices of idolaters. Leviticus 18:3, Leviticus 20:23

205. Don't pass a child through the fire to Moloch (the Canaanite god to whom parents sacrificed children) — you're the one who will get burned. Leviticus 18:21

206. Don't tolerate witchcraft. Exodus 22:17

207. Don't calculate certain times or seasons as favorable, as astrologers do. Leviticus 19:26

208. Don't do things based on signs and portents, using charms and incantations. Leviticus 19:26

209. Don't consult with mediums. Leviticus 19:31

210. Don't consult with wizards (or keep your focus off hocus-pocus). Leviticus 19:31

211. Don't practice magic using herbs, stones, or any stuff that alleged magicians use. Deuteronomy 18:10

212. In fact, don't practice magic, period (although sleight-of-hand tricks are okay). Deuteronomy 18:10

213. Don't use incantations. Deuteronomy 18:11

214. Don't seek answers from a ghost. Deuteronomy 18:11

215. Don't try to contact the dead. Deuteronomy 18:11

216. Don't seek the help of a wizard. Deuteronomy 18:11

217. Don't shave your entire beard. Do you *want* to look like those nasty idolaters? Leviticus 19:27

218. Men, don't round the corners of the hair on your head, as idolatrous priests do. Leviticus 19:27

219. Don't cut yourself or make incisions in your flesh as a sign of grief. Leviticus 19:28 and Deuteronomy 14:1

220. No tattoos — it's an idolater practice. Leviticus 19:28

221. Don't tear out your hair to make a bald spot. (It's an idolatrous custom.) Deuteronomy 14:1

222. Don't plant a tree for worship. (But feel free to hug trees.) Deuteronomy 16:21

223. Don't build a pillar for worship. Deuteronomy 16:22

224. Don't do any favors for idolaters. Deuteronomy 7:2

225. No covenants with the seven idolatrous nations. Exodus 23:32

226. Don't allow idolaters to settle in the Holy Land. Exodus 23:33

227. Burn down an idolatrous city and don't ever rebuild it. Deuteronomy 13:17

228. Don't take or use the property from destroyed idolatrous cities. Deuteronomy 13:18

Agriculture and Animal Husbandry

229. Never cross-breed cattle of different species. Leviticus 19:19

230. Never sow different kinds of seeds together in one field. Leviticus 19:19

231. After planting a fruit tree, don't eat its fruit for three years. Leviticus 19:23

232. Don't sow grains or herbs in a vineyard. Deuteronomy 22:9

233. Don't eat any grain or herbs that were sown in a vineyard. Deuteronomy 22:9

234. Don't yoke together beasts of different species. Deuteronomy 22:10

Clothing

235. Men shall not wear women's clothing (except maybe on Purim). Deuteronomy 22:5

236. Women shall not wear men's clothing (ditto). Deuteronomy 22:5

237. Don't wear garments made of wool and linen mixed together. (Cotton-poly blends, however, are fine.) Deuteronomy 22:11

The Firstborn

238. Don't pay the priesthood a symbolic amount for the firstborn of a clean animal. Numbers 18:17

The Priesthood and Holy Temple Workers

239. Don't tear the High Priest's robe. Exodus 28:32

240. A priest can't enter the Sanctuary at just any time, such as when he's not performing a service. Leviticus 16:2

241. Priests must not come in contact with any corpses other than immediate relatives. Leviticus 21:1–3

242. If a priest had to immerse himself in the mikvah during the day, he can't serve in the Sanctuary the same day until after sunset. Leviticus 22:6–7

243. Priests can't marry divorcees. Leviticus 21:7

244. Priests can't marry harlots. Leviticus 21:7

245. Priests can't marry any women forbidden to them. (It's somewhat redundant, but so it goes.) Leviticus 21:7

246. The High Priest can't come in contact with any dead, even if they're relatives. Leviticus 21:11

247. The High Priest should never be under the same roof as a dead body. Leviticus 21:11

248. The High Priest can't marry a widow. Leviticus 21:14

249. The High Priest should not have sex with a widow. Leviticus 21:15

250. If a priest has a physical blemish, he can't serve in the Sanctuary. Leviticus 21:17

251. A priest with a temporary blemish can't serve in the Sanctuary. Leviticus 21:21

252. Anyone with a physical blemish must not go up to the altar in the Sanctuary. Leviticus 21:23

253. A priest who is unclean shall not serve (because cleanliness is next to Godliness). Leviticus 22:2–3

254. Unclean priests should not enter the Courtyard. (This commandment refers to when the Israelites camped in the wilderness.) Numbers 5:2–3

255. Levites shall not occupy themselves with the service belonging to the priests, and vice versa. Numbers 18:3

256. If you're not a descendant of Aaron in the male line, you can't be a priest. Numbers 18:4–7

257. The Levites can't own any territory in Israel. Deuteronomy 18:1

258. Levites get no share of the loot from conquering the land. Deuteronomy 18:1

Tithes and Taxes

259. An uncircumcised man shall not eat of the t'rumah (priestly agricultural offering). Exodus 12:44–45 and Leviticus 22:10

260. Don't change the order of separating the t'rumah and the tithes. (The sequence is first-fruits, then the t'rumah, then the first tithe, and then the second tithe.) Exodus 22:28

261. Priests who are ritually unclean shall not eat the t'rumah. Leviticus 22:3–4

262. If you're not a priest or the wife or unmarried daughter of one, you can't eat the t'rumah. Leviticus 22:10

263. If you're a guest of a priest or one of his hired servants, you can't eat the t'rumah. Leviticus 22:10

264. Don't eat anything from which the t'rumah and tithe haven't yet been separated. Leviticus 22:15

265. Your tithed portion can't be sold. Leviticus 27:32–33

266. Don't eat the second tithe of cereals outside of Jerusalem. Deuteronomy 12:17

267. Don't drink the second tithe of wine outside of Jerusalem. Deuteronomy 12:17

268. Don't eat the second tithe of the oil outside of Jerusalem. Deuteronomy 12:17

269. Don't deprive the Levites of their due. Deuteronomy 12:19

270. Don't spend the proceeds of the second tithe on anything but food and drink. Deuteronomy 26:14

271. If you're ritually unclean, you must not eat the second tithe. Deuteronomy 26:14

272. If you're mourning, you must not eat the second tithe. Deuteronomy 26:14

The Temple, the Sanctuary, and Sacred Objects

273. Altars can't be built with hewn stones. Exodus 20:22

274. Don't go up to the altar by steps — use the ramp. Exodus 20:23

275. Don't remove the poles from the Ark. Exodus 25:15

276. Don't loosen the High Priest's breastplate from the ephod (the High Priest's linen apron). Exodus 28:28

277. Don't offer strange incense or any sacrifice upon the golden altar. Exodus 30:9

278. Don't make anointing oil for lay use. Exodus 30:32–33

279. Don't anoint a stranger with the anointing oil. Exodus 30:32

280. Don't copy the incense formula for anything else. Exodus 30:37

281. Don't extinguish the fire on the altar. Leviticus 6:6

282. The priest shall not enter the Sanctuary with disheveled hair. Leviticus 10:6

283. Don't enter the Sanctuary with torn garments. Leviticus 10:6

284. Priests may not leave the Courtyard of the Sanctuary during services. Leviticus 10:7

285. If you're drunk, you can't enter the Sanctuary or give legal decisions. Leviticus 10:9–11

286. Don't leave over any flesh of the Paschal lamb brought on the second Passover. (No doggie bags!). Numbers 9:12

287. Don't break a bone of the Paschal lamb brought on the second Passover. Numbers 9:12

288. Never allow the Sanctuary to remain unwatched. Numbers 18:5

289. Don't destroy anything of the Sanctuary, of synagogues, or of houses of study. This includes never erasing the holy names of God or destroying holy books. Deuteronomy 12:2–4

Offerings and Sacrifices

290. Don't eat the meat of the Paschal lamb if it's uncooked or sodden. Exodus 12:9

291. Don't leave any part of the Paschal sacrifice unconsumed by the morning. Exodus 12:10

292. Don't let a Jewish person who denounces Judaism eat from the Paschal lamb. Exodus 12:43

293. Don't let a stranger who lives among you eat from the Paschal lamb. Exodus 12:45

294. Don't take any of the Paschal lamb from the company's place of assembly. (That means no carryout.) Exodus 12:46

295. Don't break a bone of the Paschal lamb. Exodus 12:46

296. If you're an uncircumcised male, no Paschal lamb for you! Exodus 12:48

297. Don't slaughter the Paschal lamb while there's chametz in your home. Exodus 23:18

298. Don't leave the part of the Paschal lamb that should be burnt on the altar until the morning. Then it will be too late! Exodus 23:18

299. Don't go up to the Sanctuary without bringing an offering. Exodus 23:15

300. If you aren't a priest, you may not eat the meat from sacrifices. Exodus 29:33

301. Leaven and honey are not to be offered. Leviticus 2:11

302. Don't make an offering that's unsalted. Leviticus 2:13

303. Don't completely cut off the head of a fowl brought as a sin-offering. Leviticus 5:8

304. Don't put olive oil in a sin-offering made of flour. Leviticus 5:11

305. Don't put frankincense on a sin-offering made of flour. (Myrrh, however, is perfectly acceptable.) Leviticus 5:11

306. Don't allow the remainder of the meal offerings to become leavened. Leviticus 6:10

307. Don't eat the meal offering brought by the Priests. Leviticus 6:16

308. Don't eat any meat from sin-offerings. (It's bad karma.) Leviticus 6:23

309. Don't eat of sacrifices after the appointed time for eating them. Leviticus 7:18

310. Never eat any holy thing that has become unclean. Leviticus 7:19

311. People in a ritually unclean state can't eat things that are holy. Leviticus 7:20

312. A priest's daughter who has married a non-priest shall not eat any of the holy things. Leviticus 10:14 and Leviticus 22:12

313. Animals that have been set apart for sacrifices must not be slaughtered outside. Leviticus 17:3–4

314. Don't eat any leftover meat from a sacrifice after the appointed time for its consumption. Leviticus 19:8

315. Don't sacrifice blemished cattle. Leviticus 22:20

316. Don't make a blemish on cattle set apart for sacrifice. Leviticus 22:21

317. Don't slaughter blemished cattle as sacrifices. Leviticus 22:22

318. Don't burn the limbs of blemished cattle as sacrifices. Leviticus 22:22

319. Don't sprinkle blood from blemished cattle upon the altar. Leviticus 22:24

320. Don't sacrifice any blemished animal that comes from non-Israelites. Leviticus 22:25

321. Don't leave over any meat from the thanksgiving offering until the morning. Leviticus 22:30

322. Don't eat unleavened bread made with new grain before the offering on the second day of Passover. Leviticus 23:14

323. Don't eat roasted grain from new produce before the Omer offering. Leviticus 23:14

324. Or fresh ears of the new grain before that time. Leviticus 23:14

325. Don't exchange an animal that has been set aside to be sacrificed. Leviticus 27:10

326. Don't transfer an animal designated for one type of sacrifice to another. Leviticus 27:26

327. Don't sell a field that has been dedicated to the Lord. Leviticus 27:28

328. Don't pay the priesthood a symbolic amount for a field devoted to the Lord. Leviticus 27:28

329. Don't put olive oil in the meal-offering of a woman suspected of adultery. (Why would you even *think* of such a thing?) Numbers 5:15

330. Don't put any frankincense on that meal-offering either. Numbers 5:15

331. Don't offer up sacrifices outside the Temple. Deuteronomy 12:13

332. Don't eat meat from unblemished firstborn animals outside of Jerusalem. Deuteronomy 12:17

333. Don't eat the flesh of the burnt-offering. (Get thee to a grill.) Deuteronomy 12:17

334. Priests shouldn't eat the flesh of the sin-offering or guilt-offering outside the Temple Courtyard. Deuteronomy 12:17

335. Priests shouldn't eat meat from sacrifices before the animal's blood has been sprinkled. Deuteronomy 12:16–18

336. Priests must not eat the first fruits before they're placed in the Temple Courtyard. Deuteronomy 12:17

337. If a blemish on an animal for sacrifice has been intentionally inflicted, don't eat it. Deuteronomy 14:3

338. Don't do work with any cattle set apart for sacrifice. Deuteronomy 15:19

339. Don't shear animals that have been set apart for sacrifice. Deuteronomy 15:19

340. Don't leave over any portion of the Passover offering after the second day. Deuteronomy 16:4

341. Animals with temporary blemishes can't be sacrificed. Deuteronomy 17:1

342. If you've used an animal to hire a harlot or acquire a dog, it can't be used for sacrifice because it has been spiritually blemished. Deuteronomy 23:19

Lepers and Leprosy

343. Don't cut off the hair of the scaly eruption of the skin or scalp. (It is a way of determining leprosy.) Leviticus 13:33

344. Don't pluck out the marks of leprosy. Deuteronomy 24:8

The King

345. Don't curse the king. Exodus 22:27

346. Don't appoint a foreigner for king. Deuteronomy 17:15

347. The king shouldn't have too many horses. Deuteronomy 17:16

348. The king shouldn't have too many wives. Deuteronomy 17:17

349. . . . or too much gold and silver. (Kind of takes all the fun out of being king, doesn't it?) Deuteronomy 17:17

Nazarites

350. A Nazarite shall not drink wine or anything mixed with wine which tastes like wine. (So spritzers are definitely a no-no.) Numbers 6:3

351. A Nazarite shouldn't eat fresh grapes. Numbers 6:3

352. . . . or dried grapes. Numbers 6:3

353. . . . or grape kernels. Numbers 6:4

354. Grape skins? Sorry, none of those either. Numbers 6:4

355. Nazarites can't cut their hair. Numbers 6:5

356. Nazarites can't enter any covered structure containing a dead body. Numbers 6:6

357. Nazarites can't defile themselves by being in the presence of a corpse. Numbers 6:7

Wars

358. Those waging war for Israel shall not fear their enemies during battle. Deuteronomy 3:22, Deuteronomy 7:21, and Deuteronomy 20:3

359. Don't allow any individual of the seven Canaanite nations to live. Deuteronomy 20:16

360. Don't destroy fruit trees wantonly or when fighting a war. Deuteronomy 20:19–20

361. Don't sell a beautiful woman who has been taken captive in war. Deuteronomy 21:14

362. Don't degrade such a woman by making her a bondwoman. Deuteronomy 21:14

363. Don't offer peace to the Ammonites and the Moabites before waging war on them. Deuteronomy 23:7

364. Nobody who is ritually unclean may enter the camp of the Levites. Deuteronomy 23:11

365. Never forget the evil done to the Jews by Amalek. Deuteronomy 25:19

Index

• C •

shank bone, 188
shatnez, 57
Shavuot (holy day)
  definition, 303
  overview, 188
  priestly laws, 111
  rules, 189
Shekhinah (divine presence), 213, 249, 303
shellfish, 107, 206
Shem (Noah's son), 70
Shema (prayer)
  creation of days, 169
  definition, 303
  overview, 29
  second discourse of Moses, 133–134
  verses, 36–37
Shemini Atzeret (holy day), 185
Shemot. *See* Exodus
shepherd, 67
Shirat Ha Yam (song), 90–91
sh'lamim, 104
sh'mita, 172–173
shofar, 181
Shulchan Aruch (code of law), 54, 237, 303
sick people, 147
Simchat Torah (holy day)
  definition, 303
  overview, 185, 186
  Torah reading, 19, 212
sin. *See also specific sins*
  Aaron's golden calf, 96
  Adam and Eve, 66–67
  confession, 116–117
  offerings, 104–105
  second discourse of Moses, 137
  Sodom and Gomorrah, 73–74
  tzarat, 108–109
slavery
  communal behavior, 159
  negative commandments, 326–327
  positive commandments, 310
snake
  Garden of Evil, 66–67
  Moses's staff, 85, 86, 87
sod
  definition, 303
  interpretation of Torah, 252, 255–256
  Torah's facets, 249

Sodom (city), 72, 73–74
sodomy, 74
sofer, 231, 303
solar calendar, 170
Song at the Sea, 90–91
soul
  connection to God, 17
  creation of man, 65
  marriage, 196
  reincarnation, 112
  views of death, 198–200
spelling, 23, 244–246
spy, 120–122, 128
standing, during readings, 214
stealing, 163, 284, 312
Steinsaltz, Adin (rabbi), 1, 273–274
stoning, 163
storytelling, 53–54
stranger, 150–151
strangulation, 163
stubbornness, 96
study, of Torah
  first discourse of Moses, 130
  Orthodox Judaism, 156
  resources, 270–276
  Torah readings, 210
  Torah studies, 11, 19–20, 252–256
  Torah translations, 263–271
  Torah's infinite meanings, 250
suffering, 31–32, 153
sukkah, 183, 184, 185, 303
Sukkot (festival)
  definition, 111
  overview, 183
  priestly laws, 111
  rules, 184–186
  scheduled day, 171
sumptuary law, 206
sun, 22, 24, 168
surname, 106
symbol, 200–204, 306
synagogue
  blessings, 220–224
  conclusion of service, 226–228
  definition, 303
  holy closet ritual, 214–216
  layout, 97, 215
  overview, 209

Notes

Notes

Notes